W9-AEN-967

Chomsky on MisEducation

Critical Perspective Series

Series Editor: Donaldo Macedo, University of Massachusetts, Boston

A book series dedicated to Paulo Freire

Critical Education in the New Information Age
by Manual Castells, Ramón Flecha, Paulo Freire, Henry A. Giroux, Donaldo Macedo, and Paul Wills

Critical Ethnicity: Countering the Waves of Identity Politics
edited by Robert H. Tai and Mary L. Kenyatta

Debatable Diversity: Critical Dialogues on Change in American Universities
by Raymond V. Padilla and Miguel Montiel

Imagining Teachers: Rethinking Gender Dynamics in the Classroom
by Gustavo E. Fischman

Immigrant Voices: In Search of Education Equity
edited by Enrique (Henry) Trueba and Lilia I. Bartolomé

Latinos Unidos: From Cultural Diversity to the Politics of Solidarity
by Enrique (Henry) Trueba

Pedagogy of Freedom: Ethics, Democracy, and Civic Courage
by Paulo Freire

Pedagogy, Symbolic Control, and Identity, revised edition,
by Basil Bernstein

A Sanctuary of Their Own: Intellectual Refugees in the Academy
by Raphael Sassower

Forthcoming

Ideology Matters
by Paulo Freire and Donaldo Macedo

Paulo Freire and the Social Imagination: From Dreams to Praxis
by Maxine Greene

Chomsky on MisEducation

NOAM CHOMSKY

Edited and Introduced by Donaldo Macedo

ROWMAN & LITTLEFIELD PUBLISHERS, INC.
Lanham • Boulder • New York • Oxford

ROWMAN & LITTLEFIELD PUBLISHERS, INC.

Published in the United States of America
by Rowman & Littlefield Publishers, Inc.
4720 Boston Way, Lanham, Maryland 20706
http://www.rowmanlittlefield.com

12 Hid's Copse Road, Comnor Hill, Oxford OX2 9JJ, England

British Library Cataloguing in Publication Information Available

Library of Congress Cataloging-in-Publication Data

Chomsky, Noam.
Chomsky on miseducation / Noam Chomsky ; edited and introduced by Donaldo Macedo.
p. cm. — (Critical perspectives series)
Includes bibliographical references and index.
ISBN 0-7425-0129-9 (alk. paper)
1. Chomsky, Noam—Contributions in education. 2. Education—Philosophy. 3. Critical padagogy. I. Macedo, Donaldo P. (Donaldo Pereira), 1950– II. Title. III. Series.

LB885.C522 A3 2000
370.1—dc21 00-35297

Printed in the United States of America

∞™ The paper used in this publication meets the minimum requirements of American National Standard for Information Sciences—Permanence of Paper for Printed Library Materials, ANSI/NISO Z39.48-1992.

CONTENTS

Chomsky on MisEducation

INTRODUCTION

DONALDO MACEDO

> Democracy has failed because so many people fear it. They believe that wealth and happiness are so limited that a world full of intelligent, healthy and free people is impossible, if not undesirable. . . . Such a world, with all its contradictions can be saved, can yet be born again; but not out of capital, interest, property and gold.
>
> —W. E. B. Du Bois[1]

Schools in the so-called open and free societies face formidable paradoxical tensions. On the one hand, they are charged with the responsibility of teaching the virtues of democracy, and, on the other hand, they are complicit with the inherent hypocrisy of contemporary democracies, where, according to Noam Chomsky, the term *democracy* "refers to a system of government in which elite elements based in the business community control the state by virtue of their dominance of the private society, while the population observes quietly. So understood, democracy is a system of elite decision and public ratification, as in the United States itself. Correspondingly, popular involvement in the formation of public policy is considered a serious threat."[2]

Thus, the popular movements during the sixties and seventies that mobilized to question the criminal involvement of the United States in the Vietnam War and to demand civil rights guarantees and protection of the environment represented a real threat for the dominant ruling class. In the United States, the dominant sector of the society responded by creating the Trilateral Commission with the goal of finding ways to contain the general democratic participation of masses of people in the

Western world in questioning their governments' unethical behavior. In so doing, the Trilateral Commission dropped all pretensions concerning schools as democratic sites charged with the teaching of democratic values. The Trilateral Commission, whose members—among them the former president Jimmy Carter—belonged to the international and essentially liberal elite, resolved the paradoxical tensions of "democratic" schools by declaring them as institutions responsible for the indoctrination of the young.[3] This led Chomsky to argue that the Trilateral Commission viewed schools as institutions for indoctrination, "for imposing obedience, for blocking the possibility of independent thought, and [that] they play an institutional role in a system of control and coercion."[4]

In tandem with the Trilateral Commission's goal of seeking ways to maintain Western capitalism's cultural hegemony, a plethora of cultural commissars emerged (largely funded by conservative foundations and think tanks). Their mission was to contain what they viewed as an "excess of democracy" and blame "those who would [seek to] democratize institutions, who would change relations of power" for the "social catastrophe" of the sixties.[5] Thus, it became necessary to frontally attack the experiments in democracy that questioned the unethical (and sometimes criminal) behaviors of governments and squarely put the blame on the "great society programs not only for financial losses but also for the drop in high school test scores, drug problems and a generation of children and youth with no fathers, no faith and no dreams other than the lure of the streets."[6]

Whereas the ruling class makes no apologies for the undemocratic role of schools, cultural middle management composed of teachers, professionals, and experts is expected, through a reward system, to propagate the myth that schools are democratic sites where democratic values are learned. As cultural middle managers, teachers support "theological truths" (or unquestioned truths) so as to legitimate the institutional role schools play "in a system of control and coercion."

Nowhere is this more evident than the example I use in earlier works in which David Spritzler, a twelve-year-old student at Boston Latin School, faced a disciplinary action for his refusal to recite the Pledge of Allegiance, which he considered "a hypocritical exhortation to patriotism" in that there is not "liberty and justice for all." According to Spritzler, the Pledge is an attempt to unite the "oppressed and the oppressors. You have people who drive nice cars, live in nice houses and don't have to worry about money. Then you have the poor people, living in bad neighborhoods and going to bad schools. Somehow the Pledge makes it seem that everybody's equal when that's not happening. There's no justice for everybody."[7]

Spritzler was spared disciplinary action only after the American Civil Liberties Union wrote a letter on his behalf, citing a 1943 case, *West Virginia State Board of Education* v. *Barrett,* in which the U.S. Supreme Court upheld a student's right not to recite the Pledge of Allegiance and to remain seated.

As recorded in the first chapter of this book, entitled "Beyond a Domesticating Education: A Dialogue," I asked Chomsky why a twelve-year-old boy could see through the obvious hypocrisy contained in the Pledge of Allegiance, while his teacher and administrators, who received much higher levels of education, cannot. According to Chomsky, "What happened to David Spritzler is expected of schools, which are institutions for indoctrination and for imposing obedience. Far from creating independent thinkers, schools have always, throughout history, played an institutional role in system of control and coercion. And once you are educated, you have already been socialized in ways that support the power structure, which, in turn, rewards you immensely." In this sense, as Edward Said correctly points out, teachers are like other "professionals, experts, consultants who provide authority with their labor while gaining great profit."[8] As paid functionaries of the state, teachers are expected to engage in a form of moral, social, political, and economic reproduction designed to shape students in the image of the dominant society.

Far from the democratic education we claim to have, what we really have in place is a sophisticated colonial model of education designed primarily to train teachers in ways in which the intellectual dimension of teaching is often devalued. The major objective of a colonial education is to further de-skill teachers and students to walk unreflectively through a labyrinth of procedures and techniques. It follows, then, that what we have in place in the United States is not a system that encourages independent thought and critical thinking. On the contrary, our so-called democratic schools are based on an instrumental skills–banking approach that often prevents the development of the kind of thinking that enables one to "read the world" critically and to understand the reasons and linkages behind facts. By and large this instrumentalist approach to education is characterized by mindless, meaningless drills and exercises given "in preparation for multiple choice exams" and by teachers "writing gobbledygook in imitation of the psycho-babble that surrounds them."[9] As State Departments of Education reassert their control over the curriculum via mandated standardized tests, this form of mindless skills-based education is gaining more currency as tests guide teaching while "learning that address[es] the relationship of the self to public life, social responsibility to the broader demands of citizenship,"[10] is sidelined. In the process, teachers emphasize the mechanical learning and memorization of facts while sacrificing the critical analysis of the social and political order that generates the need for education in the first place. Seldom do teachers require students to analyze the social and political structures that inform their realities. Rarely are students allowed to engage in discovery and "to find the truth for themselves." Instead, students are expected to learn (and this never happens) "by a mere transfer of knowledge, consumed through rote memorization and later regurgitated" in state-mandated standardized tests. Far from engaging in the "development of independent and critical thought," students' minds are anesthetized, as poet John Ashbery accurately captures in "What Is Poetry?": "In School / All thoughts got combed out / What was left was like a field."[11] As our society allows the corporate cultures to reduce the priorities of education to the pragmatic requirements of the market, whereby students are trained to become "compliant workers, spectorial consumers, and passive citizens,"[12] it necessarily has to create educational structures that anesthetize students' critical abilities, in order to domesticate social order for its self-preservation.[13] Accordingly, it must create educational structures that involve "practices by which one strives to domesticate consciousness, transforming it into an empty receptacle. Education in cultural action for domination is reduced to a situation in which the educator as 'the one who knows' transfers existing knowledge to the learner as 'the one who does not know.' "[14]

More and more as the corporate culture exercises more control over schools, teachers are reduced to the role of imposing "an official truth" predetermined by "a small group of people who analyze, execute, make decisions, and run things in the political, economic and ideological system." In order to achieve this teaching task (which ironically is a form of dumbness), teachers must treat students as empty vessels to be filled with predetermined bodies of knowledge, which are often disconnected from students' social realities and from issues of equity, responsibility, and democracy. This type of education for domestication, which borders on stupidification, provides no pedagogical spaces for students, as Chomsky insightfully argues in this book, "not to be seen merely as an audience but as part of a community of common concern in which one hopes to participate constructively." Instead, students are rewarded to the degree that they become complicit with their own stupidification and become the "so-called good student who repeats, who renounces critical thinking, who adjusts to models, [who] should do nothing other than receive contents that are impregnated with the ideological character vital to the interests of the sacred order."[15]

In this education-for-domestication perspective, a good student is the one who piously recites the fossilized slogans contained in the Pledge of Allegiance. A good student is the one who willfully and unreflectively accepts big lies, as described in Tom Paxton's song "What Did You Learn in School Today?":

> What did you learn in school today, dear little boy of mine?
> What did you learn in school today, dear little boy of mine?
> I learned that Washington never told a lie,
> I learned that soldiers seldom die,
> I learned that everybody's free,
> That's what I learned in school today,
> That's what I learned in school.
> I learned that policemen are my friends,
> I learned that justice never ends,
> I learned that murderers die for their crimes
> Even if we make a mistake sometimes.
> I learned our government must be strong,
> It's always right and never wrong
> Our leaders are the finest men
> And we elect them again and again.
> I learned that war is not so bad.
> I learned about the great ones we have had.

> We've fought in Germany and in France,
> And someday I may get my chance.
> That's what I learned in school today
> That's what I learned in school.[16]

Fortunately, not all students willingly and uncritically embrace a pedagogy of big lies, and some are keenly aware of the lies their teachers tell them, to borrow a phrase from James W. Loewen. For example, history teachers try to engage students by using textbooks that "portray the past as a simple-minded morality play. 'Be a good citizen . . . you have a proud heritage. Be all that you can be. After all, look at what the United States has accomplished.'"[17] This form of false optimism, according to Loewen, "can become something of a burden for students of color, children of working-class parents, girls who notice the dearth of female historical figures, or members of any group that has not achieved socioeconomic success. No wonder children of color are alienated."[18] In their alienation, they refuse to accept the received knowledge from the ideological doctrinal system that falsifies and distorts reality in the hope that students will accommodate to life within a lie. It is for this reason that a very large segment of subordinated students resists the doctrinal education by dropping out. It is for this reason, perhaps, that many of these students resonate with Pink Floyd's song "Another Brick in the Wall": "We don't want no education / We don't want no thought control . . ."[19] As I have argued thus far, in order to maintain the present cultural and economic hegemony in the so-called open and democratic societies, schools have had to rely on the propagation of myths. According to Barbara Flores, myths "are persistent because they are not questioned; they are persuasive because they offer a simplistic view of a complex reality; and they are unrealistic because they disguise the truth."[20] It follows, then, that the teaching of truth as forcefully suggested by Chomsky presents a real threat to the doctrinal system. Teachers who are paid to safeguard the ideological doctrinal system have little interest or incentive to teach students that the United States has systematically violated the Pledge of Allegiance, from the legalization of slavery, the denial of women's rights, and the near-genocide of Native Americans to the contemporary discriminatory practices against people who, by virtue of their race, ethnicity, or gender, are not treated with the dignity and respect called for in the Pledge.

These teachers also have little incentive to teach Howard Zinn's *People's History of the United States*, from which students could learn that, once upon a time, the Massachusetts legislature promulgated a law that provided monetary rewards for dead Indians: "For every scalp of a male Indian brought in . . . forty pounds. For every scalp of such female Indian or male Indian under the age of twelve years that shall be killed . . . twenty pounds."[21] They also have little interest in teaching students that even antislavery President Abraham Lincoln did not truly uphold the U.S. Declaration of Independence propositions of equality, life, liberty, and the pursuit of happiness when he declared, "I will say, then, that I am not, nor ever have been in favor of bringing about in any way the social and political equality of the white and black races. . . . I as much as any other man am in favor of having the superior position assigned to the white race."[22]

One could argue that the incidents cited above belong to the dusty archives of our early history, but I do not believe that we have learned a great deal from historically dangerous memories considering our propensity to commit barbarism against other groups and nations in the name of democracy. It is not a mere coincidence, nor is it an innocent accident of nomenclature, that the destruction of entire villages in Vietnam that resulted in the killing of women, children, and the elderly was called by the United States a "pacification operation." Nor is it a coincidence that the invasion of Panama was named "Operation Just Cause." The latter was an invasion that killed thousands of innocent victims in order to arrest a head of state—Manuel Noriega—a thug created and supported by the U.S. government as a paid CIA informant who was considered "friendly" until he began to act too independently for our "democratic" taste. The arrest of a head of state through an invasion violates the same international laws that we claimed to protect during the Gulf War.

The U.S. defense of high principles and international laws that led to the Gulf War could only have moral currency if we were to obliterate our memory of recent history. Let me make it clear: Saddam Hussein's invasion of Kuwait was brutal, cruel, and unforgivable. But it was certainly no less brutal than the U.S. invasion of Grenada, the U.S. invasion of Panama, or the Turkish invasion of northern Cyprus—not to mention U.S. support for the right-wing totalitarianism and death squads in Chile, El Salvador, and Guatemala, among others.

Against this landscape of violation of international laws and aggression perpetrated by the United States and by other countries with U.S. support, how can we explain the ease with which President Clinton and other Western leaders convinced a supposedly highly literate and "free" citizenry that the NATO bombing of Kosovo was a "humanitarian intervention" designed to stop the ethnic cleansing of Albanians which, in reality, produced the opposite result; that is, the bombing of Kosovo by NATO forces "led directly to a radical increase in ethnic cleansing and carnage in Kosovo; it led to a sharp increase in the killings, the rapes and the torture of ethnic Albanians, hardly a great surprise."

The inability to link different historic events so as to gain a clear understanding of reality prevents those who have been ideologically domesticated through education to understand that if "we were to apply the same line of argument that justified the 'humanitarian intervention' in Kosovo, NATO should bomb other countries, Colombia for example, and also [one of] its members, Turkey." As Chomsky makes abundantly clear, in Colombia, "according to State Department estimates, the annual level of political killing by the government and its paramilitary apparatus is about the same level before the NATO bombing, and there are well over a million refugees." Instead of bombing Colombia to stop the carnage against its own citizens, the Clinton administration proposed to send $1.6 billion to strengthen the armed forces, supposedly to combat the drug war, and, according Chomsky, the "Clinton administration was particularly generous in its praise for President Cesar Gaviria of Colombia," whose tenure in office was responsible for "appalling levels of violence."

The case of Turkey is no less grotesque, involving "the flight of more than a million Kurds from the countryside to the official Kurdish capital Diyarbakir[, fleeing] Turkey's use of U.S. jets to bomb villages." The U.S. support for Indonesia and its complicity with the carnage in East Timor are well documented and would warrant the application of the same international principles that call for "humanitarian intervention." If it had not been for the denial of linkage and the social amnesia, we could have easily referred to Daniel Patrick Moynihan's role as the ambassador to the United Nations. In his memoir, *A Dangerous Place*, Moynihan discusses the invasion of East Timor by Indonesia and sheds light on his role as the U.S. ambassador to the United Nations: "The

United States wished things to turn out as they did and worked to bring this about. The Department of State desired that the United Nations prove utterly ineffective in whatever measures it undertook. This task was given to me, and I carried it forward with no inconsiderable success."[23] Moynihan added that within two months about 60,000 people had been killed, "almost the proportion of casualties experienced by the Soviet Union during the Second World War."[24] By not linking those historical events, the United States has been able to continually claim the moral high ground in the defense of international laws and the sanctity of national borders while it continues to violate these same international laws and borders at will. The inability to see through the obvious contradiction is part and parcel of the ideological manipulation that often produces a disarticulation of bodies of knowledge by dislodging observers from a critical and coherent comprehension of the world that informs and sustains them. This disarticulation of knowledge anesthetizes consciousness, without which one can never develop political clarity. As eloquently suggested by Frei Betto, clarity of reality requires that a person transcend "the perception of life as a pure biological process to arrive at a perception of life as a biographical and collective process."[25] Betto viewed his concept as a "clothesline of information." In other words, on the clothesline one may have a flux of information and yet remain unable to link one piece of information with another. Hence, it is not surprising that the western powers would so euphorically support NATO's "humanitarian intervention" in Kosovo to stop the ethnic cleansing of Albanians while turning a blind eye to the carnage in Rwanda, Colombia, Turkey, among others. Political clarity would require that a person is able to sort out the different and often fragmented pieces contained in the flux.[26] The apprehension of clarity of reality requires a high level of political clarity (something the dominant ideology tries to suppress in schools), which can be achieved by sifting through the flux of information and relating each piece to another one so as to gain a global comprehension of the facts and their raison d'être.

We can now see the reasons why people who have been educated through a domesticating model of transference (and sometimes imposition) of knowledge cannot make connections between the pieces of this knowledge to separate, for example, the mythical dimension of NATO's "humanitarian intervention" in Kosovo from factual reality. Part of the reason lies in the fact that teachers—political pundits who, like most so-called experts, have accepted blindly the dominant ideology—are technicians who, by virtue of the domesticating education they receive in an assembly line of ideas and aided by the mystification of this transferred knowledge, seldom reach the critical capacity to develop a coherent comprehension of the world. In short, this type of domesticating thinking makes it possible for us to rally behind political leaders who ritualistically call for the protection of human rights all over the world, without recognizing these same leaders' complicity in the denial of rights of human beings who live under dictatorships that we support either overtly or covertly. The selective nature of our strong support for human rights becomes glaringly clear in the cases of Colombia, Guatemala, Indonesia, Haiti, and Turkey, among other nations.

Central to a pedagogy of lies promoted by the dominant ideology to prevent the development of a "critical comprehension of reality" is the creation of "necessary illusions and emotionally potent oversimplifications . . . to keep the bewildered herd—the naïve simpleton—from being bothered with the complexity of real problems that they couldn't solve anyway." That is why schools and universities try to block the development of a more critical education along the lines suggested by Chomsky, Paulo Freire, and Henry Giroux, whereby, "as knowing subjects (sometimes of existing knowledge, sometimes of objects to be produced), our relation to knowable objects cannot be reduced to the objects themselves. We need to reach a level of comprehension of the complex of relations among objects."[27]

In an era in which we are more and more controlled by ever increasing "manufacturing of consent" through technological wizardry used by the media—ephemeral sound bites, metaphorical manipulations of language, and prepackaged ideas void of substance—it becomes that much more urgent to adhere to Chomsky's proposal to develop a critical approach to education that would serve "the general public [by] providing people with techniques of self-defense." Given the tendency for humans to construct "satisfying and often self-deceptive 'stories,' stories that often advantage themselves and their groups,"[28] particularly when these deceptive stories are rewarded by the dominant social order, the development of a critical comprehension between the meaning of words and a more coherent understanding of the meaning of the world is a prerequisite to achieving clarity of reality. As Freire suggests, it is only "through political practice [that] the less coherent sensibility of the world begins to be surpassed and more rigorous intellectual pursuits give rise to a more coherent comprehension of the world."[29]

Thus, in order to go beyond a mere word-level reading of reality (i.e., "humanitarian intervention"), we must develop a critical comprehension of psychological entities such as "memories, beliefs, values, meanings, and so forth . . . which are actually out in the social world of action and interaction."[30] We must first read the world—the cultural, social, and political practices that constitute it—before we can make sense of the word-level description of reality.

The reading of the world must precede the reading of the word, as Freire suggests. That is to say, to access the true and total meaning of an entity, we must resort to the cultural and political practices that mediate our access to the world's semantic field and its interaction with the word's semantic features. Because meaning is, at best, very leaky, we have to depend on the cultural models that contain the necessary cultural features responsible for "our stories" and, often, our "self-destructive stories."[31] A look at the proposition on "humanitarian intervention" in Kosovo reveals how cultural and political practices not only shape but also determine metaphorical manipulations of language, which are facilitated by electronically controlled images and messages through "the strategic use of doublespeak to disguise from television viewers the extent of the real terror and carnage" inherent in these "humanitarian interventions."[32] According to William Lutz, doublespeak "is a language that avoids or shifts responsibility, a language that is at variance with its real or purported meaning. It is a language that conceals or prevents thought; rather than extending the thought, doublespeak limits it."[33]

In this illuminating collection of essays, Chomsky not only urges all those who yearn to live democratically to adopt a more critical attitude toward the world, but he also provides us with insightful tools to unpack the social (dis)order so as to reveal the hypocritical and dehumanizing practices of our so-called democracies—and "this would mean teaching the truth about the world and society." Chomsky not only urges readers to embrace a language of critique necessary in unveiling obfuscated and ideologically manipulating realities, but, along the lines of Giroux and Freire, he embraces a pedagogy of hope whereby "students are invited to discover for themselves the nature of democracy and its functioning," whereby students move from their object positions as they become agents of history in a constant quest for the truth. As he energetically stresses, teachers need to sever their complicity with a technocratic training that de-intellectualizes them so they "work primarily to reproduce, legitimate and maintain the dominant social order from which they reap benefits."

Teachers need to reject becoming prey to the status of "commissars." They should become real intellectuals who "have the obligation to serve and tell the truth about things that are important, things that matter." As Chomsky so accurately stated in our dialogue, "This point is not lost on western intellectuals, who have no problem applying elementary moral principles in cases that involve official enemies." In this sense, Chomsky urges all those who want to live democratically to join the chorus of real intellectuals characterized by Edward Said as those who take

> a risk in order to go beyond the easy certainties provided us by our background, language, nationality, which so often shield us from the reality of others. It also means looking for and trying to uphold a single standard for human behavior when it comes to such matters as foreign and social policy. Thus if we condemn an unprovoked act of aggression by an enemy we should also be able to do the same when our government invades a weaker party.[34]

As real intellectuals, teachers need to appropriate a language of critique so as to denounce the hypocrisy, the social injustices, and the human misery. They need to also understand that "schools [embody] both dominant ideology and the possibility of resistance and struggle and they [should be] defended by diverse groups as fundamental for preparing students to assume the responsibilities for expanding the horizons of democracy and critical citizenship."[35] It is within the spirit of both critique and possibility that Chomsky urges the readers of *Chomsky on MisEducation* to take seriously the challenge of becoming agents of history so as to make this world less discriminatory, more democratic, less dehumanizing, and more just. Chomsky's illuminating ideas concerning humanizing the world resonate loudly with the pronouncements of another great educator, Paulo Freire, who continuously reminds all those who yearn to humanize the world that "to think of history as possibility is to recognize education as possibility. It is to recognize that if education cannot do everything, it can achieve some things. . . . One of our challenges as educators is to discover what historically is possible in the sense of contributing toward the transformation of the world, giving rise to a world that is rounder, less angular, more humane."[36]

NOTES

I would like to thank Panagiota Gounari, who patiently helped with the preparation of the manuscript and for her insightful comments and contributions during the selection of the essays included in this book.

1. W. E. B. Du Bois, *Color and Democracy: Colonies and Peace* (Milwood, N.Y.: Kraus-Thompson, 1975), 99, 142.
2. Noam Chomsky, *On Power and Ideology* (Boston: South End Press, 1987), 6.
3. Noam Chomsky, *Language and Politics*, ed. C. P. Otero (New York: Black Rose Books, 1988), 671.
4. Chomsky, *Language and Politics.*
5. Stanley Aronowitz and Henry A. Giroux, "Schooling, Culture and Literacy in the Age of Broken Dreams: A Review of Bloom and Hirsch," *Harvard Educational Review* 58, no. 2 (May 1988), 178.
6. Adam Pentman, "Buchanan Announces Presidential Candidacy," *Boston Globe* (Dec. 15, 1991), 13.
7. Diego Ribudeneira, "Taking a Stand, Seated," *Boston Globe* (Nov. 14, 1991), 40.
8. Edward W. Said, *Representations of the Intellectual* (New York: Pantheon Books, 1994), xv.
9. Patrick L. Courts, *Literacy and Empowerment: The Meaning Makers* (South Hadley, Mass.: Bergin & Garvey, 1991), 4.
10. Henry A. Giroux, *Critical Education and Cultural Studies: Making the Pedagogical More Political* (typewritten MS).
11. John Ashbery, "What Is Poetry?" *Houseboat Days: Poems* (New York: Viking, 1977), 47.
12. Giroux, *Critical Education and Cultural Studies.*
13. Paulo Freire, *The Politics of Education* (South Hadley, Mass.: Bergin & Garvey, 1985), 116.
14. Freire, *The Politics of Education*, 114.
15. Freire, *The Politics of Education*, 117.
16. Tom Paxton, "What Did You Learn in School Today?" copyright 1962 Cherry Lane Music Publishing Company, Inc. (ASCAP).

17. James W. Loewen, *Lies My Teacher Told Me* (New York: The New Press, 1945), 3.

18. Loewen, *Lies My Teacher Told Me.*

19. Pink Floyd, "Another Brick in the Wall," copyright 1979 Pink Floyd Music Limited.

20. Barbara Flores, "Language Interference on Influence: Toward a Theory for Hispanic Bilingualism" (Ph.D. dissertation, University of Arizona at Tuscon, 1982), 131.

21. Cited in Howard Zinn, *Declarations of Independence: Now Examining American Ideology* (New York: HarperCollins, 1990), 234–35.

22. Zinn, *Declarations of Independence.*

23. Cited in Noam Chomsky, *Towards a New Cold War* (New York: Pantheon, 1982), 339–40.

24. Chomsky, *Towards a New Cold War.*

25. Cited in Paulo Freire and Donaldo Macedo, *Literacy: Reading the Word and the World* (South Hadley, Mass.: Bergin & Garvey, 1987), 130.

26. Freire and Macedo, *Literacy.*

27. Freire and Macedo, *Literacy*, 131.

28. James Gee, *The Social Mind: Languages, Ideology, and Social Practices* (South Hadley, Mass.: Bergin & Garvey, 1992), vii.

29. Freire and Macedo, *Literacy*, 132.

30. Freire and Macedo, *Literacy.*

31. Gee, *The Social Mind*, xi.

32. Peter McLaren and Rhonda Hammer, "Media Knowledge, Warrior Citizenry, and Postmodern Literacies," *Journal of Urban and Cultural Studies* 1 (1992), 49.

33. William Lutz, *Doublespeak* (New York: HarperCollins, 1989), 1.

34. Said, *Representations of the Intellectual*, xiv.

35. Henry Giroux, *Radical Pedagogy and Educated Hope: Remembering Paulo Freire* (typewritten MS).

36. Paulo Freire and Donaldo Macedo, "A Dialogue: Culture, Language and Race," in *Breaking Free: The Transformative Power of Critical Pedagogy*, ed. Pepi Leistyna, Anvie Woodrum, and Stephen A. Sherblom (Cambridge, Mass.: Harvard Educational Review, 1996), 222.

1

BEYOND A DOMESTICATING EDUCATION: A DIALOGUE

Donaldo Macedo: I was intrigued some years back by a twelve-year-old student at Boston Latin School, David Spritzler, who faced disciplinary action for his refusal to recite the Pledge of Allegiance, which he considered "a hypocritical exhortation to patriotism," in that there is not "liberty and justice for all." The question that I want to ask you is why a twelve-year-old boy could readily see through the hypocrisy in the Pledge of Allegiance, while his teacher and administrators could not? I find it mind-boggling that teachers, who by the very nature of their work should consider themselves intellectuals, are unable or willfully refuse to see what is so obvious to one so young.

Noam Chomsky: This is not hard to understand. What you just described is a sign of the deep level of indoctrination that takes place in our schools, making an educated person unable to understand elementary thoughts that any twelve-year-old can understand.

Macedo: I find it mind-boggling that a highly educated teacher and a principal would sacrifice the content in the Pledge of Allegiance in order to impose obedience by demanding that a student recite the Pledge of Allegiance.

Chomsky: I don't find that mind-boggling at all. In fact, what happened to David Spritzler is expected of schools, which are institutions for indoctrination and for imposing obedience. Far from creating independent thinkers, schools have always, throughout history, played an institutional role in a system of control and coercion. And once you are well educated, you have already been socialized in ways that support the power structure, which, in turn, rewards you immensely. Let's take Harvard for example. You don't just learn mathematics at Harvard. In addition, you also learn what is expected of you as a Harvard graduate in terms of behavior and the types of questions that you never ask. You learn the nuances of cocktail parties, how to dress properly, how to develop a Harvard accent.

Macedo: And also how to network within a particular class structure and learn about the objectives, goals, and interests of the dominant class.

Chomsky: Yes. In this case, there is a sharp difference between Harvard and MIT. Although one could safely characterize MIT as a more rightist institution, it is much more open than Harvard. There is a saying around Cambridge that captures this difference: Harvard trains the people that rule the world; MIT trains those who make it work. As a result, there is much less concern with ideological control at MIT, and there is more space for independent thinking. My situation there is a testimony to what I am saying. I have never felt any interference with my political work and activism. With that said, I don't mean that MIT is a hub of political activism. It still falls under an institutional role of avoiding a good part of the truth about the world or about society. Otherwise, it couldn't survive very long if it taught the truth.

Because they don't teach the truth about the world, schools have to rely on beating students over the head with propaganda about democracy. If schools were, in reality, democratic, there would be no need to bombard students with platitudes about democracy. They would simply act and behave democratically, and we know that does not happen. The more there is a need to talk about the ideals of democracy, the less democratic the system usually is.

This is well known by those who make policy, and sometimes they don't even try to hide it. The Trilateral Commission referred to schools as "institutions" responsible for "the indoctrination of the young." The indoctrination is necessary because schools are, by and large, designed to support the interests of the dominant segment of society, those people who have wealth and power. Early on in your education you are socialized to understand the need to support the power structure, primarily corporations—the business class. The lesson you learn in the socialization through education is that if you don't support the interest of the people who have wealth and power, you don't survive very long. You are just weeded out of the system or marginalized. And schools succeed in the "indoctrination of the youth"—borrowing the Trilateral Commission's phrasing—by operating within a propaganda framework that has the effect of distorting or suppressing unwanted ideas and information.

Macedo: How can these intellectuals who operate within the propaganda framework get away with their complicity in the falsehoods they propagate in the service of the powerful interests?

Chomsky: They are not getting away with anything. They are, in fact, performing a service that is expected of them by the institutions for which they work, and they willingly, perhaps unconsciously, fulfill the requirements of the doctrinal system. This is like hiring a carpenter and, when he does the job he is contracted to do, asking how he got away with it. He performed as expected. Well, intellectuals provide a very similar service. They perform as they are expected to by giving a tolerably accurate description of reality that conforms with the interests of the people who have wealth and power—the people who own these institutions that we call schools and in fact own the society generally.

Macedo: It is clear that intellectuals have historically played an inglorious role in support of the doctrinal system. Given their less-than-honorable posture, can they be considered intellectuals in the true sense of the term? You have often referred to some Harvard professors as "commissars." I also find that term more appropriate than *intellectual,* given their complicity in the power structure and their functionary roles in support of "civilizing values" that in many instances have produced just the opposite: human misery, genocide, slavery, and wholesale exploitation of the masses.

Chomsky: Historically, that has been almost exactly the case. Going back to the time of the Bible, the intellectuals who later were called "false prophets" worked for specific interests of those in power. We know that there were dissident intellectuals at the time who had an alternative view of the world, the ones later called "prophets"—a dubious translation of an obscure word. Well, these intellectuals were marginalized, tortured, or sent into exile. Things haven't changed much in our time. Intellectuals who dissent remain marginalized in most societies, and in places like El Salvador they are just butchered. That is what happened to Archbishop Romero and the six Jesuit intellectuals who were killed by elite troops that [the United States] trained, armed, and supported with our tax dollars. One Salvadorean Jesuit correctly pointed out in his journal that, for example, in their country Václav Havel (the former political prisoner who became president of Czechoslovakia) wouldn't have been put in jail; he would have been hacked to pieces and left by the side of the road. Václav Havel, who became the darling dissident for the West, repaid his Western supporters handsomely when he addressed the U.S. Congress a few weeks after the six Jesuits in El Salvador were murdered. Instead of showing solidarity with his comrade dissidents in

El Salvador, he praised and extolled Congress as "the defender of freedom." The scandal is so obvious that it requires no comment.

A simple test will show how extraordinary this scandal is. Let's take, for example, this imaginary case: A black American Communist goes to what was then the Soviet Union, shortly after six leading Czech intellectuals were murdered by Russian-trained and -armed security forces. He goes to the Duma and praises it as "the defender of freedom." The reaction here in the United States among politicians and intellectuals would be swift and predictable. He would be denounced for supporting a murderous regime. Intellectuals in the United States need to ask why they reacted with rapture to Havel's incredible performance, which is quite comparable to this imaginary story.

How Many American intellectuals have read anything written by the Central American intellectuals who were assassinated by U.S. proxy armies? or would know of Dom Helder Camara—the Brazilian bishop who championed the cause of the poor of Brazil? That most would have difficulty even giving the names of dissidents in the brutal tyrannies in Latin America—and elsewhere—that we support and whose forces we train provides an interesting comment on our intellectual culture. Facts that are inconvenient to the doctrinal system are summarily disregarded as if they do not exist. They are just suppressed.

Macedo: This social construction of not seeing characterizes those intellectuals whom Paulo Freire described as educators who claim a scientific posture and who "might try to hide in what [they] regard as the neutrality of scientific pursuits, indifferent to how [their] findings are used, even uninterested in considering for whom or for what interests [they] are working."[1] In the name of objectivity, these intellectuals, according to Freire, "might treat [the] society under study as though [they] are not participants in it. In [their] celebrated impartiality, [they might] approach this world as if [they] were wearing 'gloves and masks' in order not to contaminate or be contaminated by it."[2] I would add that these intellectuals are wearing not just "gloves and masks" but also blinders that prevent them from seeing the obvious.

Chomsky: I'm not so sure that I agree with this postmodern critique of and attack on objectivity. Objectivity is not something that we should dismiss. On the contrary, we should work hard to embrace it in our pursuit of truth.

Macedo: I don't disagree with you. My critique of objectivity is not meant to dismiss it. What needs to be interrogated is the cover of objectivity that many intellectuals use to avoid incorporating factors in their analyses that are inconvenient and may expose their complicity in the suppression of truth in the service of the dominant ideology.

Chomsky: Yes. The pretense of objectivity as a means to distort and misinform in the service of the doctrinal system should be sharply condemned. That stance is much more easily sustained in the social sciences because the constraints imposed on researchers by the outside world are much weaker. Understanding is much more shallow, and the problems to be faced are much more obscure and complex. As a result, it is so much easier to simply ignore things that you don't want to hear. There is a marked difference between the hard sciences and the social sciences. In the natural sciences, the facts of nature do not let a researcher get away so easily with ignoring things that conflict with favored beliefs, and errors are more difficult to perpetuate. Since in the hard sciences experiments are replicated, errors are easily exposed. There's an internal discipline that guides intellectual endeavor. Still, there is plainly no guarantee even the most serious inquiry will lead to the truth.

Let's return to the initial point: that schools avoid important truths. It is the intellectual responsibility of teachers—or any honest person, for that matter—to try to tell the truth. That is surely uncontroversial. It is a moral imperative to find out and tell the truth as best one can, about things that matter, to the right audience. It is a waste of time to speak truth to power, in the literal sense of these words, and the effort can often be a form of self-indulgence. It is a waste of time, in my view, and a pointless pursuit to speak truth to Henry Kissinger, or to the CEO of AT&T, or to others who exercise power in coercive institutions—for the most part they already know these truths. Let me qualify what I just said. If and when people who exercise power in their institutional roles disassociate themselves from their institutional settings and become human beings, moral agents, then they may join everyone else. But in their roles as people who wield power, they are hardly worth addressing. It is a waste of time. It is no more worth speaking truth to power than to the worst tyrants and criminals, who are also human beings, however terrible their actions. To speak truth to power is not a particularly honorable vocation.

One should seek out an audience that matters. In teaching, it is the students. They should not be seen merely as an audience but as a part of a community of common concern in which one hopes to participate constructively. We should be speaking not *to* but *with.* That is second nature to any good teacher, and it should be to any writer and intellectual as well. A good teacher knows that the best way to help students learn is to allow them to find the truth by themselves. Students don't learn by a mere transfer of knowledge, consumed through rote memorization and later regurgitated. True learning comes about through the discovery of truth, not through the imposition of an official truth. That never leads to the development of independent and critical thought. It is the obligation of any teacher to help students discover the truth and not to suppress information and insights that may be embarrassing to the wealthy and powerful people who create, design, and make policies about schools.

Let's consider more closely what it means to teach the truth and for people to distinguish lies from truths. I don't think it requires anything more than common sense, the same common sense that enables us to adopt a critical stance toward the propaganda systems of nations that we consider to be our enemies. I earlier suggested that leading American intellectuals would not be able to name any well-known dissident in tyrannies in the sphere of our control, let's say in El Salvador. Nevertheless, those same intellectuals would have no problem providing a long list of dissidents in the former Soviet Union. They would also have no problem at all in distinguishing lies from truth and recognizing the distortions and perversions that are used to protect the population from the truth in enemy regimes. The critical skills they use in unmasking the falsehoods propagated in what they call "rogue" nations disappear when criticism of our own government and the tyrannies that we support are in order. The educated classes have mostly supported the propaganda apparatus throughout history, and when deviation from doctrinal purity is suppressed or marginalized, the propaganda machine generally enjoys great success. This was well understood by Hitler and Stalin, and to this day both closed and open societies pursue and reward the complicity of the educated class.

The educated class has been called a "specialized class," a small group of people who analyze, execute, make decisions, and run things in the political, economic, and ideological systems. The specialized class is generally a small percentage of the population; they have to be protected from the mass of the population whom Walter Lippmann called the "bewildered herd." This specialized class carries out the "executive functions," which means they do the thinking and planning and understand the "common interests," by which they mean the interests of the business class. The large majority of people, the "bewildered herd," are to function in our democracy as "spectators," not as "participants in action," according to the liberal democratic credo that Lippmann articulates clearly. In our democracy, every so often the members of the "bewildered herd" are allowed to participate in endorsing a leader through what is called "election." But once they endorse one or another member of the specialized class, they have to retreat and become once again spectators.

When the "bewildered herd" attempt to be more than spectators, when people attempt to become participants in democratic actions, the specialized class reacts to what it calls a "crisis of democracy." That is why there is so much hatred among elites for the 1960s, when groups of people who had been historically marginalized began to organize and take issue with the policies of the specialized class, particularly the war in Vietnam but also social policy at home.

One way to control the "bewildered herd" is to follow the Trilateral Commission's conception of schools as institutions responsible for the "indoctrination of the young." The members of the "bewildered herd" have to be deeply indoctrinated in the values and interests of private and state-corporate interests. Those who succeed in becoming educated in the values of the dominant ideology and who prove their loyalty to the doctrinal system can become part of the specialized class. The rest of the "bewildered herd" need to be kept in line, out of trouble, and remaining always, at most, spectators of action and distracted from the real issues that matter. The educated class considers them too stupid to run their own affairs and thus in need of the specialized class to make sure that they won't have the opportunity to act on the basis of their "misjudgments." The 70 percent or so of people who think that the Vietnam War was morally wrong need, according to the specialized class, to be protected from their "misjudgments" in opposing the war; they need to believe the official opinion that the Vietnam War was just a mistake.

To protect the "bewildered herd" from themselves and their "misjudgments," the specialized class in an open society needs to turn more and more to the technique of propaganda, euphemistically called "public relations." In totalitarian states, on the other hand, you keep the "bewildered herd" in place by holding a hammer over their heads, and if they get out of line you just smash them over the head. In a democratic society you can't rely on naked force to control the population. Therefore, you need a greater reliance on propaganda as a form of controlling the public mind. The educated class becomes indispensable in the mind-control endeavor, and schools play an important role in this process.

Macedo: Your pronouncements suggest, and I agree, that in open societies censorship is very much part of the fabric upon which the propaganda and its attempt to "control the public mind" depend. In my view, however, censorship in an open society differs substantially from the form of censorship exercised in totalitarian societies. What I have observed in the United States is that censorship not only manifests itself differently here but also depends on a form of autocensorship. What roles do the media and education play in this process?

Chomsky: What you refer to as autocensorship begins at a very early age through a socialization process that is also a form of indoctrination that works against independent thought in favor of obedience. Schools function as a mechanism of this socialization. The goal is to keep people from asking questions that matter about important issues that directly affect them and others. You don't just learn content in schools. As I mentioned, if you want to become a math teacher, you don't just learn a lot of math. In addition, you also learn how to behave, how to dress appropriately, what type of questions may be raised, how to fit in (meaning how to conform), etc. If you show too much independence and question the code of your profession too often, you are likely to be weeded out of the system of privilege. So you learn early on that to succeed you must serve the interests of the doctrinal system. You have to keep quiet and instill your students with the beliefs and doctrines that will serve the interests of those who have real power. The business class and their private interests are represented by the state-corporate nexus. But schools are by no means the only instrument of indoctrination. Other institutions work in tandem to reinforce the indoctrination process. Let's take what we are fed by television. We are offered to watch a string of empty-minded shows that are designed as entertainment but function to distract people from understanding their real problems or identifying the sources of their problems. Instead, those mindless shows socialize the viewer to become a passive consumer. One way to deal with an unfulfilled life is to buy more and more stuff. The shows exploit people's emotional needs and keep them disconnected from the needs of others. As public spaces are more and more dismantled, schools and the relatively few public spaces left work to make people good consumers.

Macedo: This fits with the overcelebration of individualism.

Chomsky: I don't agree. I don't see it as a form of individualism. Individualism, at its best, requires some form of responsibility for one's action. This mindless form of entertainment encourages people to conform and to be guided mostly by emotion and impulse. The impulse is to consume more, to be good consumers. In this sense, the media, the schools, and popular culture are divided into those who have rationality, and are the planners and the decision makers in the society, and the rest of the people. And to be successful, those who have rationality and join the specialized class have to create "necessary illusions" and "emotionally potent oversimplifications," in Reinhold Niehbuhr's words, to keep the "bewildered herd"—the naive simpleton—from being bothered with the complexity of real problems that they couldn't solve anyway. The goal is to keep people isolated from real issues and from each other. Any attempt to organize or to establish links with a collective has to be squashed. As in the totalitarian states, censorship is very real in open societies, though it takes different forms. Questions that are offensive and embarrassing to the doctrinal system are off-limits. Information that is inconvenient is suppressed. You don't have to look very far to reach this conclusion; you just have to honestly analyze what gets reported in the media and what is left out; to try to honestly understand what information is allowed in schools and what is not. Any person with average intelligence can see how the media manipulate and censor information not to their liking. It may take some work to discover the distortions and suppression of information. All you need is the desire to learn the truth.

There is no reason why the intellectuals shouldn't be able to take the same stance toward our protectorates in Latin America as they do toward enemy domains. All it takes is the willingness to use the same intelligence and common sense as they do in analyzing and dissecting atrocities committed by our enemies. If the schools were serving the general public, they would be providing people with techniques of self-defense, but this would mean teaching the truth about the world and society. They would be devoting themselves with great energy and application to precisely the kinds of things we're discussing, so that people growing up in an open and democratic society would develop techniques of self-defense against not only the propaganda apparatus in state-controlled totalitarian societies but also the privatized system of propaganda, which includes the schools, the media, the agenda-setting press, and intellectual journals and which essentially controls the educational enterprise. Those who exercise control over the educational apparatus should be referred to as a class of "commissars." Commissars are the intellectuals who work primarily to reproduce, legitimate, and maintain the dominant social order from which they reap benefits. Real intellectuals have the obligation to seek and tell the truth about things that are important, things that matter. This point is not lost on Western intellectuals, who have no problem applying elementary moral principles in cases that involve official enemies.

Macedo: This is a form of selective moralism. Participating in this selective moralism also provides these commissars with the rationale to justify their complicity in what Theodor Adorno referred to as "a callous refusal to see." I lived under two very different dictatorships, those of Antonio Salazar in Portugal and Francisco Franco in Spain, and censorship in these totalitarian regimes was naked, unmistakable, and police controlled. My experience here in the U.S. democracy is that censorship is much more diffuse and often exercised subliminally or through colleagues (including students) in the work context.

Speaking of democracy, isn't it ironic that in the United States—a country that prides itself on being the first and most democratic society in the First World—schools remain extremely undemocratic? They remain undemocratic not only in terms of their governance structures (for example, principals are appointed and not elected) but also as sites that reproduce the dominant ideology, which in turn discourages independent and critical thinking. Given the undemocratic nature of schools, how can education stimulate critical thinking in terms of students' creativity, curiosity, and needs?

Chomsky: There were alternatives to the present undemocratic schooling you just mentioned. I, for one, was very lucky to have gone to a school based on democratic ideals, where the influence of John Dewey's ideas was very much felt and where children were encouraged to study and investigate as a process of discovering the truth for themselves. Any school that has to impose the teaching of democracy is already suspect. The less democratic schools are, the more they need to teach about democratic ideals. If schools were really democratic, in the sense of providing opportunities for children to experience democracy through practice, they wouldn't feel the need to indoctrinate them with platitudes about democracy. Again, I feel lucky that my school experience was not based on memorizing falsehoods about how wonderful our democracy was. The influence of Dewey did not extend across all schools, even though he was a leading figure of North American liberalism and one of the major twentieth-century philosophers.

I also remember that, when I was a boy, I was a counselor in a summer camp, and I often witnessed the success of an indoctrination process similar to the recitation of the Pledge of Allegiance you described earlier. I remember seeing kids getting really emotional, and some would even cry, when reciting patriotic Hebrew songs that they didn't even understand. Some of the kids would get the words totally wrong, but that did not diminish their emotional state. True democratic teaching is not about instilling patriotism or rote memorization of the ideals of democracy. We know that students don't learn that way. True learning takes place when students are invited to discover for themselves the nature of democracy and its functioning.

The best way to discover how a functioning democracy works is to practice it. Well, schools don't do that very well. A good measure of functioning democracy in schools and in society is the extent to which the theory approximates reality, and we know that in both schools and society there is a large gulf between the two. In theory, in a democracy all individuals can participate in decisions that have to do with their lives, determining how public revenues are obtained and used, what foreign policy the society should follow, and so on. A simple test will show the gap between the theory, which says that all individuals can participate in decisions that involve their lives, and practice, in which the concentration of power at governmental levels works to limit individuals and groups from running their own affairs or, for example, from determining the shape of foreign policy they want to adopt.

Let's take the present bombing of Kosovo and Iraq. The situation in Kosovo prior to the bombing on March 24 was terrible, to say the least. On March 24 the bombing started, and within a few days there were thousands of refugees driven from Kosovo and a dramatic increase in rape, mass killings, and torture—a direct and in fact predicted consequence of bombing that was carried out under the guise of a humanitarian effort to protect ethnic Albanians. Well, it does not take much effort to see that a situation that had been terrible became catastrophic after the bombing, that an already horrible situation in Kosovo escalated to catastrophic proportions after NATO's "humanitarian intervention." Following the Universal Declaration of Human Rights, NATO claimed the right of "humanitarian intervention" to stop the ethnic cleansing of Albanians. As we can see, the NATO bombing led directly to a radical increase in ethnic cleansing and carnage in Kosovo; it led to a sharp increase in the killings, the rapes, and the torture of ethnic Albanians, hardly a great surprise. In fact, NATO Commander General Wesley Clark informed the press at once that this would be an "entirely predictable" effect of the bombing.

If we were to apply the same line of argument that justified the "humanitarian intervention" in Kosovo, NATO should bomb other countries, Colombia, for example, and also one of its members, Turkey. In Colombia, according to State Department estimates, the annual level of political killing by the government and its paramilitary apparatus is about at the level of Kosovo before the NATO bombing, and there are well over a million refugees, primarily fleeing from their atrocities. Colombia has been the leading Western-hemisphere recipient of U.S. arms and training as violence increased through the 1990s, and that assistance is now increasing under a "drug war" pretext dismissed by all serious observers. The Clinton administration was particularly generous in its praise for President César Gaviria of Colombia, whose tenure in office was responsible for "appalling levels of violence," according to human rights organizations.

In the case of Turkey, repression of Kurds in the 1990s is far beyond the scale of Kosovo before the NATO bombings. It peaked in the mid-1990s; one index is the flight of more than a million Kurds from the countryside to the official Kurdish capital Diyarbakir from 1990 to 1994, as the Turkish army was devastating the countryside. In 1994 two records were set: It was "the year of the worst repression in the Kurdish provinces" of Turkey, Jonathan Randal reported from the scene, and the year when Turkey became "the biggest single importer of American military hardware and thus the world's largest arms purchaser." When human rights groups exposed Turkey's use of U.S. jets to bomb villages, the Clinton administration found ways to evade laws requiring suspension of arms deliveries, much as it was doing in Indonesia and elsewhere. Again, if we were to follow the line of argument of the Universal Declaration of Human Rights, cited by NATO as justification for bombing Kosovo, NATO would be more than justified in bombing Washington.

Let's take the case of Laos. For many years, thousands of people, mostly children and poor farmers, have been killed in the Plain of Jars in northern Laos, apparently the scene of the heaviest bombing of civilian targets in history—and arguably the most cruel. Washington's furious assault on a poor peasant society had little to do with its wars in the region. The worst period began in 1968, when Washington was compelled to undertake negotiations (under popular and business pressure), ending the regular bombardment of North Vietnam. Henry Kissinger and Richard Nixon then decided to shift the planes to the bombardment of Laos and Cambodia. The deaths are from "bombies," tiny antipersonnel weapons far worse than land mines: They are designed specifically to kill people and have no effect on trucks, buildings, and so on. The plain was saturated with hundreds of millions of these murderous devices, which have a failure-to-explode rate of 20 to 30 percent, according to the manufacturer, Honeywell. These numbers suggest either remarkably poor quality control or a policy of murdering civilians by delayed action. The bombies were only a fraction of the technology deployed, which included advanced missiles to penetrate caves where families sought shelter.

Current annual casualties from bombies are estimated to be from hundreds a year to "an annual nationwide casualty rate of 20,000," more than half of them deaths, as veteran

Asia correspondent Barry Wain of the *Wall Street Journal* reported in its Asian edition. A conservative estimate, then, is that the crisis this past year alone is approximately comparable to Kosovo before the bombings. Deaths, however, are far more highly concentrated among children—more than half, according to analyses reported by the Mennonite Central Committee, which has been working there since 1977 to alleviate the continuing atrocities.

The U.S. media applauded NATO's intervention in Kosovo to stop the ethnic cleansing of Albanians, even though the bombing tragically increased ethnic cleansing and other atrocities against them. But in the case of Laos, where we are directly responsible for the deaths, the U.S. reaction was to do nothing. And the media and the commentators kept silent, following the norms under which the war against Laos was designated a "secret war"—meaning well known but suppressed, as was also the case of Cambodia after March 1969. The level of self-censorship was extraordinary then, as it still is. The relevance of this shocking example is obvious. Whereas the U.S. media were exuberant when the International Tribunal indicted Slobodan Milosevic for crimes against humanity, Kissinger, one of the architects of the carnage in Laos, remains free and celebrated as an "expert" whose "views" on the Kosovo bombing were eagerly sought by the media.

In the case of Iraq the atrocities abound, with Iraqi civilians being slaughtered by a particularly vicious form of biological warfare. Secretary of State Madeleine Albright commented on national television in 1996, when asked for her reaction to the killing of half a million Iraqi children in five years, that "we think the price is worth it." According to current estimates, about 4,000 children are still being killed a month, and the price is still "worth it."

A closer analysis of the Gulf War unveils the same guiding principles in the U.S. "humanitarian intervention" or intervention to safeguard "democracies" throughout the world. The media and the educated classes dutifully repeated

President George Bush's line that "America stands where it always has—against aggression, against those who would use force to replace the rule of law," even though he had a few months earlier violated America's principles "against aggression, against those who would use force to replace the rule of law" when he invaded Panama. President Bush was then the only head of state to have been condemned by the World Court for the "unlawful use of force"—in Washington's war against Nicaragua. Bush's claim to high principle was a joke, since the United States wasn't upholding any high principle in the Gulf, nor was any other state. The unprecedented response to Saddam Hussein wasn't because of his brutal aggression—it was because he stepped on the wrong toes, as Manuel Noriega had done a few years earlier. Both are thugs who had been friends of President Bush. Saddam Hussein is a murderous gangster—exactly as he was before the Gulf War, when he was our friend and favored trading partner. His invasion of Kuwait was certainly an atrocity, but it did not come close to the atrocities he committed with U.S. support, and it was well within the range of many similar crimes conducted by the United States and its allies.

For example, Indonesia's invasion and annexation of East Timor reached near-genocidal proportions; one-fourth of the population (700,000) were killed, a slaughter exceeding that of Pol Pot, relative to the population, in the same years. Both the United States and its allies supported these atrocities. The Australian foreign minister justified his country's acquiescence to the invasion and annexation of East Timor by saying simply that "the world is a pretty unfair place, littered with examples of acquisition by force." When Iraq invaded Kuwait, however, his government denounced the invasion with a ringing declaration that "big countries cannot invade small neighbors and get away with it." The real concerns of U.S. policy in the Gulf were that the incomparable energy resources of the Middle East remain under our control and that the enormous profits they produce help support the economies of the United States and its British client.

Macedo: It is indeed a sad statement that although the facts that you have reported are so obvious, the U.S. educated class, with the exception of a small minority, was unable to make the necessary historical linkages so as to develop a rigorous comprehension of the world. Vice President Dan Quayle read the Gulf War correctly, if unintentionally, by describing it as "a stirring victory for the forces of aggression." President Bush became trapped in a similar Freudian slip during an interview with Boston's Channel 5 TV news anchor, Natalie Jacobson. Referring to the Gulf War, Bush said, "We did fulfill our aggression," instead of what he no doubt intended, "We did fulfill our mission." The seemingly misspoken words by both Bush and Quayle denude the pedagogy of big lies to the extent that their statements more accurately capture the essence of José Ortega y Gasset's proposition that our so-called civilization, if "abandoned to its own devices" and put at the mercy of commissars such as Henry Kissinger, would bring about the rebirth of primitivism and barbarism.

Your examples of the barbarism in Kosovo, Turkey, Colombia, and Laos point to the barbarism of civilization. In many instances, the high level of technical sophistication attained by our so-called civilization has been used in the most barbaric ways, as evidenced in the gassing of the Jews and the bombing of Laos and Cambodia. It is certainly not an enlightened civilization that prides itself on reducing Iraq to a preindustrial level—killing tens of thousands of innocent victims, including women and children, while leaving Saddam Hussein, our chief for war, in power.

Chomsky: It is widely expected that U.S. military action will leave Iraq's murderous tyrant in power, continuing to pursue his weapons program, while undermining such international inspection as exists. It should also be stressed that Saddam's worst crimes were committed when he was a favored U.S. ally and trading partner and that, immediately after he was driven from Kuwait, the United States watched quietly while he turned to the slaughter of rebellious Iraqis—

first Shiites, later Kurds—even refusing to allow them access to captured Iraqi arms. Official stories rarely yield an accurate picture of what is happening. Officials stories also will not create structures to unveil the truth. An education that seeks for a democratic world ought to provide students with critical tools to make linkages that would unveil the lies and deceit. Instead of indoctrinating students with democratic myths, schools should engage them in the practice of democracy.

Macedo: It is unlikely that schools will stop indoctrinating students with myths since it is through the power of propagation of myths that the dominant ideology attempts to muffle the manifestation of a truly cultural democracy and maintain the present cultural and economic hegemony. I agree with you that schools should engage students in the practice of democracy. However, in order to do so, as you have pointed out many times, schools need to provide students with critical tools to unpack the ideological content of myths so they can begin to understand better, for example, why David Spritzler's teacher and principal, who had invested heavily in the dominant doctrinal system, went to great lengths to sacrifice the very principles of the Pledge of Allegiance in order to prevent Spritzler from living in truth, since individuals who want to live in truth represent a real threat to the dominant doctrinal system and must be weeded out or, at least, neutralized. Therefore, one should not be surprised that the teacher and the principal would try to stop David Spritzler from pointing out the hypocrisy and the class difference of our supposedly classless society.

Chomsky: The myth that we live in a classless society is a joke but believed by most people. My daughter who teaches in a state college tells me that most of her students consider themselves middle class and show no sign of class consciousness.

Macedo: The very academic discourse points to the lack of class consciousness. Whereas you find the term *working class* used in the media and also *middle class* (such as "tax break for the middle class"), you never see any mention of *ruling class* or *upper class.*

Chomsky: You will never find *ruling class* for sure. It is just suppressed. And working-class students like those in my daughter's class do not consider themselves working class. This is another sign of real indoctrination.

Macedo: The ruling elite, aided by the intelligentsia, has gone to great lengths to create mechanisms that perpetuate the myth that the United States is a classless society. With all the debate concerning the failure of education in this country, one variable that is never mentioned is class, even though class is a determinant factor in school success. Most of the students who are failing come generally from the lower class, and yet educators religiously avoid using class as a factor in their analyses and pronouncements. Instead, they create all kinds of euphemisms such as "economically marginal," "disadvantaged students," "at-risk" students, etc., as a process to avoid naming the reality of class oppression. And if you use class as a factor in your analysis, you are immediately accused of engaging in class warfare. You remember the presidential campaign of 1988 when George Bush berated his democratic opponent by saying, "I am not going to let that liberal governor divide this nation. . . . I think that's for European democracies or something else. It isn't for the United States of America. We're not going to be divided by class . . . we are the land of big dreams, of big opportunities, of fair play, and this attempt to divide America by class is going to fail because the American people realize that we are a very special country, for anybody given the opportunity can make it and fulfill the American dream."

Chomsky: Yes, it is a very special country if you are rich. To take only one current example, look at how the tax system is getting less and less progressive while enriching the rich through a large tax cut and through enormous subsidies that have been given historically to corporations. Bush is right in talking about class warfare. However, it is a class warfare designed to crush the poor even more. All indicators point out that child poverty remains very high, and malnutrition is getting worse under programs carried out to promote "family values." The assault on the welfare state is to further smash the poor, the welfare mothers, others who need help, while leaving intact the powerful nanny, subsidizing corporations with massive transfer payments. We do have a welfare state, but it is a welfare state for the rich. To maintain a well-functioning welfare state for the rich you have to have a highly conscious business class. The rest of the people have to be convinced that they live in a classless society. Schools have always played a role in keeping this myth alive.

NOTES

This dialogue took place in June of 1999.

1. Paulo Freire, *The Politics of Education: Culture, Power, and Liberation* (South Hadley, Mass.: Bergin & Garvey, 1985) 103.
2. Ibid.

2

DEMOCRACY AND EDUCATION

The topic that was suggested, which I'm very happy to talk about, is "Democracy and Education." The phrase *democracy and education* immediately brings to mind the life and work and thought of one of the outstanding thinkers of the past century, John Dewey, who devoted the greater part of his life and his thought to this array of issues. I guess I should confess a special interest. His thought was a strong influence on me in my formative years—in fact, from about age two on, for a variety of reasons that I won't go into but are real. For much of his life—later he was more skeptical—Dewey seems to have felt that reforms in early education could be in themselves a major lever of social change. They could lead the way to a more just and free society, a society in which, in his words, "the ultimate aim of production is not production of goods, but the production of free human beings associated with one another on terms of equality." This basic commitment, which runs through all of Dewey's work and thought, is profoundly at odds with the two leading currents of modern social intellectual life; one, strong in his day—he was writing in the 1920s and 1930s about these things—is associated with the command economies in Eastern Europe, the systems created by Lenin and Trotsky and turned into an even greater monstrosity by Stalin. The other, the state capitalist industrial society being constructed in the U.S. and much of the West, with the effective rule of private power. These two systems are similar in some fundamental ways, including ideologically. Both were, and one of them remains, deeply authoritarian in fundamental commitment, and both were very sharply and dramatically opposed to another tradition, the Left libertarian tradition, with roots in Enlightenment values, a tradition that included progressive liberals of the John Dewey variety, independent socialists like Bertrand Russell, leading elements of the Marxist mainstream, mostly anti-Bolshevik, and of course libertarian socialists and various anarchist movements, not to speak of major parts of the labor movement and other popular sectors.

This independent Left, of which Dewey was a part, has strong roots in classical liberalism. It grows right out of it, in my opinion, and it stands in sharp opposition to the absolutist currents of state capitalist and state socialist institutions and thought, including the rather extreme form of absolutism that's now called conservative in the U.S., terminology that would have amused Orwell and would have caused any genuine conservative to turn over in his grave, if you could find one.

I need not stress that this picture is not the conventional one, to put it rather mildly, but I think it does have one merit, at least—namely, the merit of accuracy. I'll try to explain why.

Let me return to one of Dewey's central themes, that the ultimate aim of production is not production of goods but the production of free human beings associated with one another on terms of equality. That includes, of course, education, which was a prime concern of his. The goal of education, to shift over to Bertrand Russell, is "to give a sense of the value of things other than domination," to help create "wise citizens of a free community," to encourage a combination of citizenship with liberty and individual creativeness, which means that we regard "a child as a gardener regards a young tree, as something with a certain intrinsic nature, which will develop into an admirable form, given proper soil and air and light." In fact, much as they disagreed on many other things, as they did, Dewey and Russell did agree on what Russell called this "humanistic conception," with its roots in the Enlightenment, the idea that education is not to be viewed as something like filling a vessel with water but, rather, assisting a flower to grow in its own way—an eighteenth-century view that they revived. In other words, providing the circumstances in which the normal creative patterns will flourish.

Dewey and Russell also shared the understanding that these leading ideas of the Enlightenment and classical liberalism had a revolutionary character, and retained it right at the time they were writing, in the early half of this century. If implemented, these ideas could produce free human beings whose values were not accumulation and domination but, rather, free association on terms of equality and sharing and cooperation, participating on equal terms to achieve common goals that were democratically conceived. There was only contempt for what Adam Smith called the "vile maxim of the masters of mankind, all for ourselves, and nothing for other people," the guiding principle that nowadays we're taught to admire and revere, as traditional values have eroded under unremitting attack, the so-called conservatives leading the onslaught in recent decades.

It's worth taking time to notice how sharp and dramatic is the clash of values between, on the one hand, the humanistic conception that runs from the Enlightenment up to leading twentieth-century figures like Russell and Dewey and, on the other hand, the prevailing doctrines of today, the doctrines that were denounced by Adam Smith as the "vile maxim" and also denounced by the lively and vibrant working-class press of over a century ago, which condemned what it called the "new spirit of the age, gain wealth, forgetting all but self"—Smith's vile maxim. It's quite remarkable to trace the evolution of values from a precapitalist thinker like Adam Smith, with his stress on sympathy and the goal of perfect equality and the basic human right to creative work, and contrast that and move on to the present to those who laud the "new spirit of the age," sometimes rather shamelessly invoking Adam Smith's name. For example, Nobel Prize–winning economist James Buchanan, who writes that what each person seeks in an "ideal situation" is "mastery over a world of slaves." That's what you seek, in case you hadn't noticed, something that Adam Smith would have regarded as simply pathological.

The best book I know of on Adam Smith's actual thought *(Adam Smith and His Legacy for Modern Capitalism)* is written by a professor here at Loyola, Patricia Werhane. Of course, it's always best to read the original.

One of the most dramatic illustrations of the "new spirit of the age" and its values is the commentary that's now in the press on the difficulties we face in uplifting the people of Eastern Europe. As you know, we're now extending to them, our new beneficiaries, the loving care that we've lavished on our wards elsewhere in Latin America and the Philippines and so on, with consequences that are dramatically clear and consistent in these horror chambers but also are miraculously free of any lessons about who we are and what we do. One might ask why. In any event, we are now proceeding to uplift the people liberated from communism as we've in the past liberated Haitians and Brazilians and Guatemalans and Filipinos and Native Americans and African slaves and so on. The *New York Times* is currently running an interesting series of articles on these different problems. They give some interesting insight into the prevailing values. There was an article on East Germany, for example, written by Steven Kinzer. It opens by quoting a priest who was one of the leaders of the popular protests against the communist regime in East Germany. He describes the growing concerns there about what's happening to the society. He says, "Brutal competition and the lust for money are destroying our sense of community, and almost everyone feels a level of fear or depression or insecurity" as they master the new spirit of the age in which we instruct the backward peoples of the world.

The next article turned to what we regard as the showplace, the real success story, Poland, written by Jane Perlez. The headline reads, "Fast and Slow Lanes on the Capitalist Road." The structure of the story is that some are getting the point but there are also some who are still backwards. She gives one example of a good student and one example of a slow learner. The good student is the owner of a small factory that is a "thriving example" of the best in modern capitalist Poland. It produces intricately designed wedding gowns sold mostly to rich Germans and to that tiny sector of superrich Poles. This is in a country where poverty has more than doubled since the reforms were instituted, according to a World Bank study last July, and incomes have dropped about 30 percent. However, the people who are hungry and jobless can look at the intricately designed wedding gowns in the store windows, appreciating the new spirit of the age, so it's understandable that Poland is hailed as the great success story for our achievements.

A good student explains that "people have to be taught to understand they must fight for themselves and can't rely on others." She is describing a training course she's running that's trying to instill American values among people who are still brainwashed with slogans like "I'm a miner. Who else is better?" They have got to get that out of their heads. A lot of people are better, including people who can design wedding gowns for rich Germans. That's the chosen illustration of the success story of American values. Then there are the failures, still on the slow lane on the capitalist road. Here she picks one as her example, a forty-year-old coal miner who "sits in his wood-paneled living room admiring the fruits of his labor under communism—a television set, comfortable furniture, a shiny, modern kitchen," and he wonders "why he's at home, jobless and dependent on welfare payments," having not yet absorbed the new spirit of the age, gain wealth, forgetting all but self, and not "I'm a miner. Who else is better?" The series goes on like that. It's interesting to read and to see what's taken for granted.

What's happening in Eastern Europe recapitulates what's gone on in our Third World domains for a long time and falls into place in a much longer story. It's very familiar from our own history and the history of England before us. There's a recent book, by a distinguished Yale University labor historian, David Montgomery, in which he points out that modern America was created over the protests of its working people. He's quite right. Those protests were vigorous and outspoken, particularly in the working-class and community press that flourished in the U.S. from the early nineteenth century up until the 1950s, when it was finally destroyed by private power, as its counterpart in England was about ten years later. The first major study of this topic was in 1924 by Norman Ware. It still makes very illuminating reading. It was published here in Chicago and reprinted very recently by Ivan Dee, a local publisher. It's very much worth reading. It's a work that set off very substantial study in social history.

What Ware describes, looking mostly at the labor press, is how the value system that was advocated by private power had to be beaten into the heads of ordinary people, who had to be taught to abandon normal human sentiments and to replace them with the new spirit of the age, as they called it. He reviews the mainly mid–nineteenth century working-class press, often, incidentally, run by working-class women. The themes that run through it are constant for a long period. They are concerned with what they call "degradation" and loss of dignity and independence, loss of self-respect, the decline of the worker as a person, the sharp decline in cultural level and cultural attainments as workers were subjected to what they called "wage slavery," which they regarded as not very different from the chattel slavery they had fought to uproot during the Civil War. Particularly dramatic and quite relevant to today's problems was the sharp decline in what we call "high culture," reading of classics and contemporary literature by the people who were called the factory girls in Lowell and by craftsmen and other workers. Craftsmen would hire somebody to read to them while they were working because they were interested and had libraries. All that had to go.

What they described, paraphrasing the labor press, is that when you sell your product, you retain your person. But when you sell your labor, you sell yourself, losing the rights of free men and becoming vassals of mammoth establishments of a "moneyed aristocracy" that "threatens annihilation to every man who dares to question their right to enslave and oppress." "Those who work in the mills ought to own them," not have the status of machines ruled by private "despots" who are entrenching "monarchic principles on democratic soil" as they drive downward freedom and rights, civilization, health, morals, and intellectuality in the new commercial feudalism.

Just in case you are confused, this is long before any influence of Marxism. This is American workers talking about their experiences in the 1840s. The labor press also condemned what they called the "bought priesthood," referring to the media and the universities and the intellectual class, that is, the apologists who sought to justify the absolute despotism that was the new spirit of the age and to instill its sordid and demeaning values. One of the early leaders of the AFL, Henry Demarest Lloyd, about a century ago, late nineteenth century, expressed the standard view when he described the mission of the labor movement as to overcome "the sins and superstitions of the market" and to defend democracy by extending it to control over industry by working people.

All of this would have been completely intelligible to the founders of classical liberalism, people like Wilhelm von Humboldt, for example, who inspired John Stuart Mill and who, very much like his contemporary Adam Smith, regarded creative work freely undertaken in association with others as the core value of a human life. So if a person produces an object on command, Humboldt wrote, we may admire what he did but we will despise what he is, not a true human being who acts on his own impulses and desires. The bought priesthood has the task of undermining these values and destroying them among people who sell themselves on the labor market. For similar reasons, Adam Smith warned that in any civilized society governments would have to intervene to prevent the division of labor from making people "as stupid and ignorant as it is possible for a human creature to be." He based his rather nuanced advocacy of markets on the thesis that if conditions were truly free, markets would lead to perfect equality. That was their moral justification. All of this has been forgotten by the bought priesthood, who has a rather different tale to tell.

Dewey and Russell are two of the leading twentieth-century inheritors of this tradition, with its roots in the Enlightenment and classical liberalism. Even more interesting is the inspiring record of struggle and organization and protest by working men and women since the early nineteenth century as they sought to win freedom and justice and to retain the rights that they had once had as the new despotism of state-supported private power extended its sway.

The basic issue was formulated with a good deal of clarity by Thomas Jefferson around 1816. This was before the Industrial Revolution had really taken root in the former colonies, but you could begin to see the developments. In his later years, observing what was happening, Jefferson had rather serious concerns about the fate of the democratic experiment. He feared the rise of a new form of absolutism that was more ominous than what had been overthrown in the American Revolution, in which he was of course a leader. Jefferson distinguished in his later years between what he called "aristocrats" and "democrats." The aristocrats are "those who fear and distrust the people, and wish to draw all powers from them into the hands of the higher classes." The democrats, in contrast, "identify with the people, have confidence in them, cherish and consider them as the honest and safe depository of the public interest," if not always "the most wise." The aristocrats of his day were the advocates of the rising capitalist state, which Jefferson regarded with much disdain, clearly recognizing the quite obvious contradiction between democracy and capitalism, or more accurately what we might call really existing capitalism, that is, guided and subsidized by powerful developmental states, as it was in England and the U.S. and indeed everywhere else.

This fundamental contradiction was enhanced as new corporate structures were granted increasing powers, not by democratic procedures but mainly by courts and lawyers who converted what Jefferson called the "banking institutions and monied incorporations," which he said would destroy freedom and which he could barely see the beginnings of in his day. They were converted, mainly through courts and lawyers, into "immortal persons" with powers and rights beyond the worst nightmares of precapitalist thinkers like Adam Smith or Thomas Jefferson. Half a century earlier, Adam Smith already warned against this, though he could barely see the beginnings of it.

Jefferson's distinction between aristocrats and democrats was developed about a half a century later by Bakunin, the anarchist thinker and activist. It was actually one of the few predictions of the social sciences ever to have come true. It ought to have a place of honor in any serious academic curriculum in the social sciences and the humanities for this reason alone. Back in the nineteenth century, Bakunin predicted that the rising intelligentsia of the nineteenth century would follow one of two parallel paths. One path would be to exploit popular struggles to take state power, becoming what he called a "Red bureaucracy" that will impose the most cruel and vicious regime in history. That's one strain. The other strain, he said, will be those who discover that real power lies elsewhere, and they will become its "bought priesthood," in the words of the labor press, serving the real masters in the state-supported private system of power, either as managers or apologists "who beat the people with the people's stick," as he put it, in the state capitalist democracies. The similarities are pretty striking, and they run right up to the present. They help account for the rapid transitions that people make from one to the other position. It looks like a funny transition, but in fact it's a common ideology. We're seeing it right now in Eastern Europe with the group that's sometimes called the Nomenklatura capitalists, the old communist ruling class, now the biggest enthusiasts for the market, enriching themselves as the societies become standard Third World societies. The move is very easy because it's basically the same ideology. A similar move from Stalinist apologist to "celebration of America" is quite standard in modern history, and it doesn't require much of a shift in values, just a shift in judgment as to where power lies.

Fear of democracy is deeply entrenched. Alexander Hamilton put it clearly when he described the people as a "great beast" from which governing elites have to be protected. These ideas have become ever more entrenched in educated circles as Jefferson's fears and Bakunin's predictions were increasingly realized. The basic attitudes coming into this century were expressed very clearly by Woodrow Wilson's secretary of state,

Robert Lansing—attitudes that led to Wilson's Red Scare, as it was called, which destroyed labor and independent thought for a decade. Lansing warned of the danger of allowing the "ignorant and incapable mass of humanity" to become "dominant in the earth" or even influential, as he believed the Bolsheviks intended. That's the hysterical and utterly erroneous reaction that's pretty standard among people who feel that their power is threatened.

Those concerns were articulated very clearly by progressive intellectuals of the period, maybe the leading one being Walter Lippmann in his essays on democracy, mainly in the 1920s. Lippmann was also the dean of American journalism and one of the most distinguished commentators on public affairs for many years. He advised that "the public must be put in its place" so that the "responsible men" may "live free of the trampling and the roar of a bewildered herd," Hamilton's beast. In a democracy, Lippmann held, these "ignorant and meddlesome outsiders" do have a "function." Their function is to be "interested spectators of action" but not "participants." They are to lend their weight periodically to some member of the leadership class, that's called elections, and then they are supposed to return to their private concerns. In fact, similar notions became part of mainstream academic theory at about the same time.

In the presidential address to the American Political Science Association in 1934 William Shepard argued that government should be in the hands of "an aristocracy of intellect and power," while the "ignorant, the uninformed and the antisocial elements" must not be permitted to control elections, as he mistakenly believed they had done in the past. One of the founders of modern political science, Harold Lasswell, one of the founders of the field of communications, in fact, wrote in the *Encyclopedia of Social Sciences* in 1933 or 1934 that modern techniques of propaganda, which had been impressively refined by Wilsonian liberals, provided the way to keep the public in line.

Wilson's World War I achievements in propaganda impressed others, including Adolf Hitler. But crucially they impressed the American business community. That led to a huge expansion of the public-relations industry which was dedicated to controlling the public mind, as advocates used to put it in more honest days, just as, writing in the *Encyclopedia of Social Sciences* in 1933, Lasswell described what he was talking about as propaganda. We don't use that term. We're more sophisticated.

As a political scientist, Lasswell advocated more sophisticated use of this new technique of control of the general public that was provided by modern propaganda. That would, he said, enable the intelligent men of the community, the natural rulers, to overcome the threat of the great beast who may undermine order because of, in Lasswell's terms, "the ignorance and stupidity of the masses." We should not succumb to "democratic dogmatisms about men being the best judges of their own interests." The best judges are the elites, who must be ensured the means to impose their will for the common good. Jefferson's aristocrats, in other words.

Lippmann and Lasswell represent the more liberal, progressive fringe of opinion, which grants the beast at least a spectator role. At the reactionary end you get those who are mislabeled conservatives in contemporary newspeak. So the Reaganite statist reactionaries thought that the public, the beast, shouldn't even have the spectator role. That explains their fascination with clandestine terror operations, which were not secret to anybody except the American public, certainly not to their victims. Clandestine terror operations were designed to leave the domestic population ignorant. They also advocated absolutely unprecedented measures of censorship and agitprop and other measures to ensure that the powerful and interventionist state that they fostered would serve as a welfare state for the rich and not troubled by the rabble. The huge increase in business propaganda in recent years, the recent assault on the universities by right-wing foundations, and other tendencies of the current period are other manifestations of the same concerns. These concerns were awakened by what liberal elites had called the "crisis of democracy" that developed in the 1960s, when previously marginalized and apathetic sectors of the population, like women and young people and old people and working people and so on, sought to enter the public arena, where they have no right to be, as all right-thinking aristocrats understand.

John Dewey was one of the relics of the Enlightenment classical liberal tradition who opposed the rule of the wise, the onslaught of the Jeffersonian aristocrats, whether they found their place on the reactionary or the liberal part of this very narrow ideological spectrum. Dewey understood clearly that "politics is the shadow cast on society by big business," and as long as this is so, "attenuation of the shadow will not change the substance." Meaning, reforms are of limited utility. Democracy requires that the source of the shadow be removed not only because of its domination of the political arena but because the very institutions of private power undermine democracy and freedom. Dewey was very explicit about the antidemocratic power that he had in mind. To quote him, "Power today"—this is the 1920s—"resides in control of the means of production, exchange, publicity, transportation and communication. Whoever owns them rules the life of the country," even if democratic forms remain. "Business for private profit through private control of banking, land, industry reinforced by command of the press, press agents and other means of publicity and propaganda," that is the system of actual power, the source of coercion and control, and until it's unraveled we can't talk seriously about democracy and freedom. Education, he hoped, of the kind he was talking about, the production of free human beings, would be one of the means of undermining this absolutist monstrosity.

In a free and democratic society, Dewey held, workers should be "the masters of their own industrial fate," not tools rented by employers. He agreed on fundamental issues with the founders of classical liberalism and with the democratic and libertarian sentiments that animated the popular working-class movements from the early Industrial Revolution, until they were finally beaten down by a combination of violence and propaganda. In the field of education, therefore, Dewey held that it is "illiberal and immoral" to train children to work "not freely and intelligently, but for the sake of the work earned," in which case their activity is "not free because not freely participated in." Again the conception of classical liberalism and the workers' movements. Therefore, Dewey held, industry must also change "from a feudalistic to a democratic social order" based on control by working people and free association, again, traditional anarchist ideals with their source in classical liberalism and the Enlightenment.

As the doctrinal system has narrowed under the assault of private power, particularly in the past few decades, these fundamental libertarian values and principles now sound exotic and extreme, perhaps even anti-American, to borrow one of the terms of contemporary totalitarian thought in the West. Given these changes, it's useful to remember that the kinds of ideas that Dewey was expressing are as American as apple pie. They have origins in straight American traditions, right in the mainstream; not influenced by any dangerous foreign ideologies; in a worthy tradition that's ritually lauded, though it's commonly distorted and forgotten. And all of that is part of the deterioration of functioning democracy in the current age, both at the institutional and at the ideological level, in my opinion.

Education is, of course, in part a matter of schools and colleges and the formal information systems. That's true whether the goal of education is education for freedom and democracy, as Dewey advocated, or education for obedience and subordination and marginalization, as the dominant institutions require. The University of Chicago sociologist James Coleman, one of the main students of education and effects of experience on children's lives, concludes from many studies that the total effect of home background is considerably greater than the total effect of school variables in determining student achievement. So it's therefore important to have a look at how social policy and the dominant culture are shaping these factors, home influences and so on.

That's a very interesting topic. The inquiry is much facilitated by a UNICEF study published a year ago called *Child Neglect in Rich Societies,* written by a well-known American economist, Sylvia Ann Hewlett. She studies the preceding fifteen years, the late 1970s up through the early 1990s, in the rich nations. She's not talking about the Third World but about the rich countries. She finds a sharp split between the Anglo-American societies on the one hand and continental Europe and Japan on the other hand. The Anglo-American model, spearheaded by the Reaganites and Thatcher, has been a disaster for children and families, she says. The European-Japanese model, in contrast, has improved their situation considerably, from a starting point that was already considerably higher, despite the fact that these societies lack the huge advantages of the Anglo-American societies. The U.S. has unparalleled wealth and advantages, and while the United Kingdom, Britain, has severely declined, particularly under Thatcher, it has the economic advantage, at least, of being a U.S. client as well as being a major oil exporter in the Thatcher years. That's something that makes the economic failure of Thatcherism even more dramatic, as authentic British conservatives like Lord Ian Gilmour have shown.

Hewlett describes the Anglo-American disaster for children and families as attributable "to the ideological preference for free markets." Here she's only half right, in my opinion. Reaganite conservatism opposed free markets. It did advocate markets for the poor, but it went well beyond even its statist predecessors in demanding and winning a very high level of public subsidy and state protection for the rich. Whatever you choose to call this guiding ideology, it's unfair to tarnish the good name of conservatism by applying it to this particular form of violent and lawless and reactionary statism. Call it what you like, but it's not conservatism. It's not the free market. However, Hewlett is quite right in identifying the free market for the poor as the source of the disaster for families and children. And there isn't much doubt of the effects of what Hewlett calls the "anti-child spirit that is loose in these lands," in the Anglo-American lands, most dramatically in the U.S., but also Britain. This "neglect-filled Anglo-American model" based on market discipline for the poor has largely privatized child rearing while making it effectively impossible for most of the population to rear children. That's been the combined goal and policy of Reaganite conservatism and the Thatcherite analogue. The result is, of course, a disaster for children and families.

Continuing, Hewlett points out, "in the much more supportive European model," social policy has strengthened rather than weakened support systems for families and children. It's no secret, except as usual to readers of the press. As far as I'm aware, this 1993 study, rather critically relevant to our current concerns, has yet to be reviewed anywhere. It's not been, say, featured in the *New York Times,* although the *Times* did devote last Sunday's book review section largely to this topic, with somber forebodings about the fall of IQs, the decline of SAT scores, and so on and what might be causing it. Say, in the city of New York, where the social policies that have been pursued and backed by the *Times* have driven about 40 percent of the children below the poverty level, so that they're suffering malnutrition, disease, and so on. But it turns out that that is irrelevant to the decline in IQs, as is anything that Hewlett discusses in this Anglo-American neglect-filled model. What's relevant, it turns out, is bad genes. Somehow people are getting bad genes, and then there are various speculations about why this is. For example, maybe it's because black mothers don't nurture their children, and the reason is maybe they evolved in Africa, where the climate was hostile. So those are maybe the reasons, and this is really serious, hardheaded science, and a democratic society will ignore all this at its peril, the reviewer says. Well-disciplined commissars know well enough to steer away from the obvious factors, the ones rooted in very plain and clear social policy. They are perfectly evident to anybody with their head screwed on and happen to be discussed in considerable detail by a well-known economist in a UNICEF study that's not likely to see the light of day around here.

The facts are no secret. A blue-ribbon commission of the State Boards of Education and the American Medical Association reported, "Never before has one generation of children been less healthy, less cared for or less prepared for life than their parents were at the same age." That's a big shift in an industrial society. It's only in the Anglo-American societies where this antichild, antifamily spirit has reigned for fifteen years under the guise of conservatism and family values. That's a real triumph for propaganda.

A symbolic expression of this disaster is that when Hewlett wrote her book a year ago, 146 countries had ratified the international Convention on the Rights of the Child, but one had not: the U.S. That's a standard pattern for international conventions on human rights. However, just for fairness, it's only proper to add that Reaganite conservatism is catholic in its antichild, antifamily spirit. The World Health Organization voted to condemn the Nestle Corporation for aggressive marketing of infant formula, which kills plenty of children. The vote was 118 to 1. I'll leave you to guess the one. However, this is quite minor compared with what the World Health Organization calls the "silent genocide" that's killing millions of children every year as a result of the free-market policies for the poor and the refusal of the rich to give aid. Again, the U.S. has one of the worst and most miserly records among the rich societies.

Another symbolic expression of this disaster is a new line of greeting cards by the Hallmark Corporation. One of them says, "Have a super day at school." That one, they tell you, is to be put under a box of cereal in the morning, so that when the children go off to school they'll have a warm and caring message. Another one says, "I wish I had more time to tuck you in." That's one that you stick under the pillow at night when the kid goes to sleep alone. [Laughter] There are other such examples. In part this disaster for children and families is the result simply of falling wages. State corporate policy has been designed for the last years, especially under the Reaganites and Thatcher, to enrich small sectors and to impoverish the majority, and it succeeded. It's had exactly the intended effect. That means that people have to work much longer hours to survive. For much of the population both parents have to work maybe fifty hours merely to provide necessities. Meanwhile, incidentally, corporate profits are zooming. *Fortune* magazine talks about the "dazzling" profits reaching new heights for the Fortune 500 even though sales are stagnating.

Another factor is job insecurity, what economists like to call "flexibility in the labor markets," which is a good thing under the reigning academic theology but a pretty rotten thing for human beings, whose fate doesn't enter into the calculations of sober thinking. Flexibility means you better work extra hours, without knowing whether you have a job tomorrow, or else. There are no contracts and no rights. That's flexibility. We've got to get rid of market rigidities. Economists can explain it. When both parents are working extra hours, and for many on falling incomes, it doesn't take a great genius to predict the outcome. The statistics show them. You can read them in Hewlett's UNICEF study if you like. It's perfectly obvious without reading them what's going to happen. She reports that contact time, that is, actual time spent by parents with children, has declined sharply in the last twenty-five years in the Anglo-American societies, mostly in recent years. That's actually ten to twelve hours a week. What they call "high-quality time," time when you're not just doing something else, is declining. That leads to the destruction of family identity and values. It leads to sharply increased reliance on television for child supervision. It leads to what are called "latchkey children," kids who are alone, a factor in rising child alcoholism and drug use and in criminal violence against children by children and other obvious effects in health, education, ability to participate in a democratic society, even survival, and decline in SATs and IQs, but you're not supposed to notice that. That's bad genes, remember.

None of these things is a law of nature. These are consciously selected social policies designed for particular goals, namely, enrich the Fortune 500 but impoverish others. In Europe, where conditions are more stringent but policy is not guided by the same antifamily, antichild spirit, the tendencies are in the opposite direction, and the standards for children and families are much better.

It's worth mentioning, and let me stress, that this is not just true in the Anglo-American societies themselves. We're a big, powerful state. We have influence. It's very striking to notice what happens when other countries within the range of our influence try to undertake policies that benefit families and children. There are several striking examples.

The region that we control most completely is the Caribbean and Central America. There are two countries there that did undertake such policies—Cuba and Nicaragua—and with considerable success, in fact. Something which should surprise no one is that those are the two countries that were primarily targeted for U.S. assault. And it succeeded. So in Nicaragua, the rising health standards and the improvement in literacy and the reduction in child malnutrition have been reversed thanks to the terrorist war that we fought in Nicaragua, and now it's proceeding to the level of Haiti. In the case of Cuba, of course, the terrorist war has been going on a lot longer. It was launched by John F. Kennedy. It had nothing to do with communism. There weren't any Russians around. It had to do with things like the fact that these people were devoting resources to the wrong sectors of the population. They were improving health standards. They were concerned with children, with malnutrition. Therefore we launched a huge terrorist war. A bunch of CIA documents were just released recently filling in some of the details of the Kennedy period, which was bad enough. It continues up to the present. Actually, there was another assault just a couple of days ago. On top of that there's an embargo to try to ensure that they'll really suffer. For years the pretext was that this had to do with the Russians, which is completely fraudulent, as you can see by what was going on when the policies were instituted and as is demonstrated conclusively by what happened after the Russians disappeared. Here was a real job for the bought priesthood. They have to not notice that after the Russians disappeared we harshened the attack against Cuba. Kind of odd if the reason for the attack was that they were an outpost of communism and the Russian Empire. But we can handle that.

So after the Russians disappeared from the scene and it really became possible to strangle them, the conditions got harsher. A proposal was sent through Congress by a liberal Democrat, Representative

[Robert] Torricelli, calling for a cutoff of any trade with Cuba by any subsidiary of any American corporation or any foreign corporation that used any parts produced in the U.S. That is so obviously in violation of international law that George Bush vetoed it. However, he was forced to accept it when he was outflanked from the right by the Clintonites in the last election, so he did then allow it to go through. That went right to the United Nations, where the U.S. position was denounced by just about everybody. In the final vote, the U.S. could pick up only Israel, which is automatic, and they got Rumania for some reason. Everyone else voted against it. The U.S. position was defended by no one. It is an obvious violation of international law, as even Britain and others pointed out. But it doesn't matter. It's extremely important to carry out our antichild, antifamily spirit and our insistence on highly polarized societies everywhere we can go. If a foreign country under our control tries to go a different way, we'll take care of them, too.

That's now continuing. It's the kind of thing you can actually do something about if you like. In Chicago there are the Pastors for Peace and the Chicago–Cuba Coalition, which have another caravan going to Cuba to try to undermine the embargo and bring humanitarian aid, medicines, medical books, powdered milk for infants, and other assistance. They're in the phone book under Chicago–Cuba Coalition. You can look them up. Anyone who is interested in countering the antichild, antifamily spirit that reigns here and that we're exporting by violence elsewhere can do that, just as they can do plenty of things at home.

I should say that the effects of this latest Democratic proposal, which went through, to strangle Cuba have recently been reviewed in this month's issues, October, of two leading American medical journals, *Neurology* and the *Florida Journal of Medicine*, which simply review the effects. They point out the obvious thing. It turns out that about 90 percent of the trade that was cut off by the Clinton–Torricelli bill was food and humanitarian aid, medicine, and things like that. For example, one Swedish company that was trying to export a water filtration device to create vaccines was blocked by the U.S. because there's some part in it that's American made. We really have to strangle them badly. We have to make sure that plenty of children die. One effect is a very sharp rise in infant mortality and child malnutrition. Another is a rare neurological disease that's spread over Cuba that everyone pretended they didn't know the reasons for. It's a result of malnutrition, a disease which hasn't been seen since Japanese prison camps in World War II. So we're succeeding in that one. The antichild, antifamily spirit is not just directed against kids in New York, but much more broadly.

I stress again that it is different in Europe, and there are reasons for it. One of the differences is the existence of a strong trade union movement. That's one aspect of a more fundamental difference—namely, the U.S. is a business-run society to quite an unparalleled degree, and as a result the vile maxim of the masters prevails to an unprecedented extent, pretty much as you'd expect. These are among the means that allow democracy to function formally, although by now most of the population is consumed by what the press calls "antipolitics," meaning hatred of government, disdain for political parties and the whole democratic process. That, too, is a great victory for the aristocrats in Jefferson's sense, that is, those who fear and distrust the people and wish to draw all power from them into the hands of the higher classes. By now that means into the hands of transnational corporations and the states and quasi-governmental institutions that serve their interests.

Another victory is the fact that the disillusionment, which is rampant, is antipolitics. A *New York Times* headline on this reads, "Anger and Cynicism Well Up in Voters as Hope Gives Way. Mood Turns Ugly as More People Become Disillusioned with Politics." Last Sunday's magazine section was devoted to antipolitics. Notice, not devoted to opposition to power and authority, to the easily identifiable forces that have their hands on the lever of decision making and that cast their shadow on society as politics, as Dewey put it. They have to be invisible. The *Times* has a story today again about this topic where they quote some uneducated person who doesn't get the point. He says, "Yeah, Congress is rotten, but that's because Congress is big business, so of course it's rotten." That's the story you're not supposed to see. You're supposed to be antipolitics. The reason is that whatever you think about government, it's the one part of the system of institutions that you can participate in and modify and do something about. By law and principle you can't do anything about investment firms or transnational corporations. Therefore nobody better see that. You've got to be antipolitics. That's another victory.

Dewey's observation that politics is the shadow cast on society by big business, which was incidentally also a truism to Adam Smith, has now become almost invisible. The force that casts the shadow has been pretty much removed by the ideological institutions and is so remote from consciousness that we're left with antipolitics. That's another severe blow to democracy and a grand gift to the absolutist and unaccountable systems of power that have reached levels that a Thomas Jefferson or John Dewey could scarcely imagine.

We have the usual choices. We can choose to be democrats in Thomas Jefferson's sense. We can choose to be aristocrats. The latter path is the easy one. That's the one that the institutions are designed to reward. It can bring rich rewards, given the locus of wealth and privilege and power and the ends that they very naturally seek. The other path, the path of the Jeffersonian democrats, is one of struggle, often defeat, but also rewards of a kind that can't even be imagined by those who succumb to the new spirit of the age, gain wealth, forgetting all but self. It's the same now as it was 150 years ago when there was an attempt to drive it into the heads of the factory girls in Lowell and the craftsmen in Lawrence and so on. Today's world is very far from Thomas Jefferson's. The choices it offers, however, have not changed in any fundamental way.

NOTE

This article was originally delivered as a lecture at Loyola University, Chicago, 19 October 1994.

3

THE CRAFT OF "HISTORICAL ENGINEERING"

1. THE CRAFT OF "HISTORICAL ENGINEERING"[1]

The vocation of "historical engineering" is as old as history and was recognized as a professional responsibility as the United States entered World War I. A closer look at particular cases sheds light on how the system works. Two cases will be examinated here as illustrations, drawn from a major government-media project of the 1980s: "demonizing the Sandinistas" while defending Washington's terror states.

One of the proofs that Nicaragua is a cancer causing subversion to spread through the hemisphere, as plausible as others, is that the Sandinistas supplied arms for a terrorist attack on the Palace of Justice by M-19 guerrillas in Colombia in November 1985. On January 5 and 6, 1986, the *New York Times* published stories on the Colombian charge against Nicaragua and Nicaragua's denial. The next day, January 7, Colombia officially accepted the Nicaraguan denial. The Colombian foreign minister stated in a news conference that "Colombia accepts Nicaraguan Foreign Minister Miguel D'Escoto's explanation and considers the incident closed." This news made it to page 81 of the *Boston Globe,* in the sports section. The *Times* did not report the fact at all; rather, its editorial the following day asserted that "Colombia's patience has since been strained by evidence—which Nicaragua disputes—that the Sandinistas supplied guns to terrorists who staged" the November incident. On January 15, the *Times* reported that "American officials have linked Nicaragua to the Terrorism in Bogota"—a charge denied by the Nicaraguan government—and published an opinion column by Elliott Abrams repeating the charges that both Abrams and the editors knew to be without merit. These were repeated in a news column of February 26, again ignoring the fact that Colombia had officially rejected the charges and considered the incident closed. The *Washington Post* also failed to report Colombia's acceptance of Nicaragua's disclaimer of responsibility.[2]

On March 18, a *Times* editorial entitled "The Nicaragua Horror Show" discussed Reagan's "appeal for $100 million to help the 'contras' against Nicaragua's leftist tyrants." The editorial was critical of a Reagan speech so replete with falsehoods and unsupported allegations that it elicited some discomfort. The editors urged that "Mr. Reagan should have held to [the] undeniable transgressions" of the Sandinistas; he should have asked how they can be "contained and what can the United States do to promote democracy in Nicaragua," raising it to the standards of Washington's terror states. They present a list of "the hemisphere's real grievances," namely, Nicaragua's "totalitarian" domestic policies and complication of "the region's security problems" by building the biggest military airfield in Central America and a deep-water port in the Caribbean, with Soviet-bloc aid, and its support for "guerrilla comrades in El Salvador." The list of "undeniable transgressions" concludes as follows: "more than piety explains why Tomas Borge, the Interior Minister, participated in a mass for the M-19 guerrillas who shot up the Palace of Justice in Bogota, Colombia," sure proof of Sandinista complicity in the terrorist attack. Others too were impressed by this proof of Sandinista iniquity. William Beecher, diplomatic correspondent of the *Boston Globe*, highlighted the attendance of Borge at the "memorial service for the M-19 guerrillas" who used "arms allegedly supplied by Nicaragua"; this is the kind of "mistake" that "serious analysts" hope will be caused by "rising military pressure" against Nicaragua, he observed, apparently forgetting that, nine days earlier, his newspaper had reported Colombia's dismissal of the allegation?[3]

A reader in Arizona, Dr. James Hamilton, was curious to learn the basis for the renewed charge by the *Times* editors, which he knew had been denied by the Colombian government. He wrote a series of letters to *Times* editor Max Frankel and, after receiving a dismissive form letter from foreign editor Warren Hoge, to him as well. After many attempts to obtain a response to this simple question, he finally received a letter from Hoge in mid-July. "In answer to your question about Tomas Borge,"

Hoge wrote, "Mr. Borge attended a mass in Managua celebrated by the Rev. Uriel Molina commemorating the first anniversary of the death of Enrique Schmidt, the Minister of Communications, who had been killed in a battle with the contras. During the service, a member of the congregation shouted for prayers for the M-19 and unfurled their flag."[4] Hamilton writes, "Thus, did a memorial service for a former Sandinista cabinet member become, in the hands of an editorial writer, 'a mass for the M-19 guerrillas,' permitting the *Times* to misrepresent Borge and imply an affiliation between the Sandinistas and the M-19, using the behavior of one individual in the church on that day as support for this contention." Some tales are just too useful to abandon.[5]

The remainder of the "undeniable transgressions" on the *Times* list fare no better and are, in fact, of some interest with regard to the hysteria evoked in establishment circles over Nicaragua's unwillingness to follow orders and its unconscionable efforts to survive a U.S. attack.

A more important requirement has been to establish a "symmetry" between the contras and the Salvadoran guerrillas. This "symmetry" was crucial for U.S. government propaganda, and hence a media staple. It is readily established by ignoring the scale and character of U.S. aid to the contras and direct involvement in their terror, and by the insistent claim that although rebels in El Salvador deny receiving support from Nicaragua, "ample evidence shows it exists, and it is questionable how long they could survive without it," as James LeMoyne reported after the Central American peace accords were signed in August 1987.[6] LeMoyne presented no evidence, then or ever, to support this claim. He has yet to comment on the failure of the U.S. government, which is not entirely lacking in facilities, to provide any credible evidence since early 1981—and little enough then—as was noted by the World Court, which reviewed the public materials produced by the U.S. government to establish its case, dismissing them as lacking substantive basis.[7] The claim is a propaganda necessity; therefore it is true.

Times efforts to protect the required fact are illuminating. After LeMoyne's statement appeared, the media-monitoring organization Fairness and Accuracy in Media (FAIR) wrote the *Times* asking it to share LeMoyne's "ample evidence" with its readers. Their letter was not published, but they received a private communication from foreign editor Joseph Lelyveld acknowledging that LeMoyne had been "imprecise."[8]

After the September 1987 acknowledgment that the charges were "imprecise," the *Times* had many opportunities to correct the imprecision, and used them—to repeat the charges that are privately acknowledged to be without merit. Thus, in his contribution to the media barrage organized in December in connection with the Sandinista defector Roger Miranda, LeMoyne announced that in response to Miranda's charges, Defense Minister Ortega "seemed indirectly to confirm the existence of Sandinista assistance to Salvadoran rebels." This is LeMoyne's rendition of Ortega's statement that the Reagan administration had no right to produce such charges given its arming of the contras. What Ortega went on to say, unreported, is that "the Salvadoran guerrillas have some resources and ways to get weapons" and they "are basically armed through their own efforts," not depending "on outside sources; they are self-sufficient." Thus Ortega's denial of Nicaraguan support for Salvadoran guerrillas is neatly converted by LeMoyne and the *Times* into a "confirmation" of such support.[9]

LeMoyne's *Times* colleagues also joined in the fray. Stephen Engelberg wrote that the U.S. government charge "appears to have been confirmed" by Miranda, who "said the Sandinistas were shipping the weapons to El Salvador by sea," that is, "via the Gulf of Fonseca."[10] The Gulf is thirty kilometers wide, heavily patrolled by U.S. naval vessels and SEAL teams, and covered by a radar facility on Tiger Island in the Gulf that is able to locate and track boats not only in that area but far beyond, as discussed in World Court testimony by David MacMichael, the CIA specialist responsible for analyzing the relevant material during the period to which Engelberg refers. Despite these extensive efforts, no evidence could be produced, though Nicaragua, curiously, has no difficulty providing evidence of CIA supplies in the supposedly "symmetrical" situation. It takes a measure of self-control to refrain from ridicule at this point.

After the peace accords were finally dismantled in January 1988, George Volsky wrote that the provision of the accords calling "for all countries to deny the use of their territories to insurgents in neighboring nations . . . applies mainly to Nicaragua, which is said to be helping rebels in El Salvador, and to Honduras, whose territory is reportedly an important part of the United States–directed contra supply effort."[11]

Surely a fair summary of the available evidence on the support for irregular and insurrectionist forces outlawed by the accords.

Volsky did not explain why the same provision of the accords is inapplicable to El Salvador, which is also "reportedly" involved in the U.S. support structure for the contras, or to Costa Rica, which "has long been the base for the more liberal faction of the Nicaraguan rebels" and where "the Costa Rican–based contras" continue to operate, as we regularly learn when news reports cite a "contra source in Costa Rica," and as we would learn in greater detail if there were some interest in the facts.[12]

LeMoyne later warned that if in the future "the Sandinistas [are] found still to be aiding Salvadoran guerrillas," then the peace accords will collapse; he mentioned no similar problem elsewhere. As for Honduras, LeMoyne cautiously observed several months later that its support for the contras "*appears* to be a direct violation of the accord."[13] His colleague, *Times* military correspondent Bernard Trainor, observed that "to this date, the amount of support provided by the Sandinistas to the Salvadoran guerrillas has never been established conclusively"—*Times* jargon to express the fact that no credible evidence has been presented since a trickle of aid flowed for a few months seven years earlier, well after the U.S.-backed security forces had launched a "war of extermination and genocide against a defenseless civilian population" (Bishop Rivera y Damas, the successor of the assassinated Archbishop Romero).[14]

So required doctrine is established.

No less interesting is the fact that it is taken for granted by hawks and doves alike that it would have been a major crime to provide the defenseless civilian population with means to defend themselves against a war of extermination and genocide—at least, when the war is conducted by U.S. clients, with U.S. support and, as it reached its climax, direct organization and participation. To have provided victims of Pol Pot with arms to defend themselves, had this been possible, would have been considered a sign of true nobility. It is enlightening that such simple observations as these, and their obvious import, are next to unintelligible.

In late 1988, LeMoyne completed his four-year assignment as *New York Times* correspondent in El Salvador and took the occasion to publish a comprehensive analysis of aid to the Salvadoran guerrillas.[15] Fifteen months had passed since he had written, shortly after the signing of the peace accords, of the "ample evidence" that Nicaraguan aid to the guerrillas in El Salvador was so extensive that "it is questionable how long they could survive without it." Fourteen months had passed since the foreign editor of the *Times* had agreed that the "ample evidence" did not exist, and nine months since he had instructed LeMoyne to devote an entire article to the actual evidence, such as it may be (see note 8). The results of this nine-month inquiry merit a careful look.

Gone completely is the "ample evidence" of the aid from Nicaragua on which the Salvadoran guerrillas relied for their very existence. LeMoyne makes no reference to his claims of the past, or to the request that he produce his "ample evidence," or to the contribution his unsubstantiated allegations made to the project of "demonizing the Sandinistas," protecting the murderous U.S. clients, and undercutting the peace accords.

It turns out now that the evidence is "largely circumstantial and is open to differing interpretations." It is not "ample" but is, rather, "limited evidence," of which nothing credible is provided. Furthermore, this "limited evidence" indicates that shipments "are small and probably sporadic," not the large-scale aid that kept the Salvadoran guerrillas alive according to the version of August 1987 and since—conclusions that will hardly surprise those who have been studying U.S. government propaganda on the matter during the past years. The "limited evidence" has to do with trans-shipments from the Soviet bloc, primarily Cuba, LeMoyne asserts—again without evidence. Reading on, we find that there seems to be at least as much evidence of direct arms transfers from the contras to the Salvadoran guerrillas and of Honduran army involvement in trans-shipment of arms to them. This also comes as no surprise to those who have taken the trouble to *read* government propaganda instead of simply reporting the press release; thus a State Department background paper of 1984 presented testimony of a Sandinista defector who provided no credible evidence of Sandinista arms supply but did allege that arms were coming from Mexico and Guatemala"[16] (it is also likely, but not investigated, that when the U.S. proxies broke for the border in February 1988 after their thrice-daily supply flights were curtailed, they began selling their arms to corrupt Honduran officers, who sell them in turn to Salvadoran guerrillas, a matter to which we return directly). The major Sandinista contribution to the Salvadoran guerrillas, LeMoyne now informs the reader, is a "safe haven" in Nicaragua for offices, logistics, and communications and the opportunity to travel through Nicaragua to other countries. The same is true of many other countries outside of the United States or its dependencies; and all states of the region, including Costa Rica, have always afforded such support—indeed far more—to the U.S. proxy forces attacking Nicaragua.

The careful reader will therefore discover that the whole charade of many years has collapsed. As was always obvious, the tales of "symmetry" hardly merit ridicule. The fraud was successfully maintained as long as support for the contras was an important and viable policy option; then it was necessary to present the U.S. proxy forces as authentic guerrillas, thus to insist upon the "symmetry" between the contras attacking Nicaragua and the indigenous guerrillas in El Salvador, both dependent on outside aid for survival. By late 1988, the contra option was losing its residual appeal, in part because it was no longer needed as a means to achieve the goal of maximizing civilian suffering and discontent in Nicaragua and reducing the country to ruin, in part because it was proving impossible to keep the proxy forces in the field. The tale can therefore be allowed to fade—without, however, any acknowledgment of what came before. That is to be removed from history and surely will be.

The rules of the game are that established power sets the terms of debate. The government-media system produces claims about Sandinista aid to the Salvadoran guerrillas and reiterates them insistently, in full knowledge that they are groundless, as long as they are needed for the cause. Occasionally a skeptic is allowed to intrude with the observation that the evidence is meager indeed. The question of Salvadoran aid to the U.S.-run contra forces, however, is off the agenda and is not investigated even though there is no doubt about the use of El Salvador to attack Nicaragua through 1986, and the same sources that told the truth then, but were ignored, allege that the process continues and are ignored. As long as it was serviceable, the absurd "symmetry" thesis was maintained, and the doctrine of crucial outside sustenance now put aside can be resurrected whenever it may be needed, the basis having been laid in general consciousness despite the quiet retraction.[17] Mainstream discussion is closed to the thought that Nicaragua and other governments—and individuals, were this possible—*should* send aid to people trying to defend themselves from the rampaging armies and death squads of a military regime implanted by a foreign power. A closer look at the forbidden question would yield some interesting conclusions about the prevailing moral and intellectual climate, but it would stray so far from the consensus of power that it is unthinkable.

We may note finally that not all defectors enjoy the royal treatment accorded to the Sandinista defector Miranda, critically timed in the final phase of the government-media campaign to demolish the unwanted peace accords. In the case of Miranda, the media barrage began with two long front-page articles in the *Washington Post* (13 December 1987) and continued for weeks as the media relayed State Department propaganda based upon his testimony, with its ominous warning that Nicaragua might attempt to defend the national territory from CIA supply flights to the U.S. proxy forces; the allegation that Nicaragua was thumbing its nose at the impotent U.S. Navy by merrily sending arms to El Salvador, undetected, via the Gulf of Fonseca; and the report that the Sandinistas were planning to reduce their regular military forces and provide light arms to citizens for defense against a possible U.S. invasion, a report transmuted by the independent media into a threat to "overwhelm and terrorize" their neighbors.[18]

Compare, in contrast, the media reaction to the defection of Horacio Arce, chief of intelligence of the FDN (the main contra force) from 1985. After receiving asylum in the Mexican Embassy in Tegucigalpa, Arce left for Mexico City in November 1988, then for Managua under the government amnesty program. While in Mexico City, he was interviewed and had a number of interesting things to say.

The contra chief of intelligence provided details of support for the contras by the Pentagon in violation of congressional restrictions, including training by U.S. military instructors through 1986 at a U.S. air base in a southern state, a semisecret base with seventeen airstrips, which they reached in Hercules C-130 transports without passing through immigration or customs, of course. The trainers were from Fort Bragg. After the 1982 Falklands/Malvinas war, the contras in Honduras lost their Argentine trainers and advisers, but in the U.S. base where they were being illegally trained (including Arce himself), the instructors included a specialist in psychological warfare from Chile, so the links to the neofascist states of the U.S. orbit remained.

Arce was also among those trained at the Ilopango air base near San Salvador by Salvadoran and U.S. instructors. In Honduras, they were trained directly by the Honduran military, who had been providing the essential training and logistics from 1980 and also provided pilots for supply flights into Nicaragua. Honduran immigration authorities also assisted, helping the contras gain access to refugee camps for recruitment, sometimes by force. Miskito recruits were trained separately, by a Japanese officer. Most of the supervisors of training and aid were of Hispanic origin—Cubans, Dominicans, Puerto Ricans, South Americans, and some Spaniards. The arms were mainly from Israel, as "everyone knows," much of it captured in the 1982 Lebanon war. "Cubans in the CIA are all over the place," also deeply involved in the extensive corruption. Part of the contra financing came from drug trafficking.

The United States is a global power and is thus capable of constructing elaborate systems of terror and corruption, making use of its client and mercenary states and long-standing relations with international terrorism and criminal syndicates. U.S. Embassy officials in Tegucigalpa, Arce continues, provided the contras with intelligence information and other aid. His contacts at the U.S. Embassy included "Robert McHorn of the CIA or Alexander Zunnerman who ostensibly is with AID but is CIA also." Arce was also in direct contact with the Tegucigalpa AID warehouse on the premises of the Electropura Company. AID has admittedly served as a front for CIA terrorist operations in the past, particularly in Laos during the "clandestine war."

Arce himself had fled Nicaragua with his father, a major in Somoza's National Guard, on the day of the Sandinista victory, July 19, 1979. In 1980, he was recruited for the contras, adopting the nom de guerre Mercenario ("mercenary"). By January 1981, the operation had become "something serious and something big." He went on to reach the rank of *commandante,* becoming intelligence chief after the former chief, Ricardo Lau, was dismissed (and possibly murdered by the contras, Arce believes). Lau had become an embarrassment in early 1985 when former Salvadoran Intelligence Chief Roberto Santivañez implicated him in arranging the assassination of Archbishop Romero and in having played a "key role" in organizing and training death squads in El Salvador and Guatemala, as well as in political killings in Honduras. He was "a thief among thieves," Arce reports.

Not all the contras "are rented," El Mercenario continues; some have loyalties to their chiefs. They are, however, well paid by regional standards. Without a family, Arce earned a salary of about $500 a month.

The Honduran armed forces "participate in every operation that takes place close to the border," while also providing intelligence "on military and nonmilitary targets in Nicaragua." The latter service is particularly important, Arce continues, because "we attack a lot of schools, health centers, and those sort of things. We have tried to make it so that the Nicaraguan government cannot provide social services for the peasants, cannot develop its project . . . that's the idea." Evidently, their U.S. training was successful in getting the basic idea across.

Arce also discussed the vast corruption in the contra organization, from Commander Enrique Bermúdez on down, and their sales of U.S. arms and supplies, "much of it . . . probably ending up in the hands of the guerrillas of El Salvador." In cooperation with Honduran officers, who take a cut for themselves, contras are selling assault rifles and radio-communications equipment to the FMLN in El Salvador—who therefore may be receiving aid from Nicaraguans after all, James LeMoyne and the *Times* will be happy to hear.[19]

Arce had far more of significance to report than Miranda and had a more important role within the contra organization than Miranda did in Nicaragua. Furthermore, as we have seen, the contras were favored with enormous publicity, generally receiving more than the government. But in this case, there was no way to deform the testimony into a weapon for the campaign of "demonizing the Sandinistas" and mobilizing support for the terror states; on the contrary, the message was all wrong. Editors made their choices accordingly.

2. THE OBLIGATION OF SILENCE[20]

As discussed earlier, a doctrine commonly held is that "we tend to flagellate ourselves as Americans about various aspects of our own policies and actions we disapprove of." The reality is rather different.

The prevailing pattern is one of indignant outrage over enemy crimes with much self-congratulatory appeal to high principle, combined with a remarkable ability "not to see" in the case of crimes for which we bear responsibility. In the West, there is an ample literature—much of it fraudulent—scornfully denouncing apologists or alleged apologists for the Soviet Union and Third World victims of U.S. intervention but little about the behavior that is the norm: silence and apologetics about the crimes of one's own state and its clients, when a willingness simply to face the facts might make a substantial difference in limiting or terminating these abuses. This is standard procedure elsewhere as well. In the Soviet sphere, dissidents are condemned as apologists for Western crimes that are bitterly denounced by right-thinking commissars, exactly the pattern mimicked here.

A number of examples have been mentioned, and many have been discussed elsewhere. For evaluating U.S. political culture and the media, the cases to which a serious analyst will immediately turn, apart from the crimes of the United States itself, are those of its major clients: in recent years, El Salvador and Israel. The latter case has been a particularly illuminating one ever since Israel's display of power in 1967 elicited the adulation and awe that has persisted among American intellectuals. The apologetic literature is often little more than a parody of the Stalinist period.[21]

The elaborate campaigns of defamation launched against those who do not satisfy the requirements of the faithful also strike a familiar chord. The effect, as elsewhere, has been to intimidate critics and to facilitate the exercise of violence—and also to erect barriers in the way of a political settlement that has long been feasible.[22]

Israel can be secure that as long as it is perceived as a "strategic asset," it will remain "the symbol of human decency," as the *New York Times* described it while Israeli atrocities in the occupied territories reached such a level that the media briefly took serious notice. Israel can rely upon the American labor movement bureaucracy to justify whatever it does, to explain that although "in their effort to maintain order, Israeli Defense Forces have on occasion resorted to unnecessary force, . . . no doubt such incidents can be attributed to the inexperience of the Israeli army in riot control and other police functions, and to the frustrations of Israeli soldiers as they confront young Palestinians hurling stones and petrol bombs."[23] To fully appreciate this statement and what it means, one must bear in mind that it followed one of the rare periods when the media actually gave some picture of atrocities of the kind that had been taking place for many years in the occupied territories, at a lesser but still scandalous level. John Kifner's reports in the *New York Times* were particularly good examples of professional journalism, consistent with his outstanding record over many years.

Apologetics of the AFL-CIO variety have served for twenty years to authorize harsh repression and endless humiliation, finally reaching the level of regular pogroms in which soldiers break into houses, smash furniture, break bones, and beat teenagers to death after dragging them from their homes; settler violence conducted with virtual impunity; and collective punishments, deportation, and systematic terror on orders of the Defense Ministry. As fashions change, leading figures in the campaign to protect state violence from scrutiny will doubtless create for themselves a different past, but the record is there for those who choose to see.

There has always been an Elie Wiesel to assure the reader that there are only some "regrettable exceptions—immediately corrected by Israeli authorities," while he fulminates about the real crime: the condemnation of Israeli atrocities by public opinion. He tells us of the "dreamlike eyes" of the Israeli soldiers, perhaps those who had been described a few weeks earlier by reservists returning from service in the territories. They reported the "acts of humiliation and violence against Palestinian inhabitants that have become the norm, that almost no one seeks to prevent," including "shameful acts" that they personally witnessed, while the military authorities look the other way.[24] Or perhaps Wiesel has in mind the soldiers who caught a ten-year-old boy and, when he did not respond to their demand that he identify children who had thrown stones, proceeded "to mash his head in," leaving him "looking like a steak," as soldiers put it, also beating the boy's mother when she tried to protect him, only then discovering that the child was deaf, dumb, and mentally retarded. It "didn't bother" the soldiers, one participant in the beating said, and the platoon commander ordered them on to the next chore because "we don't have time for games." Or perhaps Wiesel's point is that "a picture of an Israeli soldier kicking an old Arab woman is no longer news," as the Hebrew press bitterly comments, speaking of those who accept atrocities as readily as the author of *Against Silence,* whose words could actually mitigate suffering and abuse if he were not committed to silence as the proper course.[25] The fact that such consistent behavior over many years is treated with respect, even regarded as saintly, speaks volumes about Western culture.

Given these dispensations, Israel is free to use its phenomenal U.S. aid to send its military forces to conduct the regular operations described in the Israeli press (but rarely here) at the time when Wiesel's thoughts on "regrettable exceptions" appeared: To bar supplies from refugee camps where there is "a serious lack of food." To beat young prisoners so severely that a military doctor in the Ansar 2 detention camp refuses to admit them, one lying "battered and motionless for an hour and a half, surrounded by soldiers, without receiving any medical treatment," then "dumped" from a jeep on the way to the hospital and "brutally beaten" again "in front of dozens of soldiers" (one was allegedly censured). To break into a home and drag out a seven-year-old boy who had been hiding under his bed, then "beat him up savagely in front of his parents and the family," then to beat his father and brother too because they did not reveal the hiding place of the child, while the other children scream hysterically and "the mother cannot calm them because she is told not to move." And to mercilessly beat children of age five and up, sometimes three or four soldiers with sticks, "until [their] hands and legs are broken," or to spray gas directly into their eyes. These are among the horror stories that soldiers report from the miserable Jabaliya refugee camp, where the army has "succeeded in breaking them" so that "they are totally crushed, weak and tired." To rake a boy twelve to fifteen years old over barbed wire "in order to injure him" as prisoners arrive at the Dahariya prison, with no reaction by the officer observing, after vicious beatings of prisoners en route with clubs, plastic pipes, and handcuffs while their commanding officer looked on ("Israeli buses have become torture chambers," Knesset member Dedi Zucker reports, citing these and other atrocities). To rampage freely through Jericho, breaking into houses, brutally beating and humiliating residents. To "run amok" through the Amari refugee camp, "knocking down doors, breaking into houses, smashing furniture, and beating residents, including children," then beating an ambulance driver who arrived on the scene after dragging him by his hair—an elite paratroop unit in this case, marauding with no provocation according to witnesses. To jail a prisoner "in perfect health," leaving him "paralyzed and dumb," "apparently the result of severe beatings and torture . . . he suffered while in detention" at the Jenin interrogation center. To acquit a young Arab imprisoned for setting fire to the car of a suspected police informant when it is discovered that someone else was responsible and that his confession was extracted by torture but without any reference by the district attorney or the court to the false "confession extracted through severe beating" or what that implies. And on and on.[26]

There are other variants. The commander of an elite unit, Willy Shlap, described his first week in the El Burj refugee camp near Jabaliya. An eleven-year-old boy was found throwing a stone and was taken to his house, where his father was ordered to beat him. The father slapped him, but the officer screamed, "Is this a beating? Beat him! Beat him!" The tension mounted and the father "became hysterical," starting to beat the child brutally, knocking him on the floor and kicking him in the ribs as hard as he could. The soldiers were apparently satisfied. When atrocities became even more severe in the summer of 1988, as Wiesel published his reflections, the *Jerusalem Post* reported that, according to UNRWA relief workers and doctors at clinics, the victims of the sharp increase in brutal beatings were mostly "men aged 15 to 30," but the clinics had "also treated 24 boys and five girls aged five and younger" in the past weeks, as well as many older children, such as a seven-year-old boy brought to a clinic "with a bleeding kidney, and bearing club marks." Soldiers routinely beat, kick, and club children, according to doctors and relief officials.[27]

In a case that actually went to trial, and therefore received considerable attention (in Israel, that is), four soldiers of an elite unit of the Givati Brigade were arrested and charged with beating an inhabitant of the Jabaliya camp to death on August 22. The case was first reported in *Ha'aretz* a month later. After children had thrown stones, twenty soldiers broke into a home and began to beat the father of one of the suspected stone throwers, Hani al-Shami. He was kicked and beaten with clubs and weapons. Soldiers jumped on him from the bed while he was lying on the floor, his head bleeding from blows with clubs. His wife was also beaten up by soldiers. An officer arrived, found the severely wounded man bleeding heavily, and ordered him taken to the Military Administration offices, not to a hospital; that is routine procedure. Later, the family was informed that al-Shami was dead. Two soldiers from the same unit said, "It is true that we beat them up and very strongly too, but it is better to break bones than to shoot people," echoing the minister of defense. "We have lost our human image," they said.[28]

After the arrests were announced, other atrocities of the Brigade became public: for example, the story of a journalist from the El Bureij refugee camp, hospitalized after soldiers broke into his home, forced him to kneel on hands and knees and bray like a donkey while they beat him on the testicles, stomach, and back with clubs and electric wires for half an hour and smashed his glasses, shouting, "Now you will be a blind donkey." Soldiers described Givati as "a brigade without law," blaming the commander and the "right-wing orientation," with many units from the Hesder Yeshivot, military-religious training schools known for their ultra-Right fanaticism.[29]

The courts released the four soldiers charged with the murder while the trial proceeded, as briefly noted without comment in the *Jerusalem Post.* The Hebrew press told the story that had been omitted from the version offered to the foreign reading public. A soldier testified at the trial that "the humiliation and the beatings were because of the need to pass the time." Another added that al-Shami's protruding belly particularly amused the soldiers and was "a target for the beatings." An officer testified that he had threatened to kill al-Shami because "his groans disturbed me"; "I shouted at him that he should shut up, or I will kill him." He testified further that in the military compound to which al-Shami had been brought after the beatings, he had asked a doctor to treat al-Shami, but the doctor had refused, only giving an order to wipe the blood from his face. On that day, the witness continued, many Arabs arrived at the command post with their hands tied and eyes covered and were brutally beaten by officers and soldiers. Asked why he had not cared for al-Shami, the witness replied that "the wounded Arab did not interest me, because they are Arabs and want to kill us." Soldiers testified that "the moment you catch a rioter you beat him . . . even if he doesn't resist. It is to deter him." Troops are ordered "to break their legs so they won't be able to walk and break their hands so they won't throw stones." A company commander reported "unequivocal orders" to beat any suspect so as "to put him out of action for a month or two"; it is "necessary," he testified, because jailing suspects is "like taking them to a PLO training seminar." Beatings inside houses are "a daily matter" in Gaza.

The military court accepted the defense plea, ruling that "there is a basis to the claim that the deceased was beaten up in the military stronghold by soldiers whom to our sorrow the investigation did not succeed in identifying." Furthermore, the fact that the soldiers were detained for eighty-three days brings "a correct balance between the needs of the army and the nature of their innocence and the nature of justice." We are dealing with soldiers who "did their military duty and not with criminals," the court ruled. "Nobody had denied that they had brutally beaten an unarmed Arab inside his own home, that they had broken a club or two over his head in front of his children or jumped on him in their boots," Ziva Yariv commented; but there is no legal liability because these beatings might not have been the actual cause of death, "as if there were no law banning the brutal beating of civilians, or the breaking of a club over the body of an innocent man, as if there were no law against vicious attacks or grievous bodily harm."[30]

The military correspondent of *Ha'aretz* observed that there had been a decline in the number of "exceptions" brought to trial, the reason being that "exceptions have become the norm." The Givati soldiers, like the members of an elite paratroop unit tried for rampaging in the Kalandia refugee camp, "did not understand what the fuss is about." They had behaved no differently from soldiers in other units and had been following orders, doing exactly what is expected of them. Brutal beating of prisoners or Arab civilians in their homes or on the streets is simply part of daily life, so they were unjustly tried. Evidently, the court agreed. The Hebrew word *harig,* literally "exception," by now seems to be used to mean little other than "atrocity."[31]

Atrocities are regarded as quite routine by the authorities. Dr. Marcus Levin, who was called for military service in the reserves at the Ansar 2 detention camp Medical Center, reports that he was assigned to check the prisoners "before and after interrogation." Asking why they had to be checked "after interrogation," Levin was informed by the doctors in charge that "it is nothing special, sometimes there are some broken limbs. For example, yesterday they brought in a twelve-year-old boy with two broken legs"—after interrogation. Levin, a sixteen-year army veteran, then went to the commander to tell him, "My name is Marcus Levin and not Joseph Mengele and for reasons of conscience I refuse to serve in a place that reminds me of South American dictatorships." Most, however, find their conscience untroubled or look the other way. One doctor informed him that "in the beginning you feel like Mengele, but a few days later you become accustomed."[32]

The Israeli writer Dan Almagor recalled a TV film he had seen in England on the thirtieth anniversary of the outbreak of World War II, in which several German officers who had been released from prison after serving their sentences as war criminals were asked why they had taken such care in filming the atrocities in which they participated. "We didn't film many of them for history," one officer said, but "so that there would be something to play for the children when we went home on weekends. It was very amusing for the children," who were deprived of Mickey Mouse films because of the war. Almagor was reminded of this film when he read the testimony of the Givati soldiers who described the amusement they felt over the "attractive" protruding stomach of Hani al-Shami, which provided such a "fine target for beatings." Almagor went on to describe a visit to the West Bank with a brigade educational officer, a major, who described with pride how he beat people with a club and joined a group of other officers and enlisted men and women who were convulsed with laughter over stories told by one man from the religious ultraright with a knitted skull cap about how he had bulldozed homes designated by the secret police, including one that was not marked but was between two that were, and had destroyed a store that was in his way when he wanted to turn the bulldozer. Almagor's bitter words brought back memories to me too, among them an unforgettable incident forty years ago, when a horrifying Japanese documentary of the Hiroshima bombing was being shown, to much amusement, in the "combat zone" in downtown Boston as a pornographic film. And a story in the *New York Times* in March 1968, right after the Tet offensive, describing with some annoyance how demonstrators had disrupted an exhibit at the Chicago Museum of Science where children could "enter a helicopter for simulated firing of a machine gun at targets in a diorama of the Vietnam Central Highlands," including a peasant hut, which particularly disturbed the obnoxious peaceniks.[33]

"It is already impossible, it seems, to relate these stories, to ask for an explanation, to seek those responsible. Every other day there is a new story." These are the despairing words of Zvi Gilat, who has been recording the atrocities in the territories with care and dedication as the armed forces resort to ever more savage measures to suppress the Palestinian uprising. He is describing the village of Beita, which gained its notoriety because a Jewish girl was killed there in early April 1988. She was killed by a crazed Israeli guard accompanying hikers, after he had killed two villagers. The sister of one of the murdered men, three months pregnant, was jailed for throwing a rock at the killer of her brother and kept in prison until days before her child was due to be born; the Israeli guard who had killed three people was not charged because, army spokesman Colonel Raanan Gissen said, "I believe the tragic incident and its result are already a penalty." Other Beita residents have remained in prison for eight months, with no sentence, and only one family member permitted to attend the sessions of the military court. The sentencing of four villagers to three years imprisonment for allegedly throwing stones before the Jewish girl was killed by her guard merited a few words in paragraph eleven of an Associated Press (AP) report in the *Times*; ten days earlier, the *Times* reported the sentencing of a Jewish settler to two and a half years, the minimum sentence under law, for killing an Arab shepherd he found grazing sheep on land near his settlement. Beita residents were expelled from the country; houses were demolished, including many not specifically marked for destruction; property was destroyed; the village was not permitted to export olive oil, its main source of income, to Europe, though Israel refuses to purchase it. Two weeks before Gilat visited the village once again, a twelve-year-old boy was shot in the back of his head at close range by Israeli soldiers, killed while fleeing from soldiers whom he saw when leaving his house, left to bleed on the ground for at least five hours according to witnesses. But though he has "no more strength, no more will," Gilat goes on with more and more tales of horror, cruelty, and humiliation, while senses become dulled even among those who read them—a category that includes very few of those who pay the bills.[34]

I cite only a tiny sample of the "regrettable exceptions" that are "no doubt" attributable to "inexperience" and "frustration," atrocities that mounted through mid-1988 as the U.S. media reduced their coverage under a barrage of criticism for their unfair treatment of defenseless Israel, if not their latent anti-Semitism. Meanwhile there were quiet laments over Israel's tribulations, and occasional excesses, by some of those who helped create the basis for what they now fear. The atrocities go on, while the press looks the other way and those who might help mitigate them observe their vow of silence, assure us that nothing serious is happening, or warn of the problems Israel will face unless it takes some steps to recognize the human rights of Palestinians, not heretofore a matter of concern.

The horror stories in the Israeli (mainly Hebrew) press barely skim the surface. An official of the Israeli Ministry of Foreign Affairs, returning from reserve service, reported that "the overwhelming majority of the severe and violent events in the territories do not reach the public at all." He estimated that about one in ten events reached the public during the escalation of violence that was becoming "a real war"—one largely kept from the eyes of the American taxpayer who funds it, a further contribution to state terror.[35]

Also largely kept from those who pay the bills are the current proposals that the solution may after all be in simply "transferring" the recalcitrant population of the occupied territories, a venerable idea now again entering center stage, with opponents often objecting, in mainstream commentary and debate, on grounds that it is unfeasible. By mid-1988, some 40 percent of Israeli Jews favored expulsion of the Arab population, while 45 percent regarded Israel as too democratic, and 55 percent opposed granting equal rights to Israeli Arab citizens (contrary to much propaganda, deprivation of equal rights, such as access to most of the country's land, has always been severe). Much Zionist literature has long regarded the Palestinians as temporary visitors in the Land of Israel, perhaps recent immigrants drawn by Jewish rebuilding efforts; this has been a popular tale among American intellectuals as well. The rising ultraorthodox religious groups, with a strong base in the United States, are hardly likely to object to the removal of people who are inferior to Jews in their essential nature; thus, in the words of the revered Rav Kook, chief Ashkenazic rabbi from 1921 to 1935, "the difference between the Israelite soul . . . and the soul of all non-Jews, at any level, is greater and deeper than the difference between the soul of a human and the soul of an animal, for between the latter [two categories] there is only a quantitative difference but between the former two there is a qualitative one."[36]

Those who believe that even the transfer solution would not find acceptance in some North American quarters are seriously in error. Respected figures of the social democratic left in the U.S. have long ago explained that the indigenous inhabitants of the former Palestine are "marginal to the nation" so that their problems might be "smoothed" by "helping people to leave who have to leave." Not a whisper was heard, Alexander Cockburn noted, when the Republican Party platform of 1988 "went so far as demurely to encourage the notion of transfer" with the following words: "More jobs and more opportunities in adjoining countries might draw the energies of more young people into building a world for themselves rather than destroying someone else's"[37]—by struggling for their rights against a harsh military regime endorsed and funded by the United States.

3. THE SUMMITS[38]

In preparation for the Reagan–Gorbachev meetings at the Washington summit of December 1987, the news was carefully shaped to ensure that only proper thoughts would reach the public. Excluded were the overwhelming votes at the United Nations opposing the escalated arms race advocated by the United States in virtual isolation, definitely not a useful message at the moment when all attention was to be focused on Reagan's achievements in bringing about world peace. It was not only world opinion that had to be scrupulously censored from the independent media. The domestic peace movement is no less unworthy. In a summary of media coverage, the monitoring organization FAIR observed that "only right-wing critics of the INF Treaty were considered newsworthy." A sharp critique of the Reagan administration for reckless nuclear deployment by Republican Senator Mark Hatfield was "blacked out of the national media," as was SANE/Freeze, America's largest peace group. Its press conference on the peace movement's role in laying the basis for the INF agreement was ignored, but another the same day called by the Anti-Appeasement Alliance, where Reagan was denounced as a "Kremlin idiot," "became a big news story." Secretary of State George Shultz's denunciation of the peace movement and his call for them "to admit that they were wrong" was reported, but, SANE/Freeze Peace Secretary Brigid Shea comments, "We aren't even given one inch to tell our side of the story." Soviet charges about U.S. attempts to undermine the ABM treaty in its pursuit of star wars were dismissed as "doctrinaire" and "hostile" in TV news reports, which offered a "summit wrap-up" featuring Richard Perle, criticizing the INF Treaty from the hard Right, and the hawkish Democrat Sam Nunn, playing dove (Tom Brokaw, NBC). As usual, there is a debate, but within proper limits.[39]

The official agenda for the summit included Reagan's role as a peacemaker and his passion for human rights. The task for the media, then, was to emphasize these two notable features of the president's achievements. Proper filtering enabled the first requirement to be satisfied. The second was met with no less aplomb. As Gorbachev stepped onto American soil at the Washington airport before the TV cameras, CBS anchorman Dan Rather commented that Gorbachev will focus on arms reduction, but "Reagan will press the Soviet Union on broader issues such as human rights, Afghanistan, and Nicaragua."[40] Few were so gauche as to raise questions about Reagan's stellar human rights record (in Central America, for example), though not everyone went as far as Dan Rather, often denounced for his "ultraliberalism," in interpreting what has happened to Nicaragua as a Soviet transgression.[41]

In a front-page news story in the *New York Times*, Philip Taubman observed from Moscow that despite his promise, Gorbachev still has a good deal to learn. He continues to "articulate the orthodox Soviet view of life in the United States: A ruling class, dominated by a military-industrial complex, controls the Government and exploits the vast majority of Americans, creating a society of economic inequity and injustice." This "ideologically slanted" view is inconsistent with the "more sophisticated outlook of Soviet analysts and senior colleagues who are familiar with the United States" and therefore understand how remote this conception is from reality. The same issue of the *Times* includes an article by Adam Walinsky entitled "What It's Like to Be in Hell," describing the reality of life in the Chicago slums in this society free from economic inequity, injustice, and exploitation.[42]

The Moscow summit in June 1988 received similar treatment. With rare exceptions, commentary ranged from admiration of Reagan's courageous defense of human rights (in the Soviet Union) to criticism of his weakness for caving in to the Russians and his curious conversion to Leninism. Reagan's meeting with Soviet dissidents was featured; he is a man who "believes very firmly in a few simple principles, and his missionary work for human rights and the American way taps into his most basic values," the *New York Times* reported. In his "finest oratorical hour," the editors added, his speech to Moscow students "extended the President's persistent, laudable expressions of concern for human rights," a concern revealed, perhaps, by his fervent admiration for the genocidal killers in the Guatemalan military command and his organization of state terror in El Salvador, not to speak of his gentle treatment of the poor at home.[43]

A press conference at the Church Center near the United Nations called by a Human Rights Coalition fared differently. The national media ignored the plea for attention to human rights violations in the United States, and countries dependent on U.S. aid, presented by the legal director of the American Civil Liberties Union, representatives of the Center for Constitutional Rights, the American Indian Movement, prison-rights groups, and others.[44]

Some elements of the foreign press were more reluctant to adopt Washington's agenda. The Toronto *Globe and Mail* editors observed that just as Reagan "felt it necessary to lecture the Soviet Union on human rights" at the summit, the *New York Times* published some of the "shocking revelations" on the torturers whom the U.S. arms and advises in Honduras and the CIA's preference for inhuman methods that leave no visible trace, though the *Times* story refrained from citing the BBC report six months earlier that U.S. personnel were present at the meeting where the U.S.-trained death squad Battalion 316 ordered that an American priest, Father James Carney, be killed by throwing him from a helicopter.[45] The U.S. role in Honduras and its "quiet go-ahead" for the "dirty war" in Argentina are "not a proud record of respect for human dignity and freedom," the *Globe and Mail* editors observed, selecting some of the lesser examples that illustrate the point. Note that the *New York Times* was quite capable of publishing this account while—unlike its Canadian counterpart—it perceived no conflict here with Reagan's "laudable expressions of concern for human rights," in the Soviet bloc.

The *New Statesman* in London added that "any claim which the American President makes to moral superiority must be accounted the most macabre of hypocrisies," noting the support of this "tribune of human rights" for state terrorists in El Salvador and Guatemala and for the "bloody terrorist campaign" against defenseless civilians in Nicaragua. The editors also commented on the "obvious irony" of Reagan's presentation to Gorbachev of a videocassette of the film *Friendly Persuasion,* the only film in Hollywood history to be released with no screenplay credit because the scriptwriter was blacklisted in the days when Reagan was president of the Screen Actors Guild–Allied Artists, kicking "subversives" out of the union during the McCarthy witch hunt and later assuring us that "there was no such thing as a Hollywood blacklist." "The western media played Reagan's themes [in Moscow] for all they were worth," the editors observe; "the western media know their place." They are right with regard to the United States, where one would have to search far to find a similar discordant note.[46]

4. THE MEDIA AND INTERNATIONAL OPINION[47]

The U.N. votes at the time of the December 1987 Washington summit, and the treatment of them noted in the text, illustrate a more general pattern. In recent years, the United States has been far in the lead in vetoing Security Council resolutions. From 1967 through 1981, the United States vetoed seven resolutions condemning Israeli practices in southern Lebanon, affirming Palestinian rights, and deploring Israel's changing of the status of Jerusalem and its establishment of settlements in the occupied territories. Each time, the United States was alone in opposition. There were thirteen additional vetoes by the Reagan administration on similar issues, the U.S. standing alone.[48] The United States has also been alone or in a small minority in opposing or vetoing U.N. resolutions on South Africa, arms issues, and other matters.

These votes are often not reported or only marginally noted. The occasional reports are commonly of the kind one might find in a state-controlled press, as examples already cited illustrate. To mention another, in November 1988 the General Assembly voted 130 to 2 (the United States and Israel) for a resolution that "condemns" Israel for "killing and wounding defenseless Palestinians" in the suppression of the Palestinian uprising and "strongly deplores" its disregard for earlier Security Council resolutions condemning its actions in the occupied territories. This was reported in the *New York Times.* The first three paragraphs stated the basic facts. The rest of the article (ten paragraphs) was devoted to the U.S. and Israeli positions, to the abstainers, and to the "relatively poor showing" of the Arab states on earlier resolutions. From supporters of the resolution, all we hear are reservations of those who found it "unbalanced."[49]

The isolation of the United States has aroused some concern. In 1984, the *New York Times Magazine* devoted a major story to the topic by its U.N. correspondent Richard Bernstein.[50] He observes that "there are many voices" asking "in tones of skepticism and anguish" whether there is any value to the United Nations at all. "There is a growing sense," he continues, "that the United Nations has become repetitive, rhetorical, extremist and antidemocratic, a place where the United States is attacked with apparent impunity even by countries with which it maintains cordial bilateral relations." "There can be little doubt that, over the years, the United Nations has come to be dominated by what might be called a third-world ideology"—that is, by the views of the majority of its members—and that its attacks on the United States are "excessive and one-sided."

This judgment holds despite the annual U.N. condemnations of the Soviet Union in Afghanistan, the regular U.N. reports on its human rights violations there, and the Security Council vote condemning the Soviet downing of KAL 007 over Soviet territory. The downing by the U.S. Navy of an Iranian civilian plane over Iranian territorial waters with 290 lives lost elicited no such reaction, and the U.S. attack against South Vietnam, later all of Indochina, was neither condemned nor subjected to inquiry; in fact, Shirley Hazzard observes, "throughout these years, the war in Vietnam was never discussed in the United Nations."[51]

Continuing his review of the decline of the United Nations, Bernstein observes that both the Security Council and the General Assembly condemned the U.S. invasion of Grenada, including most NATO countries and other U.S. allies. Even the efforts of U.N. Ambassador Jeane Kirkpatrick, "perhaps the most dazzling intellect at the world body" (a comment that must have elicited a few chuckles there), have been unavailing in stemming the tide of "prefabricated jargon about racism, colonialism and fascism" and "ritualistic" attacks on the United States in place of the "reasoned debate" in the good old days when there was "an automatic majority" to support the U.S. positions. "The question," Bernstein concludes,

> is not why American policy has diverged from that of other member states, but why the world's most powerful democracy has failed to win support for its views among the participants in United Nations debates. The answer seems to lie in two underlying factors. The first and dominant one is the very structure and political culture that have evolved at the world body, tending in the process to isolate the United States and to portray it as a kind of ideological villain. The other factor is American failure to play the game of multilateral diplomacy with sufficient skill.

The question, in short, is why the world is out of step, and the answer plainly does not lie in the policies of the United States, which are praiseworthy as a matter of definition, so that argument to establish the point would be superfluous.

A different view was expressed by Senator William Fulbright in 1972, when he had become quite disaffected with U.S. policies: "Having controlled the United Nations for many years as tightly and as easily as a big-city boss controls his party machine," Fulbright remarked, "we had got used to the idea that the United Nations was a place where we could work our will." In his *History of the United Nations,* Evan Luard observes that "no doubt, if they had been in a majority, the communist states would have behaved in much the same way. The conduct of the West . . . was none the less an abuse of power. And it was an abuse that those same [Western] members were to regret more than most when the balance of power changed again and a different majority assumed control of the organization," leading to "rage, but not, as yet, regret," as Shirley Hazzard comments, reviewing Luard's study.[52]

Hazzard goes on to describe how, with the complicity of Secretary General Trygvie Lie, the United States undermined the creation of an "independent international civil service" at the U.N. that "would impartially provide exposure and propose correctives to maintain the precepts to which governments nominally subscribed at San Francisco" when the U.N. was founded. She is referring to the U.S. insistence that the FBI be permitted to conduct a "witch hunt" to control selection of staff, opening "the floodgates . . . to political appointments" and hopelessly compromising the organization.

In her own study of "the self-destruction of the United Nations," Hazzard describes the witch hunt in detail, revealing how "the *majority* of the 'international' United Nations Secretariat work force" was made subject to FBI screening and approval in a secret agreement with the State Department for which the only apparent partial precedent was an edict of Mussolini's concerning the League of Nations Secretariat. This secret agreement was "a landmark in United Nations affairs and the ascertainable point at which the international Secretariat delivered itself conclusively, in its earliest years, into the hands of national interest . . . in direct violation of the United Nations Charter." She observes that had a similar compact been discovered with the Soviet Union, "the international outcry would have been such as, in all probability, to bring down the United Nations itself"; in this case, exposure passed in silence, in accordance with the usual conventions. The U.N. submitted in fear of losing U.S. appropriations. "The United States concept of the 'international,'" Hazzard concludes, "was—as it continues to be—at best a sort of benign unilateralism through which American policies would work uncontested for everybody's benefit."[53]

This judgment explains the attitude of articulate U.S. opinion and the media toward the U.N. over the years. When the U.N. was a docile instrument of the United States, there was much indignation over Soviet negativism while distinguished social scientists reflected upon its sources in Russian culture and child-rearing practices. As the organization fell under "the tyranny of the majority"—otherwise called "democracy"—attitudes shifted to the current "skepticism and anguish," with equally profound musings on the cultural failings of the benighted majority.

The same attitudes are expressed toward other international organizations. When Latin American delegates, at a meeting of the Organization of American States (O.A.S.), refused to bend to the U.S. will over the ham-handed efforts of the Reaganites to unseat General Noriega in Panama after he had outlived his usefulness, *Times* correspondent Elaine Sciolino observed sadly that "over the years, the O.A.S. has lost much of its authority as the conscience of Latin America" (Feb. 29, 1988)—in translation, it no longer follows U.S. orders.

Throughout, it is presupposed, beyond question, that what the United States does and stands for is right and good; if others fail to recognize this moral rectitude, plainly they are at fault. The naïveté is not without a certain childlike appeal—which quickly fades, however, when we recognize how it is converted into an instrument for inflicting suffering and pain.

As the world's richest and most powerful state, the United States continues to wield the lash. The *Times* reports that the O.A.S. "is likely to suspend its aid program for the rest of the year because of the worst financial crisis in its history." Half of the $20 million shortfall for 1988 results from a cut in the U.S. contribution; two-thirds of the $46 million in outstanding dues is owed by the United States, as of November 1988. "It's so serious that the essence of the organization is in danger," the secretary general stated. O.A.S. officials warn that the fiscal crisis will cause curtailment of all development programs, adding that "the dispute grows out of sharply conflicting visions of the organization's role in the hemisphere," with the United States opposed to development programs that are favored by their beneficiaries. The drug program too "will be inoperative by the end of the year," the head of the Inter-American Drug Abuse Control Commission of the O.A.S. reported, while the Reagan administration lambasted the Latin American countries for their failure to control the flow of drugs to the United States. The U.S. cuts came against the background of criticism of the O.A.S. by administration officials and some members of Congress "for declining to take a more aggressive role against Nicaragua" and General Noriega.[54] A congressman explains that "we were not satisfied that we were getting a dollar's worth of performance for the American taxpayer." Reagan administration bully-boy tactics actually succeeded in creating hemisphere-wide support for the much-despised Noriega, in annoyance over blatant U.S. interventionism after the sudden turn against him.

The United Nations is facing the same problems now that it no longer has the wit to function as an organ of U.S. power. The United States is by far the largest debtor, owing $412 million as of September 1987; the next largest debtor was Brazil, owing $16 million. The Soviet Union had by then announced that it would pay all of its outstanding debts. In earlier years, when the U.S.S.R. was the culprit, the United States had backed a request to the World Court for a ruling on debt payment and had endorsed the court ruling that all members must pay their debts. But now the grounds have shifted, and debt payment is no longer a solemn obligation. Unreported is the fact that, according to the U.S. mission at the United Nations, the U.N. operation "funnels $400 million to $700 million per year into the U.S. and New York economies."[55]

The institutions of world order do not fare well in the media in other cases as well, when they serve unwanted ends. Efforts to resolve border tensions provide one striking illustration. These are rarely reported when the agent is an enemy state, particularly a victim of U.S. attack. Nicaraguan proposals for border monitoring are a case in point. To cite one additional example, in March 1988, during the Nicaraguan strike against the contras that apparently spilled a few kilometers into contra-held areas of Honduras, there was much indignant commentary about Sandinista aggression and their threat to peaceful Honduras. Nicaragua requested that a U.N. observer force monitor the Nicaragua–Honduras border—which would have put to rest these fears, had they been serious in the first place. Honduras rejected Nicaragua's call for U.N. observers, the U.N. spokesman told reporters. Nicaragua also asked the International Court of Justice to inquire into alleged Honduran armed incursions. There appears to have been no mention of these facts in the *New York Times,* which preferred to report that three months earlier Honduran Foreign Minister Carlos López Contreras had proposed monitoring of the border.[56]

5. DEMOLISHING THE ACCORDS[57]

Given the policies it advocates in the Third World, the United States often finds itself politically weak though militarily strong, as commonly conceded on all sides in internal documents. The result is regular opposition to diplomacy and political settlement. Since the facts do not conform to the required image, considerable talent in historical engineering is required.[58] The problem has been a persistent one during the Central American conflicts of recent years.

The United States systematically blocked all efforts to use peaceful means to resolve what *Times* correspondent Shirley Christian calls "*our* Nicaraguan agony," describing our suffering in the course of our "basically idealistic efforts to deal with the situation," in which, "on balance, we may have had the best intentions of all the players."[59] The United States succeeded in blocking the Contadora initiatives, eliminating any recourse to the World Court and United Nations as required by international law and the supreme law of the land and evading repeated Nicaraguan efforts to satisfy legitimate interests of the Central American countries—even the alleged U.S. security concerns, ludicrous as they are. The U.S. attempted to block the Arias proposals in 1987, succeeding through July with the cooperation of Salvadoran President Duarte.

The Reagan–Wright proposals of August 5 were a final effort to sabotage any meaningful agreement that might result from the planned meeting of Central American presidents the next day. But this proved "an incredible tactical error," a Guatemalan diplomat observed, arousing "the nationalistic instincts of the Costa Rican and Guatemalan delegations," which felt "insulted" by these strong-arm methods.[60] On August 7, to the dismay of the U.S. administration, the Central American presidents agreed on the Esquipulas II Accord, "inspired by the visionary and permanent desire of the Contadora and the [Latin American] Support Groups."[61]

The unexpected August 7 agreement compelled the media to backtrack quickly from their advocacy of the Reagan–Wright plan as a forthcoming gesture for peace. On August 6, James LeMoyne had reported falsely that, apart from Nicaragua, which risked isolation for its intransigence, the Central American presidents "were gratified" by the Reagan–Wright proposal—which Guatemala and Costa Rica dismissed with considerable irritation as an "insult." A day later, Washington now being isolated by the peace agreement of the Central American presidents, LeMoyne presented their Accord as sharing "the central intent of Mr. Reagan's plan, which is to demand internal political changes in Nicaragua"; the Esquipulas Accord made no mention of Nicaragua but was, rather, designed to apply simultaneously and comparably to all the Central American countries. The media proceeded to construct an interpretation that gave the United States the credit for having driven Nicaragua to negotiations by the use of force and the Reagan–Wright initiative. The purpose, apart from serving to conceal the consistent U.S. opposition to a peaceful settlement, was to legitimate state violence and thus prepare the ground for its renewal when needed, here or elsewhere.[62]

Some were unable to conceal their dismay with the developments. Former *New York Times* executive editor A. M. Rosenthal, whose regular columns since his retirement provide much insight into the thinking that animated the *Times* during his tenure, denounced "the pro-Sandinistas" in press and politics—a group that one might detect with a sufficiently powerful microscope—for their failure to stand by the Reagan–Wright plan after the Esquipulas Accord was signed. He assured the reader that the Central American presidents were "astonished" by this failure to pursue the proposal, which in Rosenthal's world they welcomed, while in the real world they had rejected it with contempt. Opponents of the Reagan–Wright plan, he wrote, are helping to kill "the peace proposals for Nicaragua"—that is, the Reagan–Wright plan, which, unlike the Esquipulas Accord, applied only to Nicaragua and therefore alone qualifies as a peace proposal for an American jingoist. Extolling the reliance on violence, Rosenthal wrote that "Secretary Shultz and Howard Baker, believing that the Sandinistas had been hurt severely enough to make negotiations feasible, got the President to agree." But now "the pro-Sandinistas in this country" are undercutting the Shultz–Baker achievements by advocacy of the Esquipulas Accord and even "acted as if it were a damnable sin to suggest that the United States should not immediately destroy the contras, whose existence brought about the opportunity for negotiations."[63]

Most, however, preferred less crude means to convert the peace agreement to the basic structure of the Reagan–Wright plan. The Esquipulas Accord set in motion a U.S. government campaign to dismantle it and maintain the option of further attacks against Nicaragua accompanied with such state terror as might be required to keep the "fledgling democracies" in line. The enthusiastic cooperation of the media ensured the success of this endeavor. The desired result was achieved by January 1988, in a brilliantly executed government-media operation.

The first task was to eliminate the provisions applying to the United States, namely, what the Accord designated as the one "indispensable element" for peace: the termination of any form of aid for indigenous guerrillas or the contras. U.S. aid for the contras attacking Nicaragua from Honduras and Costa Rica was already criminal, even in the technical legal sense, but the Esquipulas Accord raised a new barrier. By August 1987, supply flights to the contras had reached a level of one a day, in addition to the constant surveillance required to assure that barely defended targets can be safely attacked. The U.S. responded to the call for termination of such aid by escalating it. Supply flights doubled in September and virtually tripled in the following months. In late August, the CIA attempted to bribe Miskito leaders to reject Nicaraguan attempts at peaceful reconciliation and continue the war.[64]

These flagrant violations of the "indispensable element" for peace undermined the basis for the Esquipulas Accord. To assess the role of the media, we therefore ask how they dealt with these crucial facts. I will continue to keep largely to the *New York Times,* the most important newspaper and the one that provides the quasi-official record for history; the pattern elsewhere is generally similar.[65]

I was unable to find a single phrase in the *Times* referring to the bribes, the rapid U.S. escalation of supply and surveillance flights, or their success in escalating terrorist attacks against civilians. The Esquipulas Accord designated the three-month period from August 7 to early November for initial steps to realize its terms, and the period from August 7 to mid-January as the first phase, after which the International Verification and Monitoring Commission (CIVS) was to present its report on what had been achieved. During the first three-month period, *Times* Nicaragua correspondent Stephen Kinzer had forty-one articles dealing with Nicaragua. The crucial events just described were omitted entirely. In fact, there were only two references even to the existence of supply and surveillance flights.[66] On September 23, Kinzer mentioned that "thousands of contras inside Nicaragua now receive their supplies principally from clandestine airdrops run by the Central Intelligence Agency." On October 15, he wrote that "planes that fly into Nicaragua at night to drop supplies to contras take off from Honduras." In later months, there are a few scattered references to these flights.[67]

In short, we find total suppression of the most critical facts concerning the fate of the accords, not to speak of the flagrant violation of international law and the dramatic proof of the artificial character of the implanted proxy army—a conclusion never drawn, as far as I can determine. The record provides impressive evidence of the dedication of the media to state propaganda and violence.

The *Times* was not content with evasion of the supply and surveillance operations and total suppression of the escalation of U.S. aid to its forces in an effort to undermine the Esquipulas Accord. It also resorted to outright falsification. In mid-November, President Ortega attended an O.A.S. meeting in Washington, to which the U.S. brought its CIA–funded contra civilian directorate, much to the annoyance of the Latin American delegates. Ortega denounced the sharp increase in supply flights after they had been banned by the Accord, reporting 140 supply flights from August. Contra leader Adolfo Calero dismissed this estimate as far too low, stating that "his radar is not working very well." The *New York Times* reported the statements by Ortega and Calero, but with an editorial adjustment. Where they spoke of supply flights, the *Times* news report downgraded the reference to "surveillance flights," still a violation of international law and the Accord but a less serious one, thus apparently less unacceptable.[68]

A few days later, Nicaragua's U.N. Ambassador Nora Astorga reported 275 supply and surveillance flights detected from August 7 to November 3. I found no notice in the press of this not entirely trivial allegation.[69]

By such means, the media succeeded in serving Washington's goal of eliminating two central provisions of the Accord: "Aid halt to irregular forces or insurrectionist movements," and "non-use of territory to attack other states." With this implicit revision of the Accord, the United States was now free to act as it wished, with the endorsement of President Arias, according to the *Times* version, at least.[70]

The Esquipulas Accord called for "an authentic pluralistic and participatory democratic process to promote social justice, respect for human rights, sovereignty, the territorial integrity of states and the right of each nation to determine, freely and without any kind of external interference, its own economic, political and social model," as well as steps to ensure "justice, freedom and democracy," freedom of expression and political action, and opening of the communication media "for all ideological groups." It also called for "dialogue with all unarmed political opposition groups within the country" and other steps to achieve national reconciliation. Furthermore, "amnesty decrees will be issued setting out the steps to guarantee the inviolability of all forms of life and liberty, material goods and the safety of the people to benefit from said decrees."

El Salvador violated the amnesty condition at once by decreeing an amnesty that freed the state security services and their associates from the unlikely prospect of prosecution for their crimes. Human rights monitors denounced the step, predicting—accurately, as it turned out—that it would lead to an increase in state terror. The *Times*, however, lauded the amnesty. With regard to Nicaragua, the Washington media interpretation was that the amnesty must apply far more broadly than the Accord specifies. We return to these matters.

The required steps toward democracy, social justice, safeguarding of human rights, and so on, plainly could not be enacted in Washington's terror states.[71] Therefore, the provisions had to be eliminated from the operative version of the Accord. The method pursued was, again, to suppress the facts and praise the terror states for their adherence to the accords that they were increasingly violating.

In September, the Inter-American Commission on Human Rights of the O.A.S. issued a report noting a "perceptible decline in the observance of human rights" in Guatemala, expressing concern over "the resumption of methods and systems for eliminating persons in mass and the reappearance of the dreadful death squads." The Costa Rican–based Commission for the Defense of Human Rights in Central America reported to the U.N. in November on the continuing terror by the Guatemalan security services and death squads, documenting some 175 cases of abductions, disappearances, and assassinations from August 8 to November 17, 1987, in addition to grenade attacks, a bomb thrown into a church, and so on. The Guatemalan Human Rights Commission had recorded 334 extrajudicial executions and seventy-three disappearances in the first nine months of 1987. One of its directors reported in Washington that "the accords are being used as a smoke screen and the human rights situation is becoming much graver. . . . [The accords have served] to allow violations with much more impunity." He added that the documented cases represent only a fraction of the abuses because most take place outside of the capital, citing also other government atrocities. The military also launched a new offensive in the mountains to try to drive the survivors of the near-genocidal campaigns of the early 1980s into "Development Pole villages" where they could be controlled by force.[72]

American readers were spared such facts. "During the first six months after the signing of the accords," Latin Americanist Susanne Jonas observes, "not one article on Guatemalan compliance appeared in the *New York Times*, and virtually none were printed in other major U.S. media." In a review of the *Times, Christian Science Monitor, Miami Herald,* and *Wall Street Journal* from October 1987 to March 1988, Alexander Cockburn found little comment on Guatemala and no mention at all of the rising tide of political violence through November. As atrocities mounted further in December and January there were two stories on Guatemala in the journals reviewed, both in the *Monitor,* both discussing rights abuses. The totals for October through January are over 500 dead and 160 disappeared and two news stories. Combining the record of all papers reviewed over the entire period, Cockburn observes, "there is one critical story every 154 days on Guatemala in the US's most influential newspapers."[73]

In El Salvador, Tutela Legal, the human rights monitoring office of the Archdiocese of San Salvador, reported that recorded death-squad killings doubled to about ten a month immediately after the accords, continuing through January; for the year, Tutela Legal's figures were eighty-eight disappeared and ninety-six killed by death squads, the armed forces, and civil defense, in addition to 280 killed, most presumed to be civilians, during army military operations.[74] Amadeo Ramos, one of the founders of the Indian association ANIS, reported that an Indian settlement was bombed by the army and "the bodies of several Indians were found in a remote area thrown in a ditch" in mid-November; not being Miskitos in Nicaragua, their fate was of no interest. There were many other dramatic cases, ignored or barely mentioned. The Council on Hemispheric Affairs estimated eighty-seven civilians killed or "disappeared" by death squads during the August–January phase of the accords. Chris Norton, one of the few U.S. journalists based in El Salvador, reported abroad that the real numbers are unknown because, as in Guatemala, most death squad killings "have taken place in rural areas and few of them have been reported."[75]

Protection of the client regime of El Salvador is a particular imperative, reaching impressive levels. The fate of the Human Rights Commission CDHES is illustrative. The murder of its president, Herbert Anaya, was reported by James LeMoyne, with due respect for the official government story that the guerrillas were responsible. Omitted from his account was testimony to the contrary by Anaya's widow, Mirna Anaya, and others. Mirna Anaya, a Salvadoran judge until 1987, fled the country after her husband's assassination. Her statement that the security forces were responsible and that witnesses will so testify if granted protection was available to a Canadian audience, but *New York Times* readers were again spared such unpleasant facts, as well as her speech before the Human Rights Assembly of the United Nations identifying a death squad of "members of the hacienda police and National Police" as the assassins.[76]

It is of little moment that a former CDHES president, Marianela Garcia Villas, had been killed by security forces on the pretext that she was a guerrilla, while other members had been murdered or "disappeared" by the security forces. Herbert Anaya had been arrested and tortured by the Treasury Police in May 1986, along with other commission members. While in prison, they continued their work, compiling sworn testimony of torture by prisoners. They succeeded in smuggling out of the prison a document with detailed evidence on the torture of 430 prisoners along with a videotape of testimony. But this was evidence about torture by U.S. agents and clients (and a U.S. military officer in uniform, in one case), not about Cuban or Russian prisons. Hence these revelations aroused no interest, and nothing appeared in the national media. After Anaya was released in a prisoner exchange, he was denounced by the government and informed that he headed a list of commission workers to be killed. Lacking the protection that might have been afforded by some media visibility, he was assassinated, probably by the security forces or their affiliates, as indicated by Archbishop Rivera y Damas in a homily at the Metropolitan Cathedral, unreported in the *Times,* in which he cited information that "a death squad was responsible."[77]

Systematically avoiding the undesirable facts about El Salvador, LeMoyne assured his readers at the end of November that President Duarte "has gone considerably further [than the Sandinistas] in carrying out the letter of the treaty," though perhaps he too is not "particularly committed to its spirit of reconciliation," since he "is trying to split the leftist rebel alliance"—nothing more. LeMoyne also praised Duarte for having given the rebels "free access to the press"; the Council on Hemispheric Affairs, in contrast, reports that "journalists practice self-censorship to such an extent that papers will not print statements by opposition groups critical of the government."[78]

LeMoyne was also impressed with Duarte's having "permitted rebel civilian leaders to come home and actively pursue their political vision," asking whether "like the rebels in El Salvador, the contras may eventually . . . take the risk of sending some representatives back to Nicaragua to test the Sandinistas' promise to offer genuine political freedom after eight years of single-party rule"—though there is reason to "doubt their sincerity" and willingness to "tolerate some political opposition."[79] LeMoyne is well aware that respected church leaders and intellectuals who have no connection with guerrilla movements have been forced to flee El Salvador and are unable to return for fear of assassination, while in Nicaragua the opposition has never faced anything remotely comparable to the terror of Duarte's security forces and their associates and quite openly supports the U.S. forces attacking the country, regularly identifying with them in public statements in *La Prensa*, publicly denouncing the government, and implicitly calling for further military aid to the contras when visiting Washington.[80]

As LeMoyne also knows full well, not only the pro-contra internal opposition but even contra military leaders who decide to return to Nicaragua live and work there without concern for their lives. To cite only one of several cases, contra leader Fernando Chamorro returned to Nicaragua from Costa Rica and was named regional president of the Conservative Party, which openly supports the contras.[81] Consider in contrast Salvadoran Colonel Adolfo Majano, not a guerrilla leader but the army officer who led the reformist military coup in October 1979 and was described by the U.S. press as "the symbol of American policy in this country" because of his efforts to move toward democracy and reform.[82] Majano was marginalized as the traditional repressive forces took over with U.S. government backing and was removed from the junta in December 1980, when Duarte became president to preside over the slaughter then intensifying. He was forced to flee the mounting terror, returning after seven years in exile to test the "new democracy." Upon returning, he survived at least two assassination attempts by suspected death squads. A third occurred on August 25, 1988, when his car came under fire from two gunmen in a San Salvador shopping center and two bodyguards were killed. "This criminal attempt was aimed at myself and there is no doubt that it was carried out by the death squads," Majano said. The Archbishop agreed, stating in the Sunday mass three days later that the killings had been carried out by "the sinister death squads."[83] The assassination attempt took place immediately after a series of murders by security forces and presumed death squads. One suspects that similar events in Managua might have made the *New York Times*. Instead, we find philosophical reflections on the freedom and openness of El Salvador as compared with the brutal repression under the Sandinistas.

LeMoyne's zeal in applauding the encouraging developments in El Salvador as contrasted with repressive Nicaragua was sometimes excessive even by *Times* standards. Thus he reported the plans of the "rebel civilian officials" Ruben Zamora and Guillermo Ungo to return to El Salvador, where they hoped to survive by wearing bulletproof vests, constantly changing residence, and carefully restricting their movements. "The two men's planned return," LeMoyne stated, "is in sharp contrast to the situation in neighboring Nicaragua, where the ruling Sandinistas have said they will jail any rebel leader who tries to return to carry out political activities." Five days earlier, Stephen Kinzer had reported President Ortega's statement that "any contras who stop fighting," including contra leader Adolfo Calero and military commander Enrique Bermúdez, "would be allowed to participate fully in Nicaraguan political life." He quoted Ortega as saying, "A cease-fire is the immediate objective, but if the contras accept it, they can join political dialogue with other parties in Nicaragua. If Calero and Bermudez accept this, they will be free to walk the streets of Managua, hold demonstrations and join the conservative party or whichever party they choose. No one will have to sign anything. By disarming, they will automatically receive amnesty."[84]

Unreported are the facts about Fernando Chamorro, Adolfo Majano, Horacio Arce, and others or the Salvadoran government reaction when guerrilla commander Mario Aguiñada Carranza announced his intention to return to the country to take part in its political life. The government announced that it would bar his entry, and the army added that he would be captured and tried in the courts for his crimes.[85] The situation in the two countries is precisely the opposite of what LeMoyne conveys, as he can hardly fail to know.

Comparison of Zamora and Ungo with Bermúdez and Calero is a bit odd to begin with. Both Zamora (a left Christian Democrat)[86] and Ungo (a social democrat who shared the 1972 ticket with Duarte) fled from El Salvador in fear for their lives as their associates and relatives were assassinated. Among the victims was Rubén Zamora's brother, the Christian Democrat Attorney-General Mario Zamora. Two weeks after his associate was assassinated by a death squad, Duarte joined the junta, where he proceeded to legitimize the slaughter. Zamora and Ungo have maintained a political association with the Salvadoran guerrillas, most of whom were also driven to the hills by state terror. In contrast, Bermúdez is the contra military commander, formerly an officer of Somoza's National Guard; and Calero, at the right wing of the CIA-run "civilian directorate," is an avowed advocate of terror who had been excluded from visiting Costa Rica on these grounds. Furthermore, there is no comparison between the indigenous guerrillas in El Salvador and the U.S. proxy forces attacking Nicaragua. A closer comparison to Zamora and Ungo would be the internal opposition members in Nicaragua, who have always been free to take part in political life if they choose and face harassment but not state terror of the Washington/Duarte style. No hint of these truisms will be found in the *Times* or, to my knowledge, elsewhere in the mainstream, with the rarest of exceptions.

The official story throughout has been that Duarte represents the "moderate center," unable to control the "violence by both ultra-rightists and by the Marxist guerrillas" (James LeMoyne); a photo accompanying this commentary shows New York Mayor Edward Koch being greeted by Duarte's Defense Minister, General Vides Casanova, who presided over much of the slaughter. A *Times* editorial noted the Anaya assassination—as a proof of Duarte's "courage" in "defying" the death squads. Buried in a news story, the same day, is the fact that the killers were using sophisticated weapons available only to the "right-wing death squads"—that is, the assassination squads of Duarte's security forces.[87]

Honduras made virtually no pretense of observing the Esquipulas Accord. The human rights violations that had become a serious problem as the United States converted it into a military base in the 1980s increased further after the Accord was signed. Ramón Custodio, president of the Commission for Defense of Human Rights in Central America and the Honduran Human Rights Commission (CODEH), reported in late October 1987 that killings by the security forces were becoming "more blatant," citing examples. As the first three-month period of the Accord passed, he stated at an international news conference that the worsening human rights situation deteriorated further in Honduras after the Accord was signed, and in El Salvador and Guatemala as well. These and other reports on growing human rights violations after the signing of the Accord were published in Canada and Mexico but omitted from the *Times* through the August–January period.[88]

CODEH reported 263 judicial executions in Honduras in 1987, 144 more than in 1986, attributing 107 to the security forces, along with an increase in torture and illegal arrests. Honduran journalist Manuel Torres Calderón reported that economic decline in this U.S. dependency had "forced the state to intervene in the economy even more heavily than its much maligned neighbor, Nicaragua." Capital flight had reached such a level that "money leaves the country as fast as it comes in," a Honduran banker observed. Half the population has no access to health services and more than a million Hondurans live in overcrowded shantytowns, despite extensive U.S. aid and no guerrilla threat or foreign attack. Neither the increasing human rights violations nor the impact of U.S.-influenced economic management were on the media agenda.[89]

Also largely off the agenda is the hostility toward the contras in Honduras, not only among the thousands of peasants expelled from their homes in "contraland" in the south. Wire services reported that the conservative newspaper *La Prensa*, "which publishes several contra-inspired pages of information on Nicaragua, said an opinion poll carried out before the latest [March 1988] crisis erupted showed that 88.5 percent of Hondurans wanted the contras expelled." Such facts received little notice. Similarly, the media have been unable to discover the protest of the National Union of Campesinos in Honduras over contra recruitment among impoverished Honduran peasants with bribes of $500, an enormous sum by their standards, published in the major Honduran daily *El Tiempo*. Such facts, though plainly important and newsworthy, must be suppressed because they are not conducive to the portrayal of the sturdy peasants of Nicaragua organizing to resist Sandinista depredations.[90]

Growing Honduran concerns over loss of national independence and integrity under U.S. influence have also not been a popular topic. As discussed earlier, the March 1988 Nicaraguan operations against the contras elicited irate denunciations of Sandinista aggressiveness and threat to Honduras in the U.S. media and Congress, as well as a bipartisan proposal for $48 million in aid, including arms, to the beleaguered freedom fighters so unfairly attacked. When the United States sent an airlift to "defend Honduras" against Sandinista aggression, there was much jingoist fanfare at home and a reaction in Honduras that received somewhat less attention. Honduran journalists condemned the U.S. "invasion." *El Tiempo* denounced the government call for—or acquiescence in—the dispatch of U.S. troops as "not only illegal but shameful. It is telling the world that the state of Honduras does not exist." The journal described the U.S. troops as an "occupation force," while the Christian Democratic Party "said that the U.S. soldiers should fly home immediately," and its leader Rubén Palma "told reporters that Honduran

President José Azcona had acted illegally in calling in foreign troops without parliament's authorization."[91]

One could learn little about such matters from the *New York Times*,[92] and not much elsewhere. Media reporting that departed from the U.S. government agenda would have allayed the widespread shock when Hondurans attacked the U.S. Embassy a few weeks later while police stood by, in an explosion of anti-U.S. sentiment.

Apart from the barriers to U.S. terror, overcome with media complicity as discussed earlier, two central features of the Esquipulas Accord were intolerable to Washington: the role given to international monitors, the CIVS, and the "symmetry" condition on which the agreements were based, requiring steps in parallel by all Central American countries. The former condition was unacceptable because it interferes with the U.S. ability to violate the Accord as it wishes; the latter, for the same reason and because Washington's terror states cannot possibly live up to the provisions on democratization and human rights. The task of the media, then, was to eliminate these two unwanted principles. The agreement as revised by Washington must be focused solely on Nicaragua, with the international monitors dismissed. By these means, the unwanted Esquipulas Accord could be brought into line with the Reagan–Wright plan rejected by the Central American presidents in August.

The problem of international monitoring became serious in January 1988, when the CIVS was to present its findings to the Central American presidents after studying the five countries. Plainly, this was the central diplomatic event of the month; equally plainly, it was unacceptable, particularly when the commission presented its conclusions. The CIVS singled out the United States for condemnation because of its continued assistance "to the irregular forces operating against the government of Nicaragua," thus violating "an indispensable requirement for the success of the peace efforts and of this Procedure as a whole." A CIVS official informed the press that Latin American representatives were "shocked by the attitudes of patent fear" expressed by trade unionists and opposition figures in El Salvador and Guatemala. He added that the CIVS could not provide details about compliance because of objections from Honduras, El Salvador, and Guatemala—a clear indication of what the report would have said, had it not been blocked by the United States and its clients. The report praised Nicaragua's "concrete steps" toward democratization despite the difficulties it faced.

The facts were reported by several journals but eliminated from the *New York Times,* where James LeMoyne, in a dispatch focusing on denunciations of Nicaragua, dismissed the CIVS report in one sentence, stating only that its meeting ended "with little agreement" (the report was adopted unanimously). The condemnation of the United States was briefly noted in an article on another topic nine days later by Stephen Kinzer, who added that "the commission fell out of favor in some circles when it reported that Nicaragua had taken 'concrete steps toward the beginning of a democratic process'"; like the O.A.S., the CIVS had thus "lost much of its authority as the conscience of Latin America."[93] The commission was disbanded under U.S. pressure, enabling the United States to pursue its terrorist exercises unhampered and permitting Duarte to continue to serve as a front man for repression and murder.

The "symmetry" problem was overcome by focusing virtually all coverage on Nicaragua, along with the constant pretense that whatever may appear in the text of the Esquipulas Accord, "there is no doubt that [the treaty's] main provisions are principally directed at Nicaragua and will affect Nicaragua more than any of the other nations that signed the accord" (James LeMoyne). That is quite true under the conditions dictated by Washington and observed by the press, though the conclusion has no basis in the text. As LeMoyne explained further, the Sandinistas are "in a somewhat exposed position" because they, and they alone, "are under close scrutiny for their efforts to carry out the Central American peace treaty."[94] Again true, on the tacit assumption that the Free Press must follow the marching orders that issue from Washington. LeMoyne's colleague Stephen Kinzer offered the same analysis, as did the media fairly generally.

The Media Alliance in San Francisco studied press samples during two periods of peak coverage of the peace plan (August 5 through September 15, 1987; January 5 through February 7, 1988). The *New York Times* devoted ten times as many stories to Nicaragua as to all the other countries combined in the first period, and eleven times as many in the second. Other media sampled had similar proportions.[95] Efforts to gain mainstream coverage for these reports failed.

The quality of coverage also differed radically. Thus a rock-throwing incident in Nicaragua on January 23 received front-page coverage in the *Washington Post* and prominent attention elsewhere, with the *Times* warning that the incident would "strengthen the argument" of the Reagan administration that Nicaragua is not complying with the peace plan. Similarly, extensive coverage was given to the January 16 detention of four members of the Nicaraguan opposition who had met with contras and the January 19 arrest of five opposition members, all released unharmed after several hours of questioning (in the *Times*, nineteen paragraphs and a headline across the page in the first case, and a front-page above-the-fold story in the second); months later, Roy Gutman, referring to this incident, observed in the *Washington Post* that "no government ordinarily allows a legal political party to negotiate a joint program with armed forces seeking the overthrow of that government." In contrast, the murder in Honduras of a human rights leader and a Christian Democratic Party leader on January 15 received 160 words in an unheadlined story, and no conclusions were drawn about compliance with the Accord. The disruption of a "Mothers of Political Prisoners" gathering by civilian Sandinista supporters warranted a major *Times* story and photo on January 23; the disruption of a "Mothers of Political Prisoners and the Disappeared" march by the Salvadoran riot police on December 21 was ignored.[96] The examples are typical and again readily explained in terms of a propaganda model.

The readers of the Toronto *Globe and Mail* and the wire services could learn that in a one-week period in January, while compliance with the Accord was front-page news, ten people were found murdered in El Salvador in death-squad style with signs of torture, including two women who had been hanged from a tree by their hair with their breasts cut off and their faces painted red. Later in the month, there were more killings, with the tortured bodies found in a traditional death-squad dump. Foreign diplomats and Church leaders blamed the Salvadoran armed forces. Auxiliary Archbishop Rosa Chavez stated in his February 7 homily that "according to information compiled by our office [Tutela Legal], the captors [of two tortured and murdered laborers] were men in plain clothes and uniformed soldiers of the 1st Artillery Brigade's counter-insurgency section" (an elite U.S.-trained unit).[97] The readers of the *New York Times* were spared these facts, just as the *Times* had no interest in a televised mass on January 3 in which Archbishop Rivera y Damas once again denounced "the practice of torture used against many Salvadorans by the death squads," stating that bishops in several provinces reported increased death-squad murders and calling for an end to assassinations and torture.[98]

A few weeks later, as Duarte's security services and their associates extended their grim work while the *Times* obligingly looked the other way, the House of Representatives passed a resolution commending El Salvador's progress toward democracy. The proposed resolution stated that El Salvador has achieved a system "which respects human liberties," but liberal Representative Ted Weiss of New York succeeded in having it changed to say only that the country has "sought to" establish such a system. "Give them a little credit for trying, Ted," said House Foreign Affairs Committee Chairman Dante Fascell. In December, as the terror was mounting after the signing of the Esquipulas Accord, the House of Representatives had overwhelmingly passed an amendment specifying a long list of "Actions Which Should Be Undertaken" to satisfy the high ideals of Congress—in Nicaragua. Representative Weiss sought to introduce a few changes, applying the conditions to "all countries in Central America" instead of only Nicaragua. This proposal was rejected by a large majority. Congress and the media share the same agenda.[99]

In subsequent months, state terror in El Salvador escalated, rarely reported. James LeMoyne was much exercised over guerrilla terror, devoting stories to the topic with such headlines as "Salvador Rebels Kill 12 in Raid on Town," "Guerrillas in Salvador Step Up Pre-election Terrorism," and "Salvador Rebels Target Civilians, Killing 3," repeatedly referring to the same alleged atrocities.[100] Terror by U.S. clients does not pass entirely unnoticed. Thus, LeMoyne concludes one story with the words, "Such rebel violence has been reflected in a rise in political killings," its source unnamed. In a "review of the week" column, he describes a guerrilla shift to "terrorist tactics," then adds that "increasingly, the guerrillas and their sympathizers are also the targets of violence." Another report focuses on guerrilla terror, noting also that "the army appears to be returning to killing suspected leftists as an answer to sharply stepped-up guerrilla assassinations, bombings and other attacks."[101] The message is that the U.S.-installed government may not be perfect, but its deficiencies are a response to guerrilla atrocities. Readers familiar with such journalistic practice can try to read between the lines and may surmise that the government is perhaps not judiciously observing its commitment to human rights under the accords. But they will learn little about the matter from this source. They may turn to the foreign press to read, in the mainstream, that Europeans "want to see progress towards civilized politics not just in Nicaragua and Costa Rica, but also in Guatemala,

Honduras and El Salvador, which lamentably continue to be bywords for barbarity."[102]

We should again observe that these devices to conceal atrocities provide a shield behind which the state terrorists can continue their work. The contribution of disciplined journalists to murder, torture, and general misery is not small.

The media campaign, only barely sampled here,[103] succeeded in demolishing what remained of the Esquipulas Accord by January. With the CIVS abolished under U.S. pressure, Ortega agreed to go far beyond the terms of the forgotten accords, abandoning the simultaneity condition entirely. The "genius of the Arias plan," the *Times* editors explained, "is that it provides a means for Nicaragua to accommodate to neighbors without appearing to truckle to Washington," not the simultaneity requirement that was recognized to be the "genius" of the plan when it was signed.[104] They may well be correct about what Arias had in mind, to judge by the references and quotes; but if so, that would simply show that he had no more interest in the implementation of the Esquipulas Accord than the *New York Times.*

Recognizing that the powerful make the rules, Ortega agreed that Nicaragua alone would enact the provisions of the accords, even calling for an international commission, including members of both U.S. political parties, to monitor Nicaragua's adherence alone.[105] The media reported that Ortega now promises to "comply with" the accords—that is, the version fashioned in Washington, which bears little resemblance to the text—while warning that his promises plainly cannot be trusted. No one else's promises were relevant, now that the accords had been consigned to oblivion. Citing unnamed "officials," LeMoyne portrayed Nicaragua as the villain of the piece, "the country most widely accused of bad faith," now "pressed to the wall by the other four Central American leaders" to implement the peace treaty. Readers could again turn to the foreign press to read that "Nicaragua has done more to comply with the terms of the Central American peace plan than any of the other five signatories, with the exception of Costa Rica," the judgment of the editors of the *Globe and Mail,* plainly accurate but hidden by the U.S. media barrage with only an occasional glimpse of the unacceptable facts.[106]

Even critics were swept up in the propaganda campaign. Thus a *Nation* editorial (January 30) stated that Ortega "has made significant concessions to the Central American peace plan," namely, by agreeing to abandon it in conformity to U.S. demands. The terror states were now exempt, along with their sponsor.

Throughout this period, there was a simple algorithm to determine which features of the peace plan count. Violations by the United States and the "fledgling democracies" are off the agenda, as is any requirement to which Nicaragua conformed. For example, a central feature of the accords was establishment of a National Reconciliation Commission. Nicaragua alone complied in a meaningful way, selecting its severest critic, Cardinal Obando, to head the commission. Duarte, in contrast, selected U.S. presidential candidate Alvaro Magaña as the head of the commission, which did nothing. In the second U.S. dependency, Honduras, there was barely a show of forming a commission, though it was not entirely inactive. We learn from the Honduran press that the National Reconciliation Commission was supervising the distribution of U.S. supplies to the contras and thus "helping to subvert" the March 1988 cease-fire.[107]

In accord with the algorithm just presented, the provisions of the Accord with regard to the National Reconciliation Commissions disappeared. Similarly, there is no utility to the unreported conclusion of the U.N. refugee commission (UNHCR) that repatriation of refugees has been more successful in Nicaragua than elsewhere because of the "excellent disposition of the Sandinista government."[108] Off the agenda, then, is the "sense of urgency" with which the Central American presidents committed themselves to the task of refugee repatriation in the Esquipulas Accord. The pattern is close to exceptionless.

Pursuing this procedure, the media, early on, reduced the Central American agreements to "two key points" (Stephen Kinzer): (1) Will Nicaragua offer an amnesty to what the U.S. government and the media call "political prisoners"?[109] (2) Will Nicaragua agree to negotiate with the contra civilian directorate?

With regard to the first point, few readers would have been aware that, in early November 1987, the CIVS determined that amnesty provisions were to go into effect when the aggression against Nicaragua ceases, and even a real media addict would not have learned that a few weeks later in November, the Nicaraguan National Assembly decreed a complete amnesty and revoked the state of emergency, both laws to "go into effect on the date that the [CIVS certifies] compliance with" the commitments of the accords to terminate the attack against Nicaragua. These laws were formulated in terms of the simultaneity condition of the accords, which Nicaragua, in its naïveté, believed to be operative.[110] Thus, by November, Nicaragua had largely complied with the accords as they are actually written. It was alone in this regard apart from Costa Rica, as remained the case.

The U.S. government version of the accords was, however, quite different from that of the CIVS and the text. We can find it in State Department propaganda or indirectly in news reports in the *New York Times,* where Stephen Kinzer describes the contents of the accords as follows: "Under its provisions, no country in the region would be permitted to assist the contras once the Sandinistas establish full political freedom."[111] According to this useful version, as long as Nicaragua falls short of a Scandinavian democracy in peacetime, the United States is entitled to maintain its proxy army in the field attacking Nicaragua, in explicit violation of the actual accords. Since the accords do not single out Nicaragua for special treatment, it also follows that in the *Times*/State Department version of the accords, they entitle the Soviet Union to send arms and supplies to the guerrillas in El Salvador with several flights a day from Cuba until a radical restructuring of Washington's terror state has been completed. This consequence, however, is unmentioned.

As noted earlier, El Salvador also declared an amnesty, though in a form that expressly violated the terms of the Esquipulas Accord. The *New York Times* lauded the decrees as the Duarte government's "most concrete step toward complying with regional peace accord," contrasting this forthcoming move with the refusal of the Sandinistas to comply apart from the "tentative" and grudging steps[112]—steps that met the conditions of the Accord, as we have just seen, though the *Times* never reported the facts. The *Toronto Globe and Mail* chose different words, describing the Salvadoran edict as an "amnesty for the military and the death squads." This noble gesture was bitterly condemned by human rights groups, not only because it freed the assassins of tens of thousands of people from prosecution (hardly likely in any event, with the government under effective military control) but also, as María Julia Hernández of Tutela Legal observed after several more months of atrocities, because "it made the military feel secure that there would be no prosecutions for human rights" violations in the future. The amnesty "chiefly benefited the military-linked death squads," the *Globe and Mail* commented accurately.[113]

With regard to the second "key point," negotiations, the accords did not call for discussions with CIA-created front organizations of the classic Communist Party style. That the contra directorate is exactly that had long been known and is documented in detail in an important (and unmentionable) monograph by Edgar Chamorro, who was selected by the CIA to serve as spokesman for the front created for the benefit of "enemy territory" at home.[114] In a memo released during the Iran-contra hearings, Robert Owen, Oliver North's liaison with the contras, described the civilian front as "a name only," "a creation of the United States government (USG) to garner support from Congress"; power lies in the hands of the Somozist-run FDN, headed by Adolfo Calero, who "is a creation of the USG and so he is the horse we chose to ride," though he is surrounded by people who are "liars and greed- and power-motivated" for whom the war is "a business" as they hope for the marines to restore them to the power they lost.[115]

Nevertheless, applying the algorithm for interpreting the accords, the media took their key feature to be negotiations between the Sandinistas and Washington's public relations creation. The *New York Times* even went so far as to describe the Nicaraguan government and the contras as "the two factions" who must negotiate and reach a settlement, a difficult task because the government "faction" insists upon "an end to all outside support for the contras"—as the Esquipulas Accord stipulates, a fact unmentioned.[116] Another journalist, surveying the problems of the region, describes the contenders for power in Nicaragua as "the two hostile bands"; in El Salvador, in contrast, the civil war pits "the U.S.-supported government" against the "Marxist guerrilias."[117] Appropriate use of language has its role to play, alongside of careful selection, distortion, and outright falsehood.

The insistence on wide-ranging negotiations with the contra directorate was another part of the long-standing effort to establish the fiction that the proxy army is an indigenous force, comparable to the guerrillas in El Salvador who were largely mobilized by U.S.-backed state terror, have always fought within their country, receive little if any military aid from abroad, have nothing like the extraordinary intelligence and support system provided by the contras' superpower sponsor,[118] and face a military force that, on paper at least, is considerably more powerful than the army of Nicaragua. It is necessary to suppress the astonishing inability of the U.S. to construct a guerrilla army in Nicaragua despite support vastly exceeding anything available to authentic guerrillas, U.S. dominance of the media over much of the country through powerful radio stations, recruitment of mercenaries in Honduras and elsewhere, an economy that has collapsed as a result of U.S. economic warfare and terror, and denial, thanks to U.S. ideological warfare, of the right to employ the domestic measures regularly adopted by Western democracies under far less threatening circumstances. With a fraction of the outside support lavished on the U.S. proxy forces, the Salvadoran guerrillas would have quickly overthrown the U.S.-installed government, and one might suspect that a guerrilla movement could be successfully established in U.S. border regions with a comparable effort by some unimaginable superpower. This failure of the U.S. effort to organize a guerrilla force within Nicaragua or even one that could be sustained from abroad without unprecedented outside support and direction is most remarkable, and very informative, for anyone prepared to think about what it means. Therefore, the facts and their meaning must be scrupulously suppressed, as they are.

The U.S. foreign aid budget for fiscal year 1989 contained $2 million to support opposition political groups and media in Nicaragua, the *Congressional Quarterly* reported (June 25, 1988), some of which openly identify with the contra attack. None of these "democratic groups in Nicaragua," as *Congressional Quarterly* calls them, has the support of more than 3 percent of the population; combined, they have the support of 9 percent, less than one-third the support for the Sandinistas. These are among the results of polls taken under the auspices of the Centro Interamericano de Investigaciones in Mexico and the Jesuit University (UCA) in Managua. As for President Ortega himself, 42 percent ranked him "good/excellent," and 29 percent, "fair." For comparison, in a UCA poll in El Salvador that received little notice, 6 percent of the respondents supported Duarte's Christian Democrats and 10 percent supported the right-wing ARENA, while 75 percent stated that no party represented them.[119]

Other interesting results of the Salvadoran poll were that 95 percent preferred economic and humanitarian aid over any kind of military aid,

4 percent blamed "guerrilla or communist subversion" for the crisis, and only 13 percent rated Duarte as "good" or "excellent." Recall that only 10 percent of the population see any signs of a democratic process in El Salvador.[120] Another contrast between El Salvador and Nicaragua was that, in the former, pollsters have found that "certain political questions had to be carefully couched in non-incriminating language. A significant number of Salvadorans told us that they do not discuss politics—period—not even with their closest friends or relatives. By contrast, in our survey in Nicaragua in June, interviewers judged that 77 percent of some 1,129 respondents in Managua answered poll questions without apparent fear or distrust." And the interviewers reported that "their biggest problem in the field was the delay caused when respondents amplified their answers," giving explanations of their responses for or against the Sandinista regime. In polls in Honduras in November 1987, 65 percent of respondents "said they believed Hondurans were afraid of expressing their political opinions in public," and "interviewers judged that only 38 percent of their respondents answered questions without fear or distrust."[121] The difference in climate between Nicaragua and El Salvador has always been obvious, though the media have succeeded in conveying the opposite impression.

Other unreported information on public opinion in El Salvador provides a good deal of insight into U.S. policy and the real concerns of the media. In 1988, the Archbishop of San Salvador organized a national debate to consider the problems facing the country. Over sixty organizations took part, "representing the private sector, professional associations, educational and cultural bodies, labor organizations, humanitarian groups, the displaced, religious institutions and others."[122] There was near-unanimous (95–100 percent) agreement on "the failure of the Reagan Administration's project for El Salvador"; support for negotiated settlement; increasing concern over human rights violations and impoverishment of the majority "while a few have become richer"; identification of the "root cause" of the conflict not in "international communist aggression" but, rather, in "structural injustice, manifested in the unjust concentration of wealth" in land, industry, and commerce and "exhaustion of the capitalist, dependent agro-export model as part of an unjust structure of international commerce."

The same proportions (95–100 percent) condemned

1. The "subordination of political power to economic power"
2. The "direct, permanent interference by the military in the operation of the state and the society in support of the oligarchy and dominant sectors, and thus in support of North American interests" as the country is "subjugated to the interests of international capital"
3. "Mortgaging the national sovereignty and self-determination and the enormous interference of the U.S. in El Salvador's national affairs"
4. Foreign military aid
5. The "strong opposition by the United States" and its Salvadoran right-wing and military allies to the Esquipulas Accord, to which El Salvador should be pressured to conform
6. The Amnesty Law, which exculpated "those charged with war crimes and crimes against humanity."

Furthermore, 88 percent see "serious restrictions on the democratic process" and regard "Christian Democracy as a cover while North American interference became more intensified"; attribute principal responsibility for the armed conflict to "foreign intervention, especially that of the U.S."; and describe the armed struggle as a response to "the impossibility of any genuine form of popular participation." Most called for recognition of the FMLN guerrillas as a "representative political force" that emerged in response to violence and injustice (55–59 percent). The highly touted elections were described by 81 percent as "the fundamental instrument of the U.S counterinsurgency project," "legitimizing the war and neutralizing the popular movement."

The document has much to say about the "U.S. counterinsurgency project" and the likely prospects for this tortured country. It was ignored in the United States, as were the polls.

The lack of attention to public opinion in El Salvador provides interesting lessons about U.S. political culture and the societal function of the media. The United States has unleashed an enormous military and repressive apparatus in El Salvador and has poured huge sums of money into the country. If these efforts had even a remote relation to the needs and concerns of Salvadorans, then, quite obviously, their opinions would be front-page news in the U.S. media and the subject of extensive commentary. What we discover, however, is that there is not the slightest interest in their opinions. It would be misleading to say that the information is suppressed; rather, the irrelevance of the people subject to our will is as elementary as the rules of arithmetic; to consider what they think would be as absurd as trying to discover the attitudes of chickens or donkeys.

The conclusion is clear: U.S. planners, and the educated elites that comment and articulate positions on international affairs, care not a whit about the needs and concerns of the people of El Salvador. Their sole concern is the preservation of their own privilege and power. The rhetoric of "benevolence," "good intentions" that misfired, and so on, is mere deception, possibly comforting self-deception as well. The attitudes and opinions of Salvadorans are not only ignored, as of zero significance, but also happen to be diametrically opposed to those of their professed benefactors in Washington, New York, Cambridge, and elsewhere. This is a matter of no concern, not even a level of concern that would lead to attention to the facts. The disdain for subject peoples is merely a background fact, like the air we breathe.

New York Times correspondents regularly allege that polls are illegal in Nicaragua, citing no evidence and not reporting the statement of the respected Jesuit priest who is rector of UCA (which would normally be responsible for polling) that polls are permitted but that facilities are lacking—plausible, given the circumstances. The *Interamerican* report (see note 119) assumes that polls have been permitted since 1984, that the August 1987 accords further legitimize polls, and that "the present poll put that general understanding to the test." The poll was not reported in the *Times*. I noted little mention elsewhere—and that unreliable (see *Necessary Illusions*, chapter 3, note 47).

Let us return to the fate of the Central American peace negotiations after the effective demolition of the Esquipulas Accord in January 1988. In subsequent discussion, the terms of the Accord are consistently understood in the Washington version, accepted under duress by Nicaragua: the expansive interpretation devised by Washington applies to Nicaragua alone. Thus, it is possible for news columns to assert that "other countries have done somewhat better" than Nicaragua in adhering to the accords with their requirement of "freedom for the press and opposition parties, an end to support for other countries' guerrillas and negotiations with Nicaragua's rebels," as the *Boston Globe* reported in August 1988; indeed, other countries *cannot* violate the accords, whatever the facts, under the conventions of government-media newspeak.[123]

Putting aside the usual disregard for state terror in the "fledgling democracies" and Honduran support for the contras, the reference here to negotiations appears rather audacious; it was hardly a secret that Nicaragua alone had negotiated a cease-fire agreement. But one must understand the algorithm already described. When Nicaragua entered into cease-fire negotiations and reached an agreement with the contras, this "key issue" was dropped from the agenda as no longer serviceable.

It was also necessary to eliminate the inconvenient fact that El Salvador and Guatemala, in opposition to the near-unanimous will of the public,[124] were refusing to negotiate with the indigenous guerrillas. The *Times* did not interrupt its daily lambasting of the Sandinistas in January 1988, the crucial month for dismantling the accords, to report that "according to [FDR leader Guillermo] Ungo, talks have not resumed, despite FMLN requests, because of pressure exerted on Duarte by the Reagan administration as well as from the country's security forces."[125] A February 8 appeal for dialogue by Ungo was rejected by the government on grounds that it will "only dialogue with legally registered political parties"; this was reported prominently in the Mexican press but not in the *Times*.[126] The FMLN/FDR stated that this was Duarte's third rejection of renewed talks since November. Neither this nor Archbishop Rivera y Damas's homily hoping for a Duarte response appears to have been reported. Rather, the *Washington Post* editors, in a fanciful construction, condemned the guerrillas for having "rejected [Duarte's] overtures," which "went substantially beyond the obligations placed on him by the Central American peace plan." There was scant notice of subsequent rebel offers to negotiate, rejected by the government. Jeane Kirkpatrick went so far as to denounce the guerrillas for rejecting all of Duarte's "generous offers" for negotiations.[127] Again, the facts turn into their opposite as they pass through the distorting prism of the media.

In Guatemala, the Bishops' conference called for renewed negotiations on January 29: the guerrillas accepted; the army refused, backed by President Cerezo. In late February, the rebels requested talks again, to be mediated by the Archbishop; the government refused. A rebel offer of negotiations in April, supported by President Arias, who offered his country as a site, was rejected by Cerezo, and a cease-fire proposal in June was dismissed by his government.[128] All of this was unworthy of attention, on the principles already discussed.

The logic was explained further by George Shultz in a letter objecting to a congressional proposal that the president be required to submit a report on Salvadoran government efforts to achieve a cease-fire before all aid can be released. Its sponsors argued that Congress would thereby be "making clear its support for a negotiated end" to the civil war in El Salvador. Shultz replied that "it is wholly inappropriate to try to pressure the elected government to negotiate or to make concessions to the guerrillas, which would not be acceptable to any democratic government." Since Nicaragua, unlike El Salvador, has not achieved democracy and lacks an elected government, it is quite proper to subject it to terror and economic warfare to pressure it to negotiate with U.S. proxies.[129]

A cease-fire was reached in Nicaragua on March 23, 1988; again, Nicaragua was alone in implementing an element of the accords.[130] The agreement was at once undermined by congressional legislation, and the administration went still further, violating the legislation as well as the cease-fire agreement. The media went along, as discussed in the text. Further negotiations broke down in June as the contras, increasingly under hard-line leadership, followed the U.S. strategy to undermine them by constantly demanding escalation when agreement seemed near.

The Council on Hemispheric Affairs reported that

> the breakdown of the Nicaraguan talks also implemented the game plan urged several weeks ago by Assistant Secretary of State Elliott Abrams: that the administration was urging the contras not to sign a peace agreement with the Sandinistas, but go along with a prolongation of a de facto truce, hoping that some adventitious Sandinista military action, like shooting down a contra supply plane or opening fire on a contra unit, would enable the White House to seek a resumption of lethal military aid from Congress. According to Abrams this was the very least that he was hoping for. When asked what was the most that the United States would do if given such a pretext, he responded, "We'll flatten Managua."

Further elements of the "game plan" were for U.S. intelligence agencies to step up their activities within Nicaragua, "hoping to use internal opposition forces to discredit the Sandinistas and sow discontent," and to lay the basis for further military action—what is commonly and accurately referred to, outside the media, as "the Chilean method," referring to the means employed to replace Chilean democracy by a military dictatorship. As one example, the Council on Hemispheric Affairs (COHA) cited the arrest and brief detention of fifteen opposition leaders for demonstrating outside the National Assembly building after they had rejected a request that they obtain a permit. "It is widely believed in Washington," COHA continues, "that the opposition was acting at the behest of their CIA liaison to stage the unauthorized demonstration" and court arrest as proof of Sandinista bad faith.

Reviewing the situation a few weeks later, Stephen Kinzer reported that "administration officials attributed the collapse of the talks to Sandinista intransigence," mentioning no other possible explanation. The *Times* editors added that "without the war, and the damage to Nicaragua's economy, it's arguable that Managua wouldn't have signed the regional peace plan" of August 1987. They urged the administration "to work with Central Americans" to pressure the Sandinistas to accept "specific targets and timetables," against the threat of further sanctions; no suggestions are offered for other participants in the Central American drama. A few weeks earlier, James LeMoyne had observed that "there is little doubt that the pressure of the guerrillas [in El Salvador] has been the chief stimulus for positive political change here."[132] By the logic of the editors, then, we should support the indigenous guerrillas in El Salvador. Somehow, the logical consequence is not drawn.

As the first anniversary of the Esquipulas Accord approached, violations continued in the states now exempt from their terms. In El Salvador, the Church Human Rights Office documented "a startling increase" in political killings of civilians in 1988. The Archbishop, in a Sunday homily, condemned the "return to the law of the jungle" with increasing death squad violence; and Auxiliary Bishop Rosa Chávez, denouncing on national TV the killing of peasants associated with the labor union UNTS, declared that "all evidence points in only one direction—to the Salvadoran security forces." Peasants and members of the National Association of Indigenous Salvadorans were reported murdered after torture by soldiers, including a ninety-nine-year-old man and his daughter in a recently resettled village. On July 28, Rigoberto Orellana, leader of the newly founded "Movement for Bread, Land, Work and Liberty," was killed, by security forces according to spokespersons of the organization. As the anniversary of the Accord passed, killing continued. On August 21, a Swiss physician, Jurg Weiss, was detained and then killed by the National Police, shot in the face in an apparent effort to conceal his identity. He was on his way to investigate reports of the bombing of a village. The army claimed he was killed in combat, but his colleagues allege that, because of his humanitarian activity, he was targeted by security forces in their campaign of repression against humanitarian and religious volunteers. The murder was condemned in a resolution of the European Parliament on "growing escalation of state terrorism" in El Salvador. On the same day two young men were found shot to death in San Salvador, bringing the number to five for the week; all five victims showed signs of torture, according to the spokesman of the Human Rights Commission CDHES, who described the killings as intended to foster "psychological terror among the population." The attempt to assassinate Colonel Majano took place four days later.[133]

There were lesser abuses as well. The army barred the Church from providing supplies to resettled refugee villages. In rural areas, police regularly broke up political meetings (Rubén Zamora). A July 21 demonstration calling for release of an abducted trade unionist was attacked by police, who fired with automatic weapons and tear gas, leaving many wounded. On July 12, troops using tear gas, rifle butts, and clubs had attacked a march of farmers and cooperativists attempting to deliver provisions to striking electrical workers; demonstrators were detained by the police (reports ranged from one to 100 detained). Earlier, in efforts to disrupt a May Day rally, the army bombed the UNTS office, and Treasury Police abducted and severely beat the man who operated the sound system after the regular UNTS soundman had kept away under death threat. Many organizers and demonstrators were detained in prison, and a leader of the striking metalworkers' union who had directed chants at the rally "disappeared." In Honduras the army prevented workers from attending May Day demonstrations in Danlí organized by the major labor union of eastern Honduras; in mid-April, police in Tegucigalpa had shot in the air and used tear gas to prevent a protest march to the U.S. Embassy, and, according to human rights workers, "disappeared" a student, Roger González, arrested as other students were jailed in connection with the April 7 attack on the U.S. consulate while police stood by. In Costa Rica protesting farmers and cooperativists were harassed and detained by the Rural Guard; in one case, tear gas and physical force were used to prevent them from presenting a petition at the city hall.[134]

Neither the continuing atrocities nor the lesser abuses received coverage, apart from an occasional perfunctory notice. But denunciation of Sandinista iniquity continued at a fever pitch, particularly when Nicaragua briefly approached some of the regular lesser abuses of the U.S. client states in mid-July, eliciting a new round of indignant condemnations across the political spectrum and renewed support of congressional liberals for contra aid.

In her review of the first year of the Accord in August, Julia Preston observed that little was achieved apart from Nicaragua. In Honduras, Azcona remains "another caretaker president for the powerful military"; the same is true, though unstated, in El Salvador and Guatemala. She cites an August 4 Americas Watch review of human rights, which reports that "political murders by military and paramilitary forces continue on a wide scale in Guatemala and El Salvador and on a smaller scale in Honduras," along with several "reported in Nicaragua," Preston adds, "where they had not been common." "Nicaragua initially did far more than any other Central American country to comply" with the Accord until mid-July, ten months after it was signed—a long "initial" period, which terminated after the breakdown of the cease-fire negotiations, when Nicaragua "violently broke up a May 10 opposition rally [at Nandaime] and kept six leaders in jail during long trials, closed the Catholic radio [station] indefinitely, expelled U.S. ambassador Melton and expropriated the largest private sugar plantation in Nicaragua." The last two actions hardly qualify as violations of the Accord. Radio Católica reopened on August 18, leaving only the pro-Sandinista La Semana Cómica under government sanction for publishing material degrading women.[135]

The events of mid-July—in Nicaragua, that is—aroused great horror. "Sandinistas will be Sandinistas," a radio commentator observed knowingly in one of the milder reactions when the police broke up the Nandaime rally, using tear gas for the first time—after having been "pelted . . . with sticks and rocks," we learn in paragraph thirteen of Stephen Kinzer's report, a fact that disappeared from most later commentary.[136] There were front-page stories and regular reports and editorials on the Sandinista barbarity in breaking up the rally in the standard Salvadoran style, expelling the U.S. ambassador, with charges that he had been involved in organizing the pro-contra opposition, and nationalizing a private sugar plantation alleged to be nonproductive, a front-page story in the *Times.* References to the use of tear gas to break up the rally and to police violence continued to appear in the press, with appropriate horror, for months. Congress was so enraged that amidst renewed calls for arms for the contras, both Houses passed impassioned condemnations of Managua's "brutal suppression of human rights" by overwhelming margins (ninety-one to four in the Senate, 358 to eighteen in the House), the press reported approvingly.[137]

Recall that the "brutal repression of human rights" by the Sandinistas only began to approach, for a brief moment, some of the *lesser* abuses that are normal practice among the U.S. favorites in the region and does not even come close to the regular exercise of their "pedagogy of terror." Recall also that as Duarte's security services and their death squads escalated their terror after the Accord was signed, there was no condemnation in Congress but, rather, praise for their progress toward a system "which respects human liberties."

Congressional debate over how best to punish the Sandinistas for their July transgressions was no less interesting, even apart from the stirring rhetoric about our exalted libertarian standards and the pain inflicted upon our sensitive souls by any departure from them—in Nicaragua. The Senate passed the Byrd Amendment setting the conditions for renewed military aid to the contras.[138] Speaking for his colleagues, including some of the most prominent Senate liberals, Majority Leader Byrd warned the Sandinistas that they "can either fully comply with the requirements for democratization that they agreed to in the Arias peace plan and move into the mainstream of harmonious democratic relations with their neighbors," or they can continue "to blatantly violate the provisions of the peace accords," repress "the legitimate democratic aspirations of the Nicaraguan people," and face the consequences: a "return to military pressure," that is, U.S.-sponsored international terrorism. Byrd was also concerned over the failure of the Reaganites "to press the Soviet leadership to cease and desist from its military-aid program for the Government of Nicaragua," so that the only country in the region subject to foreign attack will also be the only country completely disarmed. Senator Dodd, perhaps the leading Senatorial dove with regard to Central America, was deeply impressed with these remarks and proposals and asked to "add my voice in praise of our leader," Senator Byrd. He was no less effusive in praising "the courageous leadership of President Arias, of Costa Rica; President Cerezo, of Guatemala; President Azcona, of Honduras; and President Duarte, of El Salvador, a great friend of this Congress"—though not of the people of El Salvador, who regard him with fear and contempt and see no signs of a democratic process in the country, as shown by polls that are suppressed as useless. Senator Dodd and other sponsors of the Byrd Amendment are well aware of the achievements of the military regimes of the U.S. terror states and of the escalation, in response to the Esquipulas Accord, of the terror for which the official "moderates" provide a democratic cover for the benefit of Congress and the media. It simply doesn't matter.

It is "fine" for Congress "to take a good roundhouse swing at the Sandinistas for reverting to dictatorial form" and to "remind them that Americans are not divided over democratic rights and wrongs," the *New York Times* editors commented, admonishing the Democrats "to let the Sandinistas know publicly the dangers of their bad-faith actions." The editors are not "divided over democratic rights and wrongs" in El Salvador; they have utter contempt for democratic rights in El Salvador, as their silence indicates, not to speak of their constant praise for the progress of democracy in this terror state. Stephen Kinzer, who knows Guatemala well, went so far as to quote a senior Guatemalan official on the "palpable unhappiness" of his government over the despicable behavior of the Sandinistas. "There is a liberalizing trend in the whole world, and Nicaragua is practically the only nation that is resisting it," he says, speaking for a government that is indeed liberalizing in that its murders and disappearances are down to a rate of only a few a day according to human rights groups, definitely a marked improvement over earlier years.[139]

The editors of the *Washington Post* called upon the "Central American democracies" and "Democratic critics of contra aid" to join "wholeheartedly" in condemning the Sandinista violation of "their solemnly sworn democracy pledges" as they act "very much the Communist police state, busting heads, tossing people in jail, censoring the media";

imagine what terms would apply to El Salvador or Israel for their actions at the same time, by these standards. It was surely quite proper for the American ambassador to offer "the extra help required by the opposition," the editors continue. As the Council on Hemispheric Affairs observed, few nations would tolerate such behavior; "Washington would view foreign governmental funding of U.S. dissident entities as an unfriendly if not outright illegal act" and would not be likely to "countenance the Soviet ambassador to Washington's participation in a local leftist group's rally which called for termination of the current government," let alone participation by the German or Japanese ambassador in 1942, to take a closer analogue. It is also less than likely that an ambassador from a hostile power engaged in hostilities against the United States would have been admitted in the first place, particularly one who had duplicated Melton's performance as he was sworn in as ambassador in Washington, announcing, "I want to make it crystal clear what America stands for and the values of democracy and how the Sandinistas don't meet even the minimal standards." There would be "no more compromising" with the Sandinistas, according to this protégé of Elliott Abrams, architect of the terrorist attack against Nicaragua.[140] But in the case of an official enemy, unique standards apply.

A few months earlier, Singapore had expelled a U.S. diplomat "on the grounds that he had improperly interfered in the domestic affairs of the country," Owen Harries writes in the right-wing journal he edits.[141] "Under the Vienna Convention governing diplomatic relations, such interference is impermissible," he continues, so "the United States had no option but to comply" when Singapore charged that the diplomat had "encouraged disgruntled Singaporeans in anti-government activities." Harries is writing in defense of Singapore against charges of improper behavior and police-state repression. Singapore is a semifascist country that offers a favorable investment climate, so the Vienna Convention applies. Not so, however, in the case of Nicaragua, designated by the authorities as an enemy.

Commenting further, the Council on Hemispheric Affairs observes that although Melton and members of his staff were expelled "for blatant interference in Nicaraguan internal affairs, the use of the U.S. embassy to fund, direct and coordinate disruptive activities by the civil opposition in Nicaragua in harmony with the actions of the contras . . . continues," including almost $700,000 of U.S. government funds earmarked for opposition elements. The U.S. government "is making a clear effort to create a parallel government in Nicaragua" that might assume power under escalated attack or social collapse.[142]

In October 1988, Amnesty International (AI) released a document entitled *El Salvador: "Death Squads"—A Government Strategy,* reporting that right-wing death squads had abducted, tortured, and killed hundreds of Salvadorans in the preceding eighteen months, often beheading the victims to spread fear.[143] The so-called death squads are an agency of the security forces of the U.S.-installed government, serving its strategy of intimidating any potential opposition. "Victims are customarily found mutilated, decapitated, dismembered, strangled or showing marks of torture . . . or rape," AI reported. "The death squad style is to operate in secret but to leave mutilated bodies of victims as a means of terrifying the population." The victims include trade unionists, human rights workers, judges and jurors working on human rights abuse cases, refugees, church members, teachers, and students. "There can be no recourse to the police or military when they themselves carry out death-squad killings." The killings are carried out by plainclothes gunmen and by uniformed police and military units with the apparent acquiescence of the state: "the Salvadoran death squads are simply used to shield the government from accountability for the torture, disappearances and extra-judicial executions committed in their name." Members of the death squads, some living in hiding in the United States, told AI that the squads were drawn from specially trained police units, the Treasury Police and the National Guard. Church and human rights groups estimate that about a dozen bodies bearing the marks of death-squad torture and execution were turning up every month on roadsides and in body dumps in 1987, the toll quadrupling in early 1988. AI reported that the resurgence of the death squads could be traced partly to the government amnesty of a year earlier, as had been widely predicted at the time while the *Times* hailed El Salvador's forthcoming steps toward compliance with the peace Accord.

The AI report received no notice in the *New York Times.* The Senate passed a resolution, fifty-four to twelve, warning *Nicaragua* "that continued Sandinista violation of regional peace accords would 'very likely' cause Congress to approve new military aid next year."[144] We see again the familiar pattern: U.S.-backed atrocities in its client states coupled with stern warnings to Nicaragua to improve its behavior on pain of intensified U.S. terror. Also in October 1988, the Guatemala City journal *Central America Report* took as its lead story the just released Amnesty International annual review of human rights for 1987. It reported that "some of the most serious violations of human rights are found in Central America," particularly Guatemala and El Salvador, where "kidnappings and assassinations serve as systematic mechanisms of the government against opposition from the left, the [AI] report notes"; recall that the situation deteriorated after the Esquipulas Accord and became still more grim through 1988. The human rights situation is "less dramatic" in Nicaragua and Honduras, apart from "civilian deaths at the hands of U.S.-supported contra forces." While there have been "cases of kidnappings, tortures and extrajudicial killings in Honduras, Panama and Nicaragua, these actions have not been established as systematic government mechanisms."[145]

A month later, the *New York Times* published a front-page story by Lindsey Gruson on atrocities in Guatemala.[146] In the past, Gruson observes, Guatemala City had been "a free-fire zone for political extremists" who carried out extensive terror; unmentioned is the fact that the "political extremists" responsible for the overwhelming majority of the atrocities were—and are—the agents of the U.S.-backed government. In fact, the U.S. role in Guatemala is unmentioned in this story. Gruson describes the increase in kidnappings, torture, and murder; the worsening situation in the cities; and the "de facto military dictatorship" in the countryside (quoting Americas Watch Observer Anne Manuel). The main targets in the cities are "labor leaders, union organizers and leftists." A spokesman for an independent human rights organization says that "there's a democratic façade now, nothing more. The façade hides that all the power is held by the army and that the situation is getting worse." An Americas Watch report released two weeks later accused the government of prime responsibility for the serious increase in human rights abuses, now reaching a level of about two a day, presumably a considerable underestimate, Americas Watch concludes.[147]

As 1988 came to a close, government atrocities mounted in the client states. Several new death squads appeared. The dean of the Law School in Santa Ana, Imelda Medrano, was murdered on December 16 after returning from a university demonstration in San Salvador where she was a principal speaker; her house had been watched for two days by men in a jeep with darkened windows, a death-squad trademark. Three powerful explosions destroyed the biology building of the National University on December 22. Attackers killed one watchman; a second described a heavily armed squad of about fifty men. The university rector accused the military of planting the bombs: "This is the response of the Armed Forces to the stepped up war and their impotence in containing it," he said. The attack took place as soldiers were surrounding the campus, and only the military would have been free to operate so openly, the rector added. The director of Tutela Legal agreed that "these are actions of people with military training, heavily armed and moving with total liberty." Five days later, a bomb destroyed the offices of the Lutheran Church, which the army views with suspicion because of its work with refugees. Privately, church officials, who had received death threats, blamed the army. The West German ambassador, who had condemned attacks against the Lutheran Church, received a death threat and left the country. A Western diplomat observed, "I see a military hand" behind the bombings. A source with close military contacts says the army feels it can counter the guerrillas only with "selective terror."[148] There was little news coverage, less concern, except for the possible threat to the Reagan project of bringing "democracy" to El Salvador.

The lesser abuses in the client states also continued. On September 13, soldiers and police attacked a student demonstration in San Salvador and broke up another in Santa Ana, while security forces surrounded the labor union UNTS offices. Some 250 students and university workers were arrested. The rector of the university claimed that 600 students had been arrested and that the whereabouts of over 400 were unknown. "During the demonstration riot police fired volleys of shots and canisters of tear gas into the crowd of 3,000," wounding "scores of demonstrators" and apparently killing the operator of a police water cannon (*Central America Report*). Thirty local and foreign journalists "were ordered to the ground by security agents, who warned them not to move or take photographs," and at least ten foreign observers were detained. The director of Tutela Legal "said the police actions appeared designed to intimidate urban protesters at the beginning of a crucial election period." "The patience of the security corps has its limits, faced with street provocations," Defense Minister Vides Casanova told reporters: "We'll not tolerate any more violence." The day before, COHA reported, military forces had "attacked 500 demonstrators in Usulutan who were peacefully protesting the lack of government aid following heavy flooding," injuring fifteen and arresting eight.[149]

As before, these lesser abuses pale in significance before the government strategy of intimidation through sheer terror. None of this elicited interest or concern, as distinct from the events at Nandaime that briefly approached some of the regular lesser abuses. These, as we have seen, aroused such horror that congressional doves were compelled to renew aid to their terrorist forces to punish the Sandinistas. Furthermore, the European allies of the United States refrained from more than token assistance after Hurricane Joan destroyed much of Nicaragua in October. The reason was their profound revulsion over the repression of Nandaime, which "many European governments view . . . as open defiance by the Sandinistas of the regional peace process," Julia Preston reports, noting "the current displeasure in Europe with the Sandinistas"—though not with El Salvador and Guatemala, which continue to merit their support.[150] Again we see that hypocrisy has no limits and also that Europe is far more colonized than it likes to believe.

As noted, the lesser abuses in the client states, generally ignored, were reported by Sam Dillon in the *Miami Herald.* In a later article, he reviews the increasing repression throughout the region, singling out Nicaragua as the worst offender, its most serious offence being "the gassing of a peaceful rally and jailing of top political leaders in Nandaime." He goes on to describe how the Salvadoran military attacked "large but peaceful urban protests," which "angry riot police . . . crushed . . . with tear gas, clubbings and more than 250 arrests," along with arrests of many others "in night raids on the offices of two leftist unions and peasant groups." He briefly mentions the "dramatic" increase in "political killings by the army and death squads—as well as by guerrillas." He is plainly cognizant of the facts, but, as the facts pass through the ideological filter, large-scale slaughter, terror, and repression as a government strategy of intimidation in the U.S. client states become insignificant as compared with real but far lesser abuses in a country subjected to U.S. terror and economic warfare. Note that we are considering a reporter and a journal that are at least willing to report some of the facts.[151]

The client states continued to reject negotiations, while the U.S. government and the media railed at the Sandinistas for their failure to revitalize the negotiations stalled by the obstructionist tactics of the U.S. proxies. We learn from the Mexican press that President Cerezo "reiterated his rejection of a possible dialogue with the guerrilla army," adding that as long as the "subversives . . . do not give up their belligerent position, we will not open direct talks with their leaders. . . . No dialogue can take place amidst weapons." In El Salvador, thousands of peasants, students, and workers marched through the capital city to the hotel where an O.A.S. meeting was taking place to demand that the government negotiate with the guerrillas. The guerrillas had declared a unilateral truce for the duration of the meeting and "renewed a call for negotiations with the government," AP reported. President Duarte, in his address to the O.A.S. delegates, "said the guerillas' expressed desire to resume negotiations was merely 'tactical.' He accused the rebels of pursuing 'a strategic maneuver to destroy democracy through democracy's own liberties.'"[152]

The O.A.S. meetings were covered by Lindsey Gruson in the *New York Times*. Gruson referred bleakly to the "perversion" of the peace process in Central America. Predictably, only one example is cited: the Nandaime rally and the arrests of Nicaraguan peasants on suspicion of aiding the contras. These acts of repression have "undermined efforts to reinvigorate the negotiations," Gruson reports, citing U.S. diplomats. With regard to El Salvador, his only comment is that the October 1987 amnesty closed the books on earlier army assassinations; Guatemalan and Honduran abuses are unmentioned, and nothing is said about negotiations in El Salvador and Guatemala or why they have not been "invigorated."[153] In short, a selective filter designed for the needs of government propaganda and reflecting the insignificance of terror, torture, and repression when they do not serve these ends.

Gruson also notes that no agreement could be reached on a date for the planned Central American summit, for unknown reasons. The veil is lifted by the Mexican press, which reported that the Salvadoran government cancelled the Central American summit scheduled to take place in San Salvador, pleading "lack of economic capacity." The cancellation "came only a few hours after the visit to that country of the U.S. Special Ambassador to Central America, Morris Busby," and his meeting with President Duarte. Analysts are quoted as attributing the summit difficulties to "a boycott by the U.S., in which Morris Busby will not be exempt from 'chargeability' and which might have been devised as a reply to Cerezo's refusal to support belligerent action against Nicaragua." For President Cerezo, "it is vital that the presidential summit take place, observers indicate, because with this he is trying to distract attention from the violent problems of his country and to increase the international prestige that he has gained with his policies of active neutrality."[154] The pattern is one that we have seen repeatedly: U.S. initiatives to obstruct a political settlement, Duarte's compliance, and the silence of the media.

The selection of issues and style of commentary illustrate the means employed to inculcate proper habits of thought. A particularly useful technique is uncritical citation of approved leadership elements. As the government and media sought to revitalize anti-Sandinista fervor in summer 1988, Stephen Kinzer reported on a meeting of the United States and its four Central American allies. "All four countries disapprove of the Sandinistas and have urged them to liberalize their regime," he observed, "but they do not agree on how best to exercise such pressure." President Arias is quoted as saying that "Nicaragua has unfortunately failed us," expressing "my disappointment, my pain, my sadness," as he discussed abuses in Nicaragua with his colleagues from the terror states; about their practices he has expressed no disappointment, pain, or sadness, as least so far as the U.S. media report. President Cerezo added that he is "very distressed that the Sandinistas are not following the rules of democracy." George Shultz denounced the "Communist Government of Nicaragua—and the Communist guerrillas of El Salvador and Guatemala" as "a destructive and destabilizing force in the region," as "the Sandinista regime continues to rely on Soviet arms and to amass a military machine far in excess of its defense needs." "Mr. Shultz and the Foreign Ministers of Honduras, Guatemala, El Salvador and Costa Rica expressed 'their respect for the principles of peace, democracy, security; social justice and economic development,'" Kinzer reports with no comment and no detectable shudder.[155]

An accompanying article from Washington describes the consensus of Senators to approve further aid to the contras and the concern of the Democrats that it would harm "their party's image" if the Sandinistas were to repress the internal opposition or "mount a military offensive against the contras"; "the party's image" is not damaged by its support for continuing atrocities in the terror states. A few days later, senatorial doves passed legislation permitting new military aid if the treacherous Sandinistas were to attack the contras within Nicaragua or receive more military aid than Congress considers appropriate.[156] The Associated Press quotes liberal Massachusetts Senator John Kerry, who supports "humanitarian aid to the rebels" with a vote on arms to follow in the event of "continued flow of Soviet weaponry into Nicaragua, violations of last year's regional peace Accord by the Sandinistas, and any attempt by the Nicaraguan government to militarily 'mop up' the rebel forces," Kerry said.[157]

All of this fits the standards for competent reporting. The quotes are presumably accurate, as are the descriptive statements. Lying behind the selection of facts and manner of presentation are certain unquestioned assumptions, including the following. Nicaragua alone is failing to "liberalize" and observe the Esquipulas Accord; the facts are different, but unwelcome, therefore scarcely reported. It is illegitimate for Nicaragua to defend itself from the terrorist attack of U.S. proxy forces based in Honduras by conducting military operations within its own territory or by receiving arms from the only supplier that the United States will permit; but it is legitimate for the U.S. allies to refuse any dealings with the indigenous guerrillas (generally unreported) and to attempt to destroy them with U.S arms and advisers. The president of Costa Rica, whose business-run democracy survives on a U.S. dole and who, if quoted accurately, cares little about continuing atrocities in the "fledgling democracies" or their gross violations of the minimal preconditions for democracy and of the peace treaty that bears his name in the media, is the arbiter of adherence to its provisions and of democratic practice. The president of the military-run state of Guatemala, which continues to terrorize and murder its citizens, though on a lesser scale than in earlier years, is in a position to condemn far less repressive and more open societies than his for failure to move toward "democracy." A U.S. official who bears major responsibility for the attack on Nicaragua, for traumatizing El Salvador, and for backing near-genocidal slaughter in Guatemala is, likewise, in a position to determine who is "destabilizing" Central America and what is an appropriate level of defense for the government subjected to U.S. armed attack. Aid to the U.S. proxy forces is "humanitarian," though international conventions, reiterated in the World Court ruling that the U.S. government rejects and the media ignore, are quite explicit in restricting the concept of "humanitarian aid" to aid to civilians, and civilians on both sides, without discrimination. It is only right and just for a "neutral agency" such as the State Department to administer such "humanitarian aid," and, if Nicaragua attempts measures of self-defense that would be normal and unquestioned in any Western democracy, it is proper for the CIA to supply its terrorist forces in the field within Nicaragua—unless they prove an "imperfect instrument" and thus contribute to "our Nicaraguan agony."

One can imagine a different style of reporting, not adopting these presuppositions of U.S. propaganda, citing other sources (the World Court, for example), and selecting relevant facts by different criteria (human rights and needs, democracy and freedom, the rule of law, and other values that are commonly professed). But such will rarely be found in the media. The constant barrage of properly selected material, with hardly a critical word or analytic passage, firmly instills the presuppositions that lie behind it, shaping the perceptions of the audience within the framework of acceptable doctrine more effectively than the productions of any Ministry of Truth. Meanwhile the media can plead that they are only doing their duty honestly—as they are, though not in exactly the sense they intend. As throughout this horrifying decade, the worst human rights violators in Central America by a wide margin are the outright U.S. creations—the government of El Salvador and the contras—and the U.S.-supported regime of Guatemala. If the obvious significance of these facts has been discussed in the mainstream media and journals, I have not found it. The nature of these regimes is sometimes partially revealed; but no conclusions are drawn concerning the U.S. role in Central America, U.S. political culture, and the moral standards of the privileged classes that construct and support these policies.

The conclusions that *are* drawn are quite different. *New York Times* diplomatic correspondent Robert Pear writes of the prospects for a "new policy of diplomacy in Central America" under the Bush administration. This hopeful new policy of President Bush and the pragmatic Secretary of State James Baker will emphasize working "more closely with Congress and with Latin American nations to put political pressure on the Sandinistas to allow elections [there having been none in Nicaragua by Washington edict], freedom of expression and other rights guaranteed under regional peace accords." To ensure that the reader understands the party line, Pear adds, "Nicaragua signed those accords in 1987 and 1988, but the United States and other nations say the Sandinistas have flouted many provisions." There is no hint that anything may be awry in the U.S. client states or that the actions of the United States itself might raise some questions.

The performance throughout would impress the rulers of a totalitarian state. The suffering that has resulted, and will yet ensue, is beyond measure.

NOTES

This chapter is reprinted with permission. Noam Chomsky, *Necessary Illusions: Thought Control in Democratic Societies.* Boston: South End Press, 1989, pp. 197–261. Henceforth *NI.*

1. Addendum to Chomsky, *NI,* 80.
2. Associated Press (AP), *New York Times (NYT),* Jan. 5; Stephen Kinzer, *NYT,* Jan. 6; AP, *Boston Globe (BG),* Jan. 8; editorial, *NYT,* Jan. 8; Bernard Weinraub, *NYT,* Jan. 15; Abrams, Op-Ed, *NYT,* Jan. 15; David Shipler, *NYT,* Feb. 26, 1986.
3. Beecher, "Pressuring Nicaragua," *BG,* Jan. 17, 1986.
4. Hamilton, ms., 1987.
5. For extensive documentation on how charges known to be false are maintained for propaganda purposes and the interesting reaction to the exposure of these facts, see references cited in *NI,* appendix I, section 1.
6. *NYT,* Aug. 13, 1987.
7. For a detailed review of the major State Department allegations, see Morris Morley and James Petras, *The Reagan Administration and Nicaragua* (New York: Institute of Media Analysis, 1987).
8. *Extra!* Oct.–Nov. 1987. In a letter of March 11, 1988, Lelyveld informed FAIR that he had instructed LeMoyne "to devote an entire article to what the current evidence shows on this point" (*Extra!* Sept.–Oct. 1988, pointing out that "six months later, no such article has appeared"). See below.
9. Humberto Ortega, FBIS-LAT-87-239, Dec. 14, 1987; LeMoyne, Dec. 20, 1987.
10. *NYT,* Dec. 18, 1987.
11. *NYT,* Jan. 18, 1988.
12. J. D. Gannon, *Christian Science Monitor (CSM),* Aug. 26, 1988.
13. *NYT,* Feb. 7, July 4, 1988, emphasis added.

14. Trainor, *NYT,* April 3, 1988; Rivera y Damas, Oct. 26, 1980, cited by Bonner, *Weakness and Deceit* (New York: Times Books, 1984), 207.

15. "Salvador Rebels: Where Do They Get the Arms?" *NYT,* Nov. 24, 1988. Whether by accident or not, this article appeared a month after FAIR had made public the failure of the *Times* to deal with the issue despite the promise of the foreign editor; see note 8.

16. See my introduction to Morley and Petras, *Reagan Administration and Nicaragua.*

17. Others too have put the doctrine aside. *Newsweek* Central America correspondent Charles Lane writes in the *Wall Street Journal (WSJ)* (always irate about Sandinista attempts to overthrow the government of El Salvador and others) that the Salvadoran guerrillas "capture or make most of their own weapons." Still, history has passed them by, he writes, in part because of the "disillusioning Sandinista experiment," a "once-promising revolution" (we now read) that "turned into an embarrassing Cuban-style economic basket case [for unstated reasons] and a U.S.–Soviet battleground" (*WSJ,* Dec. 23, 1988).

18. On the Miranda testimony and the media/State Department version of it, see my article in *Z Magazine,* March 1988; Holly Sklar, *Washington's War on Nicaragua* (Boston: South End, 1988), 383f.

19. Marcio Vargas, Mexico City, interview with Arce, *Central America Information Bulletin* (Guatemala City), Dec. 21, 1988; Rubén Montedonico, *El Día* (Mexico City), Nov. 6, 7, 1988, reprinted in translation in *Honduras Update,* Nov.–Dec. 1988. On Lau, see Chomsky, *Turning the Tide* (Boston: South End, 1985), 104.

20. Addendum to *NI,* 81.

21. For discussion of one example, see my review of Saul Bellows's *To Jerusalem and Back,* reprinted in *Towards a New Cold War* (New York: Pantheon, 1982), a review that aroused such anger that it caused the suspension of the journal in which it originally appeared, so I was informed. For many more examples, see other chapters in the same book, my *Peace in the Middle East?* (New York: Pantheon, 1974, chapter 5), and *Fateful Triangle* (Boston: South End, 1983; extended edition, 1999).

22. See *NI,* appendix V, section 4.

23. "Statement by the AFL-CIO Executive Council on Israel," Feb. 16, 1988.

24. Wiesel, Op-Ed, *NYT,* June 23; Reuven Padhatzur, *Ha'aretz,* May 16, 1988. On Wiesel's long-held doctrine that it is obligatory to maintain silence in the face of atrocities of the state one loves, and that only those in power are in a position to know so that he must refrain from comment on atrocities, see *Fateful Triangle* and *Turning the Tide.* For his reiteration of the obligation of silence at the peak of the recent repression, see his article in *Yediot Ahronot,* Jan. 22, 1988, where he explains, "I refuse to criticize Israel, I have always refused

to do this," among other similar sentiments, familiar from apologists for other states in earlier days. It would be unfair, however, to note Wiesel's practice without reference to those who now condemn him for his silence while effacing their own much worse records over many years. On the unacceptable facts, see the references of note 21. Wiesel, at least, had the integrity to adhere to his long-held position when it became unpopular.

25. Zeev Sachor, "Getting Accustomed to Atrocities," *Hotam*, April 1, 1988; one of many items translated from the Israeli press in the 1988 Report of the Israeli League for Human Rights, Tel Aviv, which give the flavor of the pogroms organized by the Defense Ministry to teach the beasts of burden a lesson. This highly informative material is next to unknown in the United States, though it is arguably of some relevance to those who are expected to pay the bills.

26. *Ha'aretz*, July 15, 4; *Jerusalem Post (JP)*, July 6; Ya'akov Lazar, *Hotam*, July 15, reporting from Jabaliya; William Montalbano, *Los Angeles Times (LAT)*, May 31, 1988, AP, May 30, on Dahariya, one of the atrocities reported by Dedi Zucker based on testimony by reservists, *Yediot Ahronot*, June 10; *Yerushalayim*, June 17, on Jericho; AP, June 22, 24, citing charges by Knesset member Ran Cohen; *JP*, Aug. 3, 1988, on the release of Mohammed Dari after three months in prison. For extensive documentation, see *Punishing a Nation: Human Rights Violations during the Palestinian Uprising, December 1987–December 1988* (Al Haq-Law in the Service of Man, Ramallah, December 1988).

27. Yizhar Be'er, *Kol Ha'ir*, Aug. 26, 1988; Joshua Brilliant, *JP*, Aug. 26, 1988.

28. Eitan Rabin, *Ha'aretz*, Sept. 23, 1988.

29. Shimon Elkavetz, *Hadashot*, Sept. 28; Tali Zelinger, *JP*, Sept. 29, 1988.

30. *JP*, Nov. 17; *Ha'aretz*, Dec. 2, Nov. 15, 16; Yariv, *Yediot Ahronot*, Nov. 18, 1988. Michal Sela, *JP*, Jan. 26, Feb. 3; *JP*, Feb. 10, 1989. See also Glenn Frankel, *Washington Post (WP)*, Feb. 12; George Moffett, *CSM*, Feb. 15, 1989.

31. Reuven Padhatzur, *Ha'aretz*, Nov. 30, 1988. See also Eitan Rabin, *Ha'aretz Supplement*, Dec. 2, 1988, making the same points.

32. *Hadaf Hayarok*, supplement to *Al Hamishmar*, Aug. 23, 1988.

33. Almagor, *Ha'ir*, Dec. 16, 1988; *NYT*, March 18, 1968.

34. Gilat, *Hadashot*, Dec. 16; Gissen, Joel Brinkley, *NYT*, April 28; AP, *NYT*, Dec. 15; special, *NYT*, Dec. 5, 1988. Eiran Taus, *Al-Hamishmar*, Nov. 19; Judith Green, *News from Within (Jerusalem)*, Dec. 14, 1988. Green, a Jerusalem architect working with the "Beita Committee," which hopes to reconstruct the houses destroyed by the army, visited the village with a member of the U.S. consulate on the day when the child was killed and reported this story as well as the destruction caused by rampaging soldiers in a village that was quiet, with almost no villagers on the streets when the soldiers entered with riot control equipment. See my article in *Z Magazine*, July 1988, for more on the background, based in part on a personal visit a week after the incident with the hikers in April, while the village was still under military siege (reprinted in *Fateful Triangle*, 1999 edition).

35. Gad Lior, *Yediot Ahronot,* July 10, 1988.

36. For a few references to current discussion on transfer, see my article in *Z Magazine,* May 1988. Poll, *Ha'aretz,* June 8, 1988; the poll, excluding settlers and kibbutz members, found 41 percent in favor. A poll taken shortly after found 49 percent favoring "transfer" of Arabs from the occupied territories; *JP,* Aug. 12, 1988. Rav Kook, quoted by Eyal Kafkafi, *Davar,* Sept. 26, 1988. See Yehoshafat Harkabi, *Israel's Fateful Hour* (New York: Harper and Row, 1988), the first readily available source to deal with these important matters.

37. Michael Walzer, "Nationalism, Internationalism, and the Jews," in Irving Howe and Carl Gershman, eds., *Israel, the Arabs and the Middle East* (Bantam, 1972); Cockburn, *Nation,* Nov. 21, 1988.

38. Addendum to *NI,* 84.

39. *Extra!* Dec. 1987.

40. CBS News, 6:30 p.m., Dec. 7, 1987. The phrase in quotes is either an exact quote or a very close paraphrase; I do not have the transcript available.

41. Many did, however; see *NI,* chapter 2.

42. *NYT,* Dec. 4, 1987.

43. Steven Roberts, *NYT,* May 31; editorial, *NYT,* June 1.

44. Alexander Cockburn, *Nation,* June 18, 1988.

45. Editorial, *Globe and Mail,* June 10, 1988; James LeMoyne, *New York Times Magazine,* June 5, 1988. With regard to Father Carney, LeMoyne notes only the report that he was executed. On the follow-up to LeMoyne's account of torture, see *NI,* appendix V, section 6.

46. *New Statesman,* June 3, 10, 1988. For some exceptions, see a forthright editorial in *BG,* June 1, and Michael Parks, *LAT,* May 28, 1988.

47. Addendum to *NI,* 89.

48. *American-Arab Affairs,* Winter 1987–88.

49. Paul Lewis, *NYT,* Nov. 4, 1988.

50. "The U.N. versus the U.S.," *NYT Magazine,* Jan. 22, 1984.

51. Shirley Hazzard, *Defeat of an Ideal* (Atlantic Monthly Press, Little, Brown, 1973), 201. The only exceptions, she notes, were a Lao government initiative of 1959 and the Tonkin Gulf incident of 1964, when Adlai Stevenson falsely claimed that the alleged attacks on U.S. naval vessels were "a calculated, a deliberate act of military aggression against the United States."

52. *Times Literary Supplement* (London), Sept. 17, 1982.

53. *Defeat of an Ideal,* 9, 14ff., 60f., 65, 71.

54. Here named "General Ortega," in a slip of the pen; David Johnston, *NYT,* June 25, 1988. Lindsey Gruson, *NYT,* Nov. 14, 1988.

55. Paul Lewis, *NYT,* Oct. 16, 1987; AP, Feb. 28, 1988.

56. AP, March 22; *CSM,* March 25, 43 words; Treaster, *NYT,* March 27, 1988. See also Mary McGrory, *BG,* March 23, noting that Honduras refused to admit a U.N. observer team.

57. Addendum to *NI,* 90.

58. For discussion of how the problem was addressed in the case of Indochina from 1950 until today, see Edward Herman and Noam Chomsky, *Manufacturing Consent* (New York: Pantheon, 1988), chapters 5–6. On similar problems with regard to the Arab–Israeli conflict, see *NI,* appendix V, section 4.

59. *New Republic,* Aug. 29, 1988; my emphasis. Christian, regarded as a specialist on Nicaragua, goes on to argue that the contras are a typical Latin American guerrilla movement, "largely a Central American creation," since "aside from a few individual Americans with nebulous government ties the key players were the Argentine colonels" (transmuted into Central Americans), the Honduran military chief Gustavo Alvarez, a noted killer, "and an assortment of former Nicaraguan National Guardsmen." Plainly, "the classic pattern of guerrilla armies in Latin America," even putting aside a few notable omissions. She does not elaborate on the significance of this interesting collection of "key players." Such contributions are apparently taken seriously.

60. Michael Allen, *WSJ,* Aug. 10; *Central America Report* (Guatemala City), Aug. 14, 1987. See Chomsky, *Culture of Terrorism* (Boston: South End, 1988), 141f., 18–19, on the events and the media reaction.

61. Here and below, I will use the Guatemalan version of the English translation; Special Document, Esquipulas II Accord, *Central America Report,* August 14, 1987.

62. LeMoyne, *NYT,* Aug. 6, 7. On the actual reaction of Presidents Cerezo and Arias, see *Central America Report,* Aug. 14. See *Culture of Terrorism,* 141f., for further details.

63. Rosenthal, *NYT,* Aug. 21, 1987.

64. Brian Barger, UPI, *Philadelphia Inquirer,* Oct. 9, 1987; *Excelsior* (Mexico City), Oct. 22, 1987. On the supply flights and other matters, see the footnoted versions of my articles in *Z Magazine,* January, March 1988.

65. For some exceptions, see *NI,* chapter 4, notes 34, 37.

66. Note that this review is based on the library edition of the *Times.* The earlier (Boston) edition sometimes differs. Thus in the last paragraph (par. 25) of an October 24 story on contra attacks, omitted in the library edition, Kinzer mentions that the contras are using Redeye missiles and other supplies provided by "clandestine" CIA flights from Honduras, which Nicaragua cannot intercept without jet fighters.

67. In a December 6 interview with a contra commander, Kinzer quotes him as saying that the contras cannot supply themselves within Nicaragua (the sharp contrast with El Salvador is unmentioned, following standard convention) and have received, intact, 52 CIA supply drops. In a report the following day, he cites a Nicaraguan government report of 82 supply flights and 21 surveillance missions from November 5 to December 5. A January 25 story notes that "clandes-

tine night supply flights into Nicaragua are a vital lifeline for the contras," citing an American official who says that there were more than 350 such flights in 1987. A brief AP report on October 30, 1987, notes the crash of a contra supply plane in Honduras.

68. Neil Lewis, *NYT,* Nov. 12, 1987. Others stated the facts correctly. See references cited in note 64.

69. U.N. General Assembly, A/42/PV.67, Nov. 16, 1987. On the reporting of this U.N. session, see *NI,* chapter 4.

70. Stephen Kinzer, *NYT,* Oct. 15, 1987. He claims that President Arias "said Honduras could not be expected to close contra camps and ban clandestine supply flights if the Sandinistas do not negotiate a cease-fire with the contras and issue a broad amnesty." The Esquipulas Accord set no such condition on cessation of contra aid. Neither Arias nor anyone else has held that foreign aid to the guerrillas in El Salvador and Guatemala is legitimate until the governments negotiate a cease-fire with these indigenous forces or live up to the terms of the accords. If Kinzer's statement is correct, it follows that Arias too was committed to the failure of the accords that are mislabeled "the Arias plan." There are repeated references in the *Times* to alleged positions of Arias that lead to the same conclusion, but it is difficult to know how much is accurate, how much wishful thinking. For more on Arias's role and the reason for his relative acceptability in the United States, see my article in *Z Magazine,* November 1988. For comment on his "shocking record" in "only superficially promoting his own plan while responding to pressures from Washington and the powerful right-wing elements within Costa Rica," see COHA, "News and Analysis," Feb. 10, 1989.

71. Questions also arise about Costa Rica, generally regarded as exempt from the accords. Thus the Spanish-language press is firmly under right-wing control, barring access of "all ideological groups," among other questions that would arise if Costa Rican affairs were reported. See *NI,* appendix V, section 6. Also, *Culture of Terrorism,* 243, for one critical case.

72. COHA, *Washington Report on the Hemisphere,* Feb. 3, 1988; *Update,* Central American Historical Institute, Dec. 28, 1987; *Cultural Survival* 12, no. 3, 1988.

73. Jonas, *San Francisco Bay Guardian*; Cockburn, *Anderson Valley Advertiser*; both June 8, 1988.

74. Human Rights Watch (Americas Watch/Asia Watch/Helsinki Watch) and Lawyers Committee for Human Rights, *Critique: Review of the Department of State's Country Reports on Human Rights Practices for 1987,* June 1988. The review particularly condemns the State Department reports on the Central American countries and their denigration and misrepresentation of the work of the "highly respected" Tutela Legal. These have been regular features of State Department productions.

75. COHA, *Washington Report on the Hemisphere,* Feb. 17, 1988; *Latinamerica Press* (Peru), Nov. 19, 1987.

76. See my article in *Z Magazine,* March 1988, for further details; U.N. testimony, *La Voz,* CDHES, March 24, 1988.

77. AP, Nov. 15, 1987; the Archbishop also noted other death-squad killings. On February 20, the *Times* ran a brief AP report noting that the Archbishop attributed the murder to death squads and that the alleged killer retracted his confession.

78. LeMoyne, *NYT,* Nov. 29, 1987; COHA, *Washington Report on the Hemisphere,* Feb. 17, 1988. Access to radio and TV later became much more free, but to speak of "free access to the press" in November 1987 was outlandish, and there has never been anything corresponding to the U.S.-funded pro-contra journal *La Prensa.* On the media in Central America, see *NI,* appendix V.

79. *NYT,* Nov. 29, 1987; Feb. 22, June 5, 1988.

80. See *NI,* appendix V, section 6.

81. Ibid. On Chamorro's return, see COHA, "News and Analysis," Feb. 20, 1988.

82. See *Turning the Tide,* 109–10.

83. *El Sol* (El Salvador On Line, Center for Central American Studies, Washington), Aug. 29, 1988; Sam Dillon, "El Salvador's Violent Past Returns in Poverty, Death," *Miami Herald (MH),* Sept. 6, 1988.

84. LeMoyne, *NYT,* Nov. 21; Stephen Kinzer, *NYT,* Nov. 16, 1987. LeMoyne duly noted the risks that Zamora and Ungo faced from "extreme leftists and rightists" who "enforce their views with bullets and bloodshed," concealing the fact that the major risk by far has always been the behavior of the state security services and their associates. The "terror of left and right" technique is a common literary device to conceal the terror of the "centrists" whom the U.S. supports.

85. *El Norte* (Mexico), July 17, 1988; Central America NewsPak.

86. His party is the Social Christian Popular Movement. For his assessment of the current situation, with no "functioning democracy" or even "a democratic opening," see COHA, *Washington Report on the Hemisphere,* Aug. 31, 1988.

87. LeMoyne, photo, *NYT,* Nov. 4, 1987; *NYT,* October 28, 1987.

88. For further information, see references of note 64.

89. *Central America Report,* July 15, 1988; *Latinamerica Press* (Peru), July 21, 1988, datelined Tegucigalpa.

90. Reuters and AP, *Toronto Globe and Mail,* March 23; Pamela Constable, *BG,* March 20, 1988; *El Tiempo,* July 14, 1987.

91. *Toronto Globe and Mail,* March 23, 1988. See *NI,* appendix III, on the integrity of the concerns angrily expressed over the Sandinista border violation. On the aid proposal, see Susan Rasky, *NYT,* March 19, 1988.

92. From Tegucigalpa, Joseph Treaster reported only that "ordinary Hondurans" generally feel that with the contras out of Honduras, tensions between the two countries will end, referring to the fear in Honduras that they will "get stuck with" the contras; *NYT,* March 21, 27.

93. See *NI,* 221. Peter Ford, *CSM,* Jan. 15; Richard Boudreaux, *LAT,* Jan. 14; LeMoyne, *NYT,* Jan. 16; Kinzer, *NYT,* Jan. 25, 1988.

94. *NYT,* Nov. 10, 1987.

95. *San Francisco Bay Guardian,* Jan. 6, April 20, 1988.

96. Ibid.; FAIR questionnaire submitted to *Times* editors on their Central American coverage, Jan. 23, 1988. Gutman, *WP,* Aug. 7, 1988.

97. AP, Feb. 2, 3; *Globe and Mail,* Feb. 3, 1988; Amnesty International, El Salvador, "Death Squads—a Government Strategy" (October 1988). See my article in *Z Magazine,* Jan. 1988, for further details.

98. Douglas Farah, *WP,* Jan. 4; COHA, *Washington Report on the Hemisphere,* Jan. 20, 1988.

99. AP, Feb. 23, 26, 1988; Congressional Record, House, Dec. 8, 1987, H11037f. See *Envío,* Jan. 1988, for a reaction by Jesuits in Nicaragua.

100. Feb. 18, March 20, April 20, 1988. On the credibility of LeMoyne's reports of guerrilla atrocities, see *NI,* appendix V, section 4.

101. March 20, "Review of the Week"; Feb. 29, 1988. LeMoyne's successor Lindsey Gruson follows basically the same script. Thus a dispatch with the headline "Rebel Attacks on the Rise in Salvador" begins with ten paragraphs on the violence of the "Marxists committed to redistributing the nation's wealth and overthrowing the American-backed government," including attacks on army headquarters, ambushing police, and two car bombs in a wealthy neighborhood; and in paragraph eleven, we learn that human rights monitors report "a sharp increase in terrorism and massacres attributed to right-wing death squads, the army and the guerrillas" (*NYT,* Oct. 20, 1988).

102. Editorial, *Observer* (London), Feb. 7, 1988.

103. For details, see my articles in *Z Magazine,* January, March 1988.

104. Editorial, *NYT,* Jan. 31.

105. LeMoyne, *NYT,* Jan. 22, 1988.

106. LeMoyne, *NYT,* Jan. 18; *Globe and Mail,* Feb. 5, 1988.

107. Editorial, *El Tiempo,* May 5, 1988, reprinted in Hondupress, May 18.

108. *Central America Report,* June 17, 1988.

109. Human rights monitors have repeatedly condemned this technique of ideological warfare, but to no avail. See my article in *Z Magazine,* Jan. 1988, for details.

110. Reuters, *NYT,* Nov. 9, 1987, citing the CIVS report of November 8 and Latin American officials; *Amnesty Law and Bill to suspend the State of Emergency,* promulgated in November 1987, unofficial translation, Nicaraguan Foreign

Ministry, given to me in December by Foreign Minister Miguel D'Escoto, who appeared genuinely to believe that the Accord would be permitted to survive.

111. Nov. 18, 1987.

112. Lindsey Gruson, *NYT,* Oct. 29; LeMoyne, *NYT,* Nov. 29, 1987.

113. Chris Norton, *Globe and Mail,* Feb. 10, 1988.

114. Chamorro, *Packaging the Contras: A Case of CIA Disinformation* (New York: Institute for Media Analysis, 1987).

115. *Harper's,* Oct. 1987.

116. Lindsey Gruson, *NYT,* Dec. 15, 1987.

117. Tad Szulc, *Parade Magazine,* Aug. 28, 1988.

118. Julia Preston notes that the Sandinistas have captured "state-of-the-art equipment, so modern that not even all U.S. units have them" (*WP,* Feb. 4, 1988), quite apart from the sheer mass of regular supply and the crucial assistance of U.S. aerial and naval surveillance. On the high quality of contra military and communication systems, extraordinary by the standards of the region, see *Culture of Terrorism,* 91. The illegal "humanitarian" aid sent to the contras in their Honduran bases provides them with a level of sustenance beyond what they could find within Nicaragua, not only food and supplies but even first-class sports equipment (see Joe Gannon, *CSM,* Feb. 13, 1989). The "humanitarian" aid is presumably designed not only to maintain the terrorist forces in the field but also to draw people from Nicaragua as the economic situation worsens.

119. *Interamerican*'s Public Opinion Series, no. 7, June 4–5, 1988, Interamerican Research Center, Los Angeles; *Alert!* (CISPES), March 1988.

120. See *NI,* 16.

121. William Bollinger and David M. Lund, *Latinamerica Press* (Peru), Sept. 22, 1988. Bollinger is the director of the Interamerican Research Center; Lund is chair of the history department at the Universidad Autónoma in Mexico City. Both are involved in polling in Central America, including the polls they discuss.

122. Conclusions of the National Debate for Peace in El Salvador, called by Archbishop Arturo Rivera y Damas, Sept. 1988. Distributed by National Agenda for Peace in El Salvador, Box 192, Cardinal Station, Washington, DC 20064.

123. Katherine Ellison, Knight-Ridder Service, *BG,* Aug. 1, 1988. Others understand that "Nicaragua has gone further in complying with the Arias peace plan than Guatemala, Honduras and El Salvador," but Nicaragua's ties to the Soviet bloc provide "a reason, if not an excuse," for ignoring the fact, and recognition of it in no way influences continuing news coverage or opinion; editorial, *NYT,* March 11, 1988.

124. In El Salvador at least; in Guatemala, evidence is not available. Ellison's report is unusual in at least acknowledging that Guatemala "broke off talks with the guerrillas."

125. COHA, "News and Analysis," Jan. 14, 1988. The FDR is the political group allied with the FMLN guerrillas.

126. *Excelsior,* Feb. 9; *Central America Report,* Feb. 26. There were brief notices in *BG,* Feb. 9, 11; *CSM,* Feb. 10, 1988.

127. *El Sol,* Feb. 22; editorial, *WP Weekly,* March 28; AP, May 13; *BG,* May 1; Tad Szulc, *LAT,* May 22, 1988.

128. *Central America Report,* March 4, June 24; AP, Feb. 24, March 30, 1988.

129. *Congressional Quarterly,* June 25, 1988.

130. To be precise, we refer now to the revised accords, modified by the dictates of the U.S. government, and relayed by the media in conformity to these dictates.

131. COHA press release, June 11, 1988.

132. Kinzer and editorial, *NYT,* June 25; LeMoyne, *NYT,* June 7, 1988.

133. COHA, *Washington Report on the Hemisphere,* July 20, citing Tutela Legal. Archbishop Rivera y Damas, May 29; Bishop Chávez, denouncing April 14 killings; *Alert!* (CISPES), July, June; *El Sol,* Aug. 8; Orellana, *El Sol,* Aug. 1; *Guardian* (New York), Aug. 17; *El Sol,* Aug. 29, 1988. European Parliament, *Excelsior* (Mexico), Oct 7, 1988; *Central America News Update.*

134. Brook Larmer, *CSM,* Aug. 16; Zamora, NPR, July 19; *El Sol,* July 25; AP, *BG,* June 22, 100 words. *El Sol,* July 18; AP, *NYT,* July 14, 125 words. Joel Bleifuss, *In These Times,* May 18. Hondupress, May 4; editorial, *El Tiempo,* May 4; Hondupress, May 18, June 15; *Central America Report,* Nov. 18, 1988. María Verónica Frenkel, reporting on a visit to striking farmers in Costa Rica, *Nicaragua through Our Eyes (Americans Working in Nicaragua),* July 1988.

135. *WP Weekly,* Aug. 15–21; *NYT,* Aug. 19; COHA, *Washington Report on the Hemisphere,* Aug. 31, 1988.

136. *NYT,* July 11, 1988.

137. Robert Pear, *NYT,* July 15, 1988, and many further references.

138. See *NI,* 57.

139. Editorials, *NYT,* July 18, Aug. 7; Kinzer, *NYT* "Week in Review," July 17, 1988.

140. *WP Weekly,* July 18–24, 25–31; COHA press release, July 14; *Update,* Central American Historical Institute (Georgetown U., Washington), Aug. 17, 1988.

141. *The National Interest,* Fall 1988.

142. COHA, "News and Analysis," Sept. 8, 1988.

143. Reuters, *Toronto Globe and Mail,* Oct. 26; *MH,* Oct. 26; a briefer report appears in *BG,* AP, same day. See also Americas Watch, *Nightmare Revisited,* September 1988.

144. Pamela Constable, *BG,* Oct. 27, 1988.

145. *Central America Report,* Oct. 14, 1988.

146. *NYT,* Nov. 13, 1988.

147. *LAT–BG,* Nov. 25, 1988.

148. Chris Norton, *CSM,* Jan. 13; *El Sol,* Jan. 9, 1989.

149. UPI, *BG,* Sept. 14; *El Sol,* Sept. 19; *Central America Report,* Sept. 23; Sam Dillon, *MH,* Sept. 20; COHA, "News and Analysis," Oct. 19, 1988.

150. Preston, *WP,* Nov. 8, 1988.

151. Sam Dillon, *MH,* Oct. 1, 1988.

152. *Excelsior* (Mexico City), Aug. 31; Central America NewsPak; AP, Nov. 15; a few words were excerpted in *BG,* noting that there had been a march for unstated purposes, Nov. 16, 1988.

153. Lindsey Gruson, *NYT,* Nov. 18, 1988.

154. *Excelsior,* Oct. 19, 21, 1988; Central America NewsPak.

155. Kinzer, *NYT,* Aug. 2, 1988.

156. See note 138.

157. Rasky, *NYT,* Aug. 2; AP, *BG,* Aug. 3, 1988.

4

MARKET DEMOCRACY IN A NEOLIBERAL ORDER: DOCTINES AND REALITY

I have been asked to speak on some aspect of academic or human freedom, an invitation that offers many choices. I will keep to some simple ones.

Freedom without opportunity is a devil's gift, and the refusal to provide such opportunities is criminal. The fate of the more vulnerable offers a sharp measure of the distance from here to something that might be called "civilization." While I am speaking, 1,000 children will die from easily preventable disease, and almost twice that many women will die or suffer serious disability in pregnancy or childbirth for lack of simple remedies and care.[1] UNICEF estimates that to overcome such tragedies, and to ensure universal access to basic social services, would require a quarter of the annual military expenditures of the "developing countries," about 10 percent of U.S. military spending. It is against the background of such realities as these that any serious discussion of human freedom should proceed.

It is widely held that the cure for such profound social maladies is within reach. The hopes have foundation. The past few years have seen the fall of brutal tyrannies, the growth of scientific understanding that offers great promise, and many other reasons to look forward to a brighter future. The discourse of the privileged is marked by confidence and triumphalism: the way forward is known, and there is no other. The basic theme, articulated with force and clarity, is that "America's victory in the Cold War was a victory for a set of political and economic principles: democracy and the free market." These principles are "the wave of the future—a future for which America is both the gatekeeper and the model." I am quoting the chief political commentator of the *New York Times,* but the picture is conventional, widely repeated throughout much of the world, and accepted as generally accurate even by critics. It was also enunciated as the "Clinton Doctrine," which declared that our new mission is to "consolidate the victory of democracy and open markets" that had just been won. There remains a range of disagreement: at one extreme, "Wilsonian idealists" urge continued dedication to the traditional mission of benevolence; at the other, "realists" counter that we may lack the means to conduct these crusades of "global meliorism" and should not neglect our own interests in the service of others.[2] Within this range lies the path to a better world.

Reality seems to me rather different. The current spectrum of public-policy debate has as little relevance to actual policy as its numerous antecedents: neither the United States nor any other power has been guided by "global meliorism." Democracy is under attack worldwide, including the leading industrial countries—at least, democracy in a meaningful sense of the term, involving opportunities for people to manage their own collective and individual affairs. Something similar is true of markets. The assaults on democracy and markets are furthermore related. Their roots lie in the power of corporate entities that are totalitarian in internal structure, increasingly interlinked and reliant on powerful states, and largely unaccountable to the public. Their immense power is growing as a result of social policy that is globalizing the structural model of the Third World, with sectors of enormous wealth and privilege alongside an increase in "the proportion of those who will labor under all the hardships of life, and secretly sigh for a more equal distribution of its blessings," as the leading framer of American democracy, James Madison, predicted 200 years ago.[3] These policy choices are most evident in the Anglo-American societies but extend worldwide. They cannot be attributed to what "the free market has decided, in its infinite but mysterious wisdom," "the implacable sweep of 'the market revolution,'" "Reaganesque rugged individualism," or a "new orthodoxy" that "gives the market full sway."[4] The quotes are liberal-to-left, in some cases quite critical. The analysis is similar across the rest of the spectrum but generally euphoric. The reality, on the contrary, is that state intervention plays a decisive role, as in the past, and the basic outlines of policy are hardly novel. Current versions reflect "capital's clear subjugation of labor" for more than fifteen years, in the words of the business press,[5] which often frankly articulates the perceptions of a highly class-conscious business community, dedicated to class war.

If these perceptions are valid, then the path to a world that is more just and more free lies well outside the range set forth by privilege and power. I cannot hope to establish such conclusions here but only to suggest that they are credible enough to consider with care. And to suggest further that prevailing doctrines could hardly survive were it not for their contribution to "regimenting the public mind every bit as much as an army regiments the bodies of its soldiers," to borrow the dictum of the respected Roosevelt–Kennedy liberal Edward Bernays in his classic manual for the public-relations industry, of which he was one of the founders and leading figures.

Bernays was drawing from his experience in Woodrow Wilson's state propaganda agency, the Committee on Public Information. "It was, of course, the astounding success of propaganda during the war that opened the eyes of the intelligent few in all departments of life to the possibilities of regimenting the public mind," he wrote. His goal was to adapt these experiences to the needs of the "intelligent minorities," primarily business leaders, whose task is "the conscious and intelligent manipulation of the organized habits and opinions of the masses." Such "engineering of consent" is the very "essence of the democratic process," Bernays wrote shortly before he was honored for his contributions by the American Psychological Association in 1949. The importance of "controlling the public mind" has been recognized with increasing clarity as popular struggles succeeded in extending the modalities of democracy, thus giving rise to what liberal elites call "the crisis of democracy," as when normally passive and apathetic populations become organized and seek to enter the political arena to pursue their interests and demands, threatening stability and order. As Bernays explained the problem, with "universal suffrage and universal schooling, . . . at last even the bourgeoisie stood in fear of the common people. For the masses promised to become king," a tendency fortunately reversed—so it has been hoped—as new methods "to mold the mind of the masses" were devised and implemented.[6]

Quite strikingly, in both of the world's leading democracies there was a growing awareness of the need to "apply the lessons" of the highly successful propaganda systems of World War I "to the organization of political warfare," as the chairman of the British Conservative Party put the matter seventy years ago. Wilsonian liberals in the U.S. drew the same conclusions in the same years, including public intellectuals and prominent figures in the developing profession of political science. In another corner of Western civilization, Adolf Hitler vowed that next time Germany would not be defeated in the propaganda war and also devised his own ways to apply the lessons of Anglo-American propaganda for political warfare at home.[7] Meanwhile the business world warned of "the hazard facing industrialists" in "the newly realized political power of the masses," and the need to wage and win "the everlasting battle for the minds of men" and "indoctrinate citizens with the capitalist story" until "they are able to play back the story with remarkable fidelity" and so on, in an impressive flow, accompanied by even more impressive efforts, and surely one of the central themes of modern history.[8]

To discover the true meaning of the "political and economic principles" that are declared to be "the wave of the future," it is of course necessary to go beyond rhetorical flourishes and public pronouncements and to investigate actual practice and the internal documentary record. Close examination of particular cases is the most rewarding path, but these must be chosen carefully to give a fair picture. There are some natural guidelines. One reasonable approach is to take the examples chosen by the proponents of the doctrines themselves, as their "strongest case." Another is to investigate the record where influence is greatest and interference least, so that we see the operative principles in their purest form. If we want to determine what the Kremlin meant by "democracy" and "human rights," we will pay little heed to Pravda's solemn denunciations of racism in the United States or state terror in Washington's client regimes, even less to protestation of noble motives. Far more instructive is the state of affairs in the "people's democracies" of Eastern Europe. The point is elementary and applies to the self-designated "gatekeeper and model" as well. Latin America is the obvious testing ground, particularly the Central America–Caribbean region. Here Washington has faced few external challenges for almost a century, so the guiding principles of policy, and of today's neoliberal "Washington consensus," are revealed most clearly when we examine the state of the region and how that came about.

It is of some interest that the exercise is rarely undertaken and, if proposed, castigated as extremist or worse. I leave it as an "exercise for the reader," merely noting that the record teaches useful lessons about the political and economic principles that are to be "the wave of the future."

Washington's "crusade for democracy," as it is called, was waged with particular fervor during the Reagan years, with Latin America the chosen terrain. The results are commonly offered as a prime illustration of how the U.S. became "the inspiration for the triumph of democracy in our time," to quote the editors of the leading intellectual journal of American liberalism.[9] The most recent scholarly study of democracy describes "the revival of democracy in Latin America" as "impressive" but not unproblematic; the "barriers to implementation" remain "formidable" but can perhaps be overcome through closer integration with the United States.[10] The author, Sanford Lakoff, singles out the "historic North American Free Trade Agreement (NAFTA)" as a potential instrument of democratization. In the region of traditional U.S. influence, he writes, the countries are moving toward democracy, having "survived military intervention" and "vicious civil war."

Let us begin by looking more closely at these recent cases, the natural ones given overwhelming U.S. influence, and the ones regularly selected to illustrate the achievements and promise of "America's mission."

The primary "barriers to implementation" of democracy, Lakoff suggests, are the "vested interests" that seek to protect "domestic markets"—that is, to prevent foreign (mainly U.S.) corporations from gaining even greater control over the society. We are to understand, then, that democracy is enhanced as significant decision making shifts even more into the hands of unaccountable private tyrannies, mostly foreign based. Meanwhile, the public arena is to shrink still further as the state is "minimized" in accordance with the neoliberal "political and economic principles" that have emerged triumphant. A study of the World Bank points out that the new orthodoxy represents "a dramatic shift away from a pluralist, participatory ideal of politics and towards an authoritarian and technocratic ideal . . . ," one that is very much in accord with leading elements of twentieth-century liberal and progressive thought and, in another variant, the Leninist model; the two are more similar than often recognized.[11]

Thinking through the tacit reasoning, we gain some useful insight into the concepts of democracy and markets, in the operative sense. Lakoff does not look into the "revival of democracy" in Latin America, but he does cite a scholarly source that includes a contribution on Washington's crusade in the 1980s. The author is Thomas Carothers, who combines scholarship with an "insider's perspective," having worked on "democracy enhancement" programs in Reagan's State Department.[12] Carothers regards Washington's "impulse to promote democracy" as "sincere" but largely a failure. Furthermore, the failure was systematic: where Washington's influence was least, in South America, there was real progress toward democracy, which the Reagan administration generally opposed, later taking credit for it when the process proved irresistible. Where Washington's influence was greatest, progress was least, and where it occurred, the U.S. role was marginal or negative. His general conclusion is that the U.S. sought to maintain "the basic order of . . . quite undemocratic societies" and to avoid "populist-based change," "inevitably [seeking] only limited, top-down forms of democratic change that did not risk upsetting the traditional structures of power with which the United States has long been allied."

The last phrase requires a gloss. The term *United States* is conventionally used to refer to structures of power within the United States; the "national interest" is the interest of these groups, which correlates only weakly with interests of the general population. So the conclusion is that Washington sought top-down forms of democracy that did not upset traditional structures of power with which the structures of power in the United States have long been allied. Not a very surprising fact or much of a historical novelty.

To appreciate the significance of the fact, it is necessary to examine more closely the nature of parliamentary democracies. The United States is the most important case, not only because of its power but because of its stable and long-standing democratic institutions. Furthermore, the United States was about as close to a model as one can find. America can be "as happy as she pleases," Thomas Paine remarked in 1776: "she has a blank sheet to write upon."[13] The indigenous societies were largely eliminated. There is little residue of earlier European structures, one reason for the relative weakness of the social contract and of support systems, which often had their roots in precapitalist institutions. And to an unusual extent, the sociopolitical order was consciously designed. In studying history, one cannot construct experiments, but the U.S. is as close to the "ideal case" of state capitalist democracy as can be found.

Furthermore, the leading Framer of the constitutional system was an astute and lucid political thinker, James Madison, whose views largely prevailed. In the debates on the Constitution, Madison pointed out that in England, if elections "were open to all classes of people, the property of landed proprietors would be insecure. An agrarian law would soon take place," giving land to the landless. The system that he and his associates were designing must prevent such injustice, he urged, and "secure the permanent interests of the country," which are property rights. It is the responsibility of government, Madison declared, "to protect the minority of the opulent against the majority." To achieve this goal, political power must rest in the hands of "the wealth of the nation," men who would "sympathize sufficiently" with property rights and "be safe depositories of power over them," while the rest are marginalized and fragmented, offered only limited public participation in the political arena. Among Madisonian scholars, there is a consensus that "the Constitution was intrinsically an aristocratic document designed to check the democratic tendencies of the period," delivering power to a "better sort" of people and excluding "those who were not rich, well born, or prominent from exercising political power."[14]

These conclusions are often qualified by the observation that Madison, and the constitutional system generally, sought to balance the rights of persons against the rights of property. But the formulation is misleading. Property has no rights. In both principle and practice, the phrase "rights *of* property" means the right *to* property, typically material property, a personal right that must be privileged above all others and is crucially different from others in that one person's possession of such rights deprives another of them. When the facts are stated clearly, we can appreciate the force of the doctrine that "the people who own the country ought to govern it," "one of [the] favorite maxims" of Madison's influential colleague John Jay, his biographer observes.[15]

One may argue, as some historians do, that these principles lost their force as the national territory was conquered and settled, the native population driven out or exterminated. Whatever one's assessment of those years, by the late nineteenth century the founding doctrines took on a new and much more oppressive form. When Madison spoke of "rights of persons," he meant humans. But the growth of the industrial economy, and the rise of corporate forms of economic enterprise, led to a completely new meaning of the term. In a current official document, "'Person' is broadly defined to include any individual, branch, partnership, associated group, association, estate, trust, corporation or other organization (whether or not organized under the laws of any State), or any government entity,"[16] a concept that doubtless would have shocked Madison and others with intellectual roots in the Enlightenment and classical liberalism—precapitalist and anticapitalist in spirit.

These radical changes in the conception of human rights and democracy were not introduced primarily by legislation but, rather, by judicial decisions and intellectual commentary. Corporations, which previously had been considered artificial entities with no rights, were accorded all the rights of persons, and far more, since they are "immortal persons" and "persons" of extraordinary wealth and power. Furthermore, they were no longer bound to the specific purposes designated by state charter but could act as they chose, with few constraints. The intellectual backgrounds for granting such extraordinary rights to "collectivist legal entities" lie in neo-Hegelian doctrines that also underlie Bolshevism and fascism: the idea that organic entities have rights over and above those of persons. Conservative legal scholars bitterly opposed these innovations, recognizing that they undermine the traditional idea that rights inhere in individuals and undermine market principles as well.[17] But the new forms of authoritarian rule were institutionalized and, along with them, the legitimation of wage labor, which was considered hardly better than slavery in mainstream American thought through much of the nineteenth century, not only by the rising labor movement but also by such figures as Abraham Lincoln, the Republican Party, and the establishment media.[18]

These are topics with enormous implications for understanding the nature of market democracy. Again, I can only mention them here. The material and ideological outcome helps explain the understanding that "democracy" abroad must reflect the model sought at home: "top-down" forms of control, with the public kept to a "spectator" role, not participating in the arena of decision making, which must exclude these "ignorant and meddlesome outsiders," according to the mainstream of modern democratic theory. I happen to be quoting the essays on democracy by Walter Lippmann, one of the most respected American public intellectuals and journalists of the century.[19] But the general ideas are standard and have solid roots in the constitutional tradition, radically modified, however, in the new era of collectivist legal entities.

Returning to the "victory of democracy" under U.S. guidance, neither Lakoff nor Carothers asks how Washington maintained the traditional power structure of highly undemocratic societies. Their topic is not the terrorist wars that left tens of thousands of tortured and mutilated corpses, millions of refugees, and devastation perhaps beyond recovery—in large measure wars against the Church, which became an enemy when it adopted "the preferential option for the poor," trying to help suffering people to attain some measure of justice and democratic rights. It is more than symbolic that the terrible decade of the 1980s opened with the murder of an Archbishop who had become "a voice for the voiceless" and closed with the assassination of six leading Jesuit intellectuals who had chosen the same path, in each case by terrorist forces armed and trained by the victors of the "crusade for democracy." One should take careful note of the fact that the leading Central American dissident intellectuals were doubly assassinated: both murdered and silenced. Their words, indeed their very existences, are scarcely known in the United States, unlike dissidents in enemy states, who are greatly honored and admired—another cultural universal, I presume.

Such matters do not enter history as recounted by the victors. In Lakoff's study, which is not untypical in this regard, what survives are references to "military intervention" and "civil wars," with no external factor identified. These matters will not so quickly be put aside, however, by those who seek a better grasp of the principles that are to shape the future, if the structures of power have their way.

Particularly revealing is Lakoff's description of Nicaragua, again standard: "a civil war was ended following a democratic election, and a difficult effort is underway to create a more prosperous and self-governing society." In the real world, the superpower attacking Nicaragua escalated its assault after the country's first democratic election: the election of 1984, closely monitored and recognized as legitimate by the professional association of Latin American scholars (LASA), Irish and British parliamentary delegations, and others, including a hostile Dutch government delegation that was remarkably supportive of Reaganite atrocities, as well as the leading figure of Central American democracy, José Figueres of Costa Rica, also a critical observer, though regarding the elections as legitimate in this "invaded country" and calling on Washington to allow the Sandinistas "to finish what they started in peace; they deserve it." The U.S. strongly opposed the holding of the elections and sought to undermine them, concerned that democratic elections might interfere with its terrorist war. But that concern was put to rest by the good behavior of the doctrinal system, which barred the reports with remarkable efficiency, reflexively adopting the state propaganda line that the elections were meaningless fraud.[20]

Overlooked as well is the fact that, as the next election approached on schedule,[21] Washington left no doubt that unless the results came out the right way, Nicaraguans would continue to endure the illegal economic warfare and "unlawful use of force" that the World Court had condemned and ordered terminated, of course in vain. This time the outcome was acceptable and hailed in the U.S. with an outburst of exuberance that is highly informative.[22]

At the outer limits of critical independence, columnist Anthony Lewis of the *New York Times* was overcome with admiration for Washington's "experiment in peace and democracy," which showed that "we live in a romantic age." The experimental methods were no secret. Thus *Time* magazine, joining in the celebration as "democracy burst forth" in Nicaragua, outlined them frankly: to "wreck the economy and prosecute a long and deadly proxy war until the exhausted natives overthrow the unwanted government themselves," with a cost to us that is "minimal," leaving the victim "with wrecked bridges, sabotaged power stations, and ruined farms," and providing Washington's candidate with "a winning issue," ending the "impoverishment of the people of Nicaragua," not to speak of the continuing terror, better left unmentioned. To be sure, the cost to them was hardly "minimal": Carothers notes that the toll "in per capita terms was significantly higher than the number of U.S. persons killed in the U.S. Civil War and all the wars of the twentieth century *combined*."[23] The outcome was a "Victory for U.S. Fair Play," a headline in the *New York Times* exulted, leaving Americans "United in Joy," in the style of Albania and North Korea.

The methods of this "romantic age," and the reaction to them in enlightened circles, tell us more about the democratic principles that have emerged victorious. They also shed some light on why it is such a "difficult effort" to "create a more prosperous and self-governing society" in Nicaragua. It is true that the effort is now under way and is meeting with some success for a privileged minority, while most of the population faces social and economic disaster, all in the familiar pattern of Western dependencies.[24] Note that it is precisely this example that led editors to laud themselves as "the inspiration for the triumph of democracy in our time," joining the enthusiastic chorus.

We learn more about the victorious principles by recalling that these same representative figures of liberal intellectual life had urged that Washington's wars must be waged mercilessly, with military support for "Latin-style fascists, . . . regardless of how many are murdered," because "there are higher American priorities than Salvadoran human rights." Elaborating, editor Michael Kinsley, who represented "the left" in mainstream commentary and television debate, cautioned against unthinking criticism of Washington's official policy of attacking undefended civilian targets. Such international terrorist operations cause "vast civilian suffering," he acknowledged, but they may be "perfectly legitimate" if "cost–benefit analysis" shows that "the amount of blood and misery that will be poured in" yields "democracy," as the world rulers define it. Enlightened opinion insists that terror is not a value in itself, but must meet the pragmatic criterion. Kinsley later observed that the desired ends had been achieved: "impoverishing the people of Nicaragua was precisely the point of the contra war and the parallel policy of economic embargo and veto of international development loans," which "wreck[ed] the economy" and "creat[ed] the economic disaster [that] was probably the victorious opposition's best election issue." He then joined in welcoming the "triumph of democracy" in the "free election" of 1990.[25]

Client states enjoy similar privileges. Thus, commenting on yet another of Israel's attacks on Lebanon, foreign editor H. D. S. Greenway of the *Boston Globe,* who had graphically reported the first major invasion fifteen years earlier, commented that "if shelling Lebanese villages, even at the cost of lives, and driving civilian refugees north would secure Israel's border, weaken Hezbollah, and promote peace, I would say go to it, as would many Arabs and Israelis. But history has not been kind to Israeli adventures in Lebanon. They have solved very little and have almost always caused more problems." By the pragmatic criterion, then, the murder of many civilians, expulsion of hundreds of thousand of refugees, and devastation of southern Lebanon is a dubious proposition.[26]

It would not be too hard, I presume, to find comparable examples here in South Africa in the recent past. Bear in mind that I am keeping to the dissident sector of tolerable opinion, what is called "the left," a fact that tells us more about the victorious principles and the intellectual culture within which they find their place.

Also revealing was the reaction to periodic Reagan administration allegations about Nicaraguan plans to obtain jet interceptors from the Soviet Union (the U.S. having coerced its allies into refusing to sell them). Hawks demanded that Nicaragua be bombed at once. Doves countered that the charges must first be verified, but if they were, the U.S. would have to bomb Nicaragua. Sane observers understood why Nicaragua might want jet interceptors: to protect its territory from CIA overflights that were supplying the U.S. proxy forces and providing them with up-to-the-minute information so that they could follow the directive to attack undefended "soft targets." The tacit assumption is that no country has a right to defend civilians from U.S. attack. The doctrine, which reigned challenged, is an interesting one. It might be illuminating to seek counterparts elsewhere.

The pretext for Washington's terrorist wars was self-defense, the standard official justification for just about any monstrous act, even the Nazi Holocaust. Indeed, Ronald Reagan, finding "that the policies and actions of the Government of Nicaragua constitute an unusual and extraordinary threat to the national security and foreign policy of the United States," declared "a national emergency to deal with that threat," arousing no ridicule.[27] Others react differently. In response to John F. Kennedy's efforts to organize collective action against Cuba in 1961, a Mexican diplomat explained that Mexico could not go along because, "if we publicly declare that Cuba is a threat to our security, forty million Mexicans will die laughing."[28] Enlightened opinion in the West takes a more sober view of the extraordinary threat to national security. By similar logic, the USSR had every right to attack Denmark, a far greater threat to its security, and surely Poland and Hungary when they took steps toward independence. The fact that such pleas can regularly be put forth is again an interesting comment on the intellectual culture of the victors and another indication of what lies ahead.

The substance of the Cold War pretexts is greatly illuminated by the case of Cuba, as are the real operative principles. These have emerged with much clarity once again in the past few weeks, with Washington's refusal to accept World Trade Organization (W.T.O.) adjudication of a European Union challenge to its embargo, which is unique in its severity and had already been condemned as a violation of international law by the Organization of American States (OAS) and repeatedly by the United Nations, with near unanimity, more recently extended to severe penalties for third parties that disobey Washington's edicts, yet another violation of international law and trade agreements. The official response of the Clinton administration, as reported by the Newspaper of Record, is that "Europe is challenging 'three decades of American Cuba policy that goes back to the Kennedy Administration,' and is aimed entirely at forcing a change of government in Havana."[29] The administration also declared that the W.T.O. "has no competence to proceed" on an issue of American national security and cannot "force the U.S. to change its laws."

At the very same moment, Washington and the media were lauding the W.T.O. telecommunications agreement as a "new tool of foreign policy" that compels other countries to change their laws and practices in accord with Washington's demands, incidentally handing over their communications systems to mainly U.S. megacorporations in yet another serious blow against democracy.[30] But the W.T.O. has no authority to compel the U.S. to change its laws, just as the World Court has no authority to compel the U.S. to terminate its international terrorism and illegal economic warfare. Free trade and international law are like democracy: fine ideas, but to be judged by outcome, not process.

The reasoning with regard to the W.T.O. is reminiscent of the official U.S. grounds for dismissing World Court adjudication of Nicaragua's charges. In both cases, the U.S. rejected jurisdiction on the plausible assumption that rulings would be against the U.S.; by simple logic, then, neither is a proper forum. The State Department Legal Adviser explained that when the U.S. accepted World Court jurisdiction in the 1940s, most members of the U.N. "were aligned with the United States and shared its views regarding world order." But now "a great many of these cannot be counted on to share our view of the original constitutional conception of the U.N. Charter," and "this same majority often opposes the United States on important international questions." Lacking a guarantee that it will get its way, the U.S. must now "reserve to ourselves the power to determine whether the Court has jurisdiction over us in a particular case," on the principle that "the United States does not accept compulsory jurisdiction over any dispute involving matters essentially within the domestic jurisdiction of the United States, as determined by the United States." The "domestic matters" in question were the U.S. attack against Nicaragua.[31]

The media, along with intellectual opinion generally, agreed that the Court discredited itself by ruling against the United States. The crucial parts of its decision were not reported, including its determination that all U.S. aid to the contras is military and not humanitarian; it remained "humanitarian aid" across the spectrum of respectable opinion until Washington's terror, economic warfare, and subversion of diplomacy brought about the "Victory for U.S. Fair Play."[32]

Returning to the W.T.O. case, we need not tarry on the allegation that the existence of the United States is at stake in the strangulation of the Cuban economy. More interesting is the thesis that the U.S. has every right to overthrow another government, in this case, by aggression, large-scale terror over many years, and economic strangulation. Accordingly, international law and trade agreements are irrelevant. The fundamental principles of world order that have emerged victorious again resound, loud and clear.

The Clinton administration declarations passed without challenge, though they were criticized on narrower grounds by historian Arthur Schlesinger. Writing "as one involved in the Kennedy Administration's Cuban policy," Schlesinger maintained that the Clinton administration had misunderstood Kennedy's policies. The concern had been Cuba's "troublemaking in the hemisphere" and "the Soviet connection," Schlesinger explained.[33] But these are now behind us, so the Clinton policies are an anachronism, though otherwise unobjectionable, so we are to conclude.

Schlesinger did not explain the meaning of the phrases "troublemaking in the hemisphere" and "the Soviet connection," but he has elsewhere, in secret. Reporting to incoming President Kennedy on the conclusions of a Latin American mission in early 1961, Schlesinger spelled out the problem of Castro's "troublemaking"—what the Clinton administration calls Cuba's effort "to destabilize large parts of Latin America": it is "the spread of the Castro idea of taking matters into one's own hands," a serious problem, Schlesinger added later, when "the distribution of land and other forms of national wealth greatly favors the propertied classes . . . [and] the poor and underprivileged, stimulated by the example of the Cuban revolution, are now demanding opportunities for a decent living." Schlesinger also explained the threat of the "Soviet connection": "Meanwhile, the Soviet Union hovers in the wings, flourishing large development loans and presenting itself as the model for achieving modernization in a single generation."[34] The "Soviet connection" was perceived in a similar light far more broadly in Washington and London, from the origins of the Cold War eighty years ago.

With these (secret) explanations of Castro's "destabilization" and "troublemaking in the hemisphere" and of the "Soviet connection," we come closer to an understanding of the reality of the Cold War, another important topic I will have to put aside. It should come as no surprise that basic policies persist with the Cold War a fading memory, just as they were carried out before the Bolshevik revolution: the brutal and destructive invasion of Haiti and the Dominican Republic, to mention just one illustration of "global meliorism" under the banner of "Wilsonian idealism."

It should be added that the policy of overthrowing the government of Cuba antedates the Kennedy administration. Castro took power in January 1959. By June, the Eisenhower administration had determined that his government must be overthrown. Terrorist attacks from U.S. bases began shortly after. The formal decision to overthrow Castro in favor of a regime "more devoted to the true interests of the Cuban people and more acceptable to the U.S." was taken in secret in March 1960, with the addendum that the operation must be carried out "in such a manner as to avoid any appearance of U.S. intervention" because of the expected reaction in Latin America and the need to ease the burden on doctrinal managers at home. At the time, the "Soviet connection" and "troublemaking in the hemisphere" were nil, apart from the Schlesingerian version. The CIA estimated that the Castro government enjoyed popular support (the Clinton administration has similar evidence today).

The Kennedy administration also recognized that its efforts violated international law and the Charters of the U.N. and OAS, but such issues were dismissed without discussion, the declassified record reveals.[35]

Let us move on to NAFTA, the "historic" agreement that may help to advance U.S.-style democracy in Mexico, Lakoff suggests. A closer look is again informative. The NAFTA agreement was rammed through Congress over strenuous popular opposition but with overwhelming support from the business world and the media, which were full of joyous promises of benefits for all concerned, also confidently predicted by the U.S. International Trade Commission and leading economists equipped with the most up-to-date models (which had just failed miserably to predict the deleterious consequences of the U.S.–Canada Free Trade Agreement but were somehow going to work in this case). Completely suppressed was the careful analysis by the Office of Technology Assessment (OTA) (the research bureau of Congress), which concluded that the planned version of NAFTA would harm most of the population of North America, proposing modifications that could render the agreement beneficial beyond small circles of investment and finance. Still more instructive was the suppression of the official position of the U.S. labor movement, presented in a similar analysis. Meanwhile, labor was bitterly condemned for its "backward, unenlightened" perspective and "crude threatening tactics," motivated by "fear of change and fear of foreigners"; I am again sampling only from the far left of the spectrum, in this case, Anthony Lewis. The charges were demonstrably false, but they were the only word that reached the public in this inspiring exercise of democracy. Further details are most illuminating, have been reviewed in the dissident literature at the time and since but kept from the public eye, and are unlikely to enter approved history.[36]

By now, the tales about the wonders of NAFTA have quietly been shelved, as the facts have been coming in. One hears no more about the hundreds of thousands of new jobs and other great benefits in store for the people of the three countries. These good tidings have been replaced by the "distinctly benign economic viewpoint"—the "experts' view"—that NAFTA had no significant effects. The *Wall Street Journal* reports that "administration officials feel frustrated by their inability to convince voters that the threat doesn't hurt them" and that job loss is "much less than predicted by Ross Perot," who was allowed into mainstream discussion (unlike the OTA, the labor movement, economists who didn't echo the party line, and of course dissident analysts) because his claims were sometimes extreme and easily ridiculed. "'It's hard to fight the critics' by telling the truth—that the trade pact 'hasn't really done anything,'" an administration official observes sadly. Forgotten is what "the truth" was going to be when the impressive exercise in democracy was roaring full-steam ahead.[37]

While the experts have downgraded NAFTA to "no significant effects," dispatching the earlier "experts' view" to the memory hole, a less than "distinctly benign economic viewpoint" comes into focus if the "national interest" is widened in scope to include the general population. Testifying before the Senate Banking Committee in February 1997, Federal Reserve Board Chair Alan Greenspan was highly optimistic about "sustainable economic expansion" thanks to "atypical restraint on compensation increases [which] appears to be mainly the consequence of greater worker insecurity"—an obvious desideratum for a just society. The February 1997 *Economic Report of the President,* taking pride in the administration's achievements, refers more obliquely to "changes in labor market institutions and practices" as a factor in the "significant wage restraint" that bolsters the health of the economy.

One reason for these benign changes is spelled out in a study commissioned by the NAFTA Labor Secretariat "on the effects of the sudden closing of the plant on the principle of freedom of association and the right of workers to organize in the three countries." The study was carried out under NAFTA rules in response to a complaint by telecommunications workers on illegal labor practices by Sprint. The complaint was upheld by the U.S. National Labor Relations Board, which ordered trivial penalties after years of delay, the standard procedure. The NAFTA study, by Cornell University labor economist Kate Bronfenbrenner, has been authorized for release by Canada and Mexico but not by the Clinton administration. It reveals a significant impact of NAFTA on strikebreaking. About half of union organizing efforts are disrupted by employer threats to transfer production abroad, for example, by placing signs reading "Mexico Transfer Job" in front of a plant where there is an organizing drive. The threats are not idle: when such organizing drives nevertheless succeed, employers close the plant in whole or in part at triple the pre-NAFTA rate (about 15 percent of the time). Plant-closing threats are almost twice as high in more mobile industries (e.g., manufacturing versus construction).

These and other practices reported in the study are illegal, but that is a technicality, on a par with violations of international law and trade agreements when outcomes are unacceptable. The Reagan administration had made it clear to the business world that its illegal anti-union activities would not be hampered by the criminal state, and successors have kept to this stand. There has been a substantial effect on destruction of unions—or in more polite words, "changes in labor market institutions and practices" that contribute to "significant wage restraint" within an economic model offered with great pride to a backward world that has not yet grasped the victorious principles that are to lead the way to freedom and justice.[38]

What was reported all along outside the mainstream about the goals of NAFTA is also now quietly conceded: the real goal was to "lock Mexico in" to the "reforms" that had made it an "economic miracle," in the technical sense of this term: a "miracle" for U.S. investors and the Mexican rich, while the population sank into misery. The Clinton administration "forgot that the underlying purpose of NAFTA was not to promote trade but to cement Mexico's economic reforms," *Newsweek* correspondent Marc Levinson loftily declares, failing only to add that the contrary was loudly proclaimed to ensure the passage of NAFTA, while critics who pointed out this "underlying purpose" were efficiently excluded from the free market of ideas by its owners. Perhaps some day the reasons will be conceded too. "Locking Mexico in" to these reforms, it was hoped, would deflect the danger detected by a Latin America Strategy Development Workshop in Washington in September 1990. It concluded that relations with the brutal Mexican dictatorship were fine, though there was a potential problem: "a 'democracy opening' in Mexico could test the special relationship by bringing into office a government more interested in challenging the US on economic and nationalist grounds"[39]—no longer a serious problem now that Mexico is "locked into the reforms" by treaty. The U.S. has the power to disregard such obligations at will; not Mexico.

In brief, the threat is democracy, at home and abroad, as the chosen example again illustrates. Democracy is permissible, even welcome, but again, as judged by outcome, not process. NAFTA was considered to be an effective device to diminish the threat of democracy. It was implemented at home by effective subversion of the democratic process and in Mexico by force, again over vain public protest. The results are now presented as a hopeful instrument to bring American-style democracy to benighted Mexicans. A cynical observer aware of the facts might agree.

Once again, the chosen illustrations of the triumph of democracy are natural ones and are interesting and revealing as well, though not quite in the intended manner.

Markets are always a social construction, and in the specific form being crafted by current social policy they should serve to restrict functioning democracy, as in the case of NAFTA, the W.T.O. agreements, and other instruments that may lie ahead. One case that merits close attention is the Multilateral Agreement on Investment (MAI) that is now being forged by the OECD, the rich men's club, and the W.T.O. (where it is the MIA). The apparent hope is that the agreement will be adopted without public awareness, as was the initial intention for NAFTA, not quite achieved, though the "information system" managed to keep the basic story under wraps. If the plans outlined in draft texts are implemented, the whole world may be "locked into" treaty arrangements that provide transnational corporations with still more powerful weapons to restrict the arena of democratic politics, leaving policy largely in the hands of huge private tyrannies that have ample means of market interference as well. The efforts may be blocked at the W.T.O. because of the strong protests of the "developing countries," notably India and Malaysia, which are not eager to become wholly owned subsidiaries of great foreign enterprises. But the OECD version may fare better, to be presented to the rest of the world as a fait accompli, with the obvious consequences. All of this proceeds in impressive secrecy, so far.[40]

The announcement of the Clinton Doctrine was accompanied by a prize example to illustrate the victorious principles: what the administration had achieved in Haiti. Since this is again offered as the strongest case, it would only be appropriate to look at it.

True, Haiti's elected president was allowed to return but only after the popular organizations had been subjected to three years of terror by forces that retained close connections to Washington throughout; the Clinton administration still refuses to turn over to Haiti 160,000 pages of documents on state terror seized by U.S. military forces—"to avoid embarrassing revelations" about U.S. government involvement with the coup regime, according to Human Rights Watch.[41] It was also necessary to put President Aristide through "a crash course in democracy and capitalism," as his leading supporter in Washington described the process of civilizing the troublesome priest.

The device is not unknown elsewhere, as an unwelcome transition to formal democracy is contemplated.

As a condition on his return, Aristide was compelled to accept an economic program that directs the policies of the Haitian government to the needs of "Civil Society, especially the private sector, both national and foreign": U.S. investors are designated to be the core of Haitian Civil Society, along with wealthy Haitians who backed the military coup, but not the Haitian peasants and slum dwellers who organized a civil society so lively and vibrant that they were even able to elect their own president against overwhelming odds, eliciting instant U.S. hostility and efforts to subvert Haiti's first democratic regime.[42]

The unacceptable acts of the "ignorant and meddlesome outsiders" in Haiti were reversed by violence, with direct U.S. complicity, not only through contacts with the state terrorists in charge. The O.A.S. declared an embargo. The Bush and Clinton administrations undermined it from the start by exempting U.S. firms and also by secretly authorizing the Texaco Oil Company to supply the coup regime and its wealthy supporters in violation of the official sanctions, a crucial fact that was prominently revealed the day before U.S. troops landed to "restore democracy" but has yet to reach the public and is an unlikely candidate for the historical record.[43]

Now democracy has been restored. The new government has been forced to abandon the democratic and reformist programs that scandalized Washington and to follow the policies of Washington's candidate in the 1990 election, in which he received 14 percent of the vote.

The prize example tells us more about the meaning and implications of the victory for "democracy and open markets."

Haitians seem to understand the lessons, even if doctrinal managers in the West prefer a different picture. Parliamentary elections in April 1997 brought forth "a dismal 5 percent" of voters, the press reported, thus raising the question "Did Haiti Fail US Hope?"[44] We have sacrificed so much to bring them democracy, but they are ungrateful and unworthy.

One can see why "realists" urge that we stay aloof from crusades of "global meliorism."

Similar attitudes hold throughout the hemisphere. Polls show that in Central America, politics elicits "boredom," "distrust," and "indifference" in proportions far outdistancing "interest" or "enthusiasm" among "an apathetic public . . . which feels itself a spectator in its democratic system" and has "general pessimism about the future." The first Latin America survey, sponsored by the EU, found much the same: "the survey's most alarming message," the Brazilian coordinator commented, was "the popular perception that only the elite had benefited from the transition to democracy."[45] Latin American scholars observe that the recent wave of democratization coincided with neoliberal economic reforms, which have been very harmful for most people, leading to a cynical appraisal of formal democratic procedures. The introduction of similar programs in the richest country in the world has had similar effects. By the early 1990s, after fifteen years of a domestic version of structural adjustment, over 80 percent of the U.S. population had come to regard the democratic system as a sham, with business far too powerful, and the economy as "inherently unfair." These are natural consequences of the specific design of "market democracy" under business rule.

Natural and not unexpected. Neoliberalism is centuries old, and its effects should not be unfamiliar. The well-known economic historian Paul Bairoch points out that "there is no doubt that the Third World's compulsory economic liberalism in the nineteenth century is a major element in explaining the delay in its industrialization," or even "deindustrialization," while Europe and the regions that managed to stay free of its control developed by radical violation of these principles.[46] Referring to the more recent past, Arthur Schlesinger's secret report on Kennedy's Latin American mission realistically criticized "the baleful influence of the International Monetary Fund," then pursuing the 1950s version of today's "Washington Consensus" ("structural adjustment," "neoliberalism"). Despite much confident rhetoric, not much is understood about economic development. But some lessons of history seem reasonably clear and not hard to understand.

Let us return to the prevailing doctrine that "America's victory in the Cold War" was a victory for democracy and the free market. With regard to democracy, the doctrine is partially true, though we have to understand what is meant by *democracy*: top-down control "to protect the minority of the opulent against the majority." What about the free market? Here, too, we find that doctrine is far removed from reality, as several examples have already illustrated.

Consider again the case of NAFTA, an agreement intended to lock Mexico into an economic discipline that protects investors from the danger of a "democracy opening." Its provisions tell us more about the economic principles that have emerged victorious. It is not a "free trade agreement." Rather, it is highly protectionist, designed to impede East Asian and European competitors. Furthermore, it shares with the global agreements such antimarket principles as "intellectual property rights" restrictions of an extreme sort that rich societies never accepted during their period of development but that they now intend to use to protect home-based corporations: to destroy the pharmaceutical industry in poorer countries, for example—and, incidentally, to block technological innovations, such as improved production processes for patented products. Progress is no more a desideratum than markets, unless it yields benefits for those who count.

There are also questions about the nature of "trade." Over half of U.S. trade with Mexico is reported to consist of intrafirm transactions, up about 15 percent since NAFTA. Already a decade ago, mostly U.S.-owned plants in northern Mexico employing few workers and with virtually no linkages to the Mexican economy produced more than one-third of engine blocks used in U.S. cars and three-fourths of other essential components. The post-NAFTA collapse of the Mexican economy in 1994, exempting only the very rich and U.S. investors (protected by U.S. government bailouts), led to an increase of U.S.–Mexico trade as the new crisis, driving the population to still deeper misery, "transformed Mexico into a cheap [i.e., even cheaper] source of manufactured goods, with industrial wages one-tenth of those in the US," the business press reports. According to some specialists, half of U.S. trade worldwide consists of such centrally managed transactions, and much the same is true of other industrial powers,[47] though one must treat with caution conclusions about institutions with limited public accountability. Some economists have plausibly described the world system as one of "corporate mercantilism," remote from the ideal of free trade. The

OECD concludes that "oligopolistic competition and strategic interaction among firms and governments rather than the invisible hand of market forces condition today's competitive advantage and international division of labor in high-technology industries,"[48] implicitly adopting a similar view.

Even the basic structure of the domestic economy violates the neoliberal principles that are hailed. The main theme of the standard work on U.S. business history is that "modern business enterprise took the place of market mechanisms in coordinating the activities of the economy and allocating its resources," handling many transactions internally, another large departure from market principles.[49] There are many others. Consider, for example, the fate of Adam Smith's principle that free movement of people is an essential component of free trade—across borders, for example. When we move on to the world of transnational corporations, with strategic alliances and critical support from powerful states, the gap between doctrine and reality becomes substantial.

Free market theory comes in two varieties: the official doctrine and what we might call "really existing free market doctrine"—market discipline is good for you, but I need the protection of the nanny state. The official doctrine is imposed on the defenseless, but it is "really existing doctrine" that has been adopted by the powerful since the days when Britain emerged as Europe's most advanced fiscal-military and developmental state, with sharp increases in taxation and efficient public administration as the state became "the largest single actor in the economy" and its global expansion,[50] establishing a model that has been followed to the present in the industrial world, surely by the United States, from its origins.

Britain did finally turn to liberal internationalism in 1846, after 150 years of protectionism, violence, and state power had placed it far ahead of any competitor. But the turn to the market had significant reservations. Forty percent of British textiles continued to go to colonized India, and much the same was true of British exports generally. British steel was kept from U.S. markets by very high tariffs that enabled the United States to develop its own steel industry. But India and other colonies were still available and remained so when British steel was priced out of international markets. India is an instructive case; it produced as much iron as all of Europe in the late 18th century, and British engineers were studying more advanced Indian steel manufacturing techniques in 1820 to try to close "the technological gap." Bombay was producing locomotives at competitive levels when the railway boom began. But "really existing free market doctrine" destroyed these sectors of Indian industry just as it had destroyed textiles, shipbuilding, and other industries that were advanced by the standards of the day. The U.S. and Japan, in contrast, had escaped European control and could adopt Britain's model of market interference.

When Japanese competition proved to be too much to handle, England simply called off the game: the empire was effectively closed to Japanese exports, part of the background of World War II. Indian manufacturers asked for protection at the same time—but against England, not Japan. No such luck, under really existing free market doctrine.[51]

With the abandonment of its restricted version of laissez-faire in the 1930s, the British government turned to more direct intervention into the domestic economy as well. Within a few years, machine tool output increased five times, along with a boom in chemicals, steel, aerospace, and a host of new industries, "an unsung new wave of industrial revolution," Will Hutton writes. State-controlled industry enabled Britain to outproduce Germany during the war, even to narrow the gap with the U.S., which was then undergoing its own dramatic economic expansion as corporate managers took over the state-coordinated wartime economy.[52]

A century after England turned to a form of liberal internationalism, the U.S. followed the same course. After 150 years of protectionism and violence, the U.S. had become by far the richest and most powerful country in the world and, like England before it, came to perceive the merits of a "level playing field" on which it could expect to crush any competitor. But like England with crucial reservations.

One was that Washington used its power to bar independent development elsewhere, as England had done. In Latin America, Egypt, South Asia, and elsewhere, development was to be "complementary" not "competitive." There was also large-scale interference with trade. For example, Marshall Plan aid was tied to purchase of U.S. agricultural products, part of the reason why the U.S. share in world trade in grains increased from less than 10 percent before the war to more than half by 1950, while

Argentine exports reduced by two-thirds. U.S. Food for Peace aid was also used both to subsidize U.S. agribusiness and shipping and to undercut foreign producers, among other measures to prevent independent development.[53] The virtual destruction of Colombia's wheat growing by such means is one of the factors in the growth of the drug industry, which has been further accelerated throughout the Andean region by the neoliberal policies of the past few years. Kenya's textile industry collapsed in 1994 when the Clinton administration imposed a quota, barring the path to development that has been followed by every industrial country, while "African reformers" are warned that they "must make more progress" in improving the conditions for business operations and "sealing in free-market reforms" with "trade and investment policies" that meet the requirements of Western investors. In December 1996 Washington barred exports of tomatoes from Mexico in violation of NAFTA and W.T.O. rules (though not technically, for it was a sheer power play and did not require an official tariff), at a cost to Mexican producers of close to $1 billion annually. The official reason for this gift to Florida growers is that prices were "artificially suppressed by Mexican competition" and Mexican tomatoes were preferred by U.S. consumers. In other words, free-market principles were working but with the wrong outcome.[54]

These are only scattered illustrations.

One revealing example is Haiti, along with Bengal the world's richest colonial prize and the source of a good part of France's wealth, largely under U.S. control since Wilson's Marines invaded eighty years ago and by now such a catastrophe that it may scarcely be habitable in the not-too-distant future. In 1981, a USAID–World Bank development strategy was initiated, based on assembly plants and agroexport, shifting land from food for local consumption. USAID forecast "a historic change toward deeper market interdependence with the United States" in what would become "the Taiwan of the Caribbean." The World Bank concurred, offering the usual prescriptions for "expansion of private enterprises" and minimization of "social objectives," thus increasing inequality and poverty and reducing health and educational levels. It may be noted, for what it is worth, that these standard prescriptions are offered side by side with sermons on the need to reduce inequality and poverty and improve health and educational levels, while World Bank technical studies recognize that relative equality and high health and educational standards are crucial factors in economic growth.

In the Haitian case, the consequences were the usual ones: profits for U.S. manufacturers and the Haitian superrich and a decline of 56 percent in Haitian wages through the 1980s—in short, an "economic miracle." Haiti remained Haiti, not Taiwan, which had followed a radically different course, as advisers must surely know.

It was the effort of Haiti's first democratic government to alleviate the growing disaster that called forth Washington's hostility and the military coup and terror that followed. With "democracy restored," USAID is withholding aid to ensure that cement and flour mills are privatized for the benefit of wealthy Haitians and foreign investors (Haitian "Civil Society," according to the orders that accompanied the restoration of democracy) while barring expenditures for health and education. Agribusiness receives ample funding, but no resources are made available for peasant agriculture and handicrafts, which provide the income of the overwhelming majority of the population. Foreign-owned assembly plants that employ workers (mostly women) at well below subsistence pay under horrendous working conditions benefit from cheap electricity, subsidized by the generous supervisor. But for the Haitian poor—the general population—there can be no subsidies for electricity, fuel, water, or food; these are prohibited by International Monetary Fund rules on the principled grounds that they constitute "price control." Before the "reforms" were instituted, local rice production supplied virtually all domestic needs, with important linkages to the domestic economy. Thanks to one-sided "liberalization," it now provides only 50 percent, with the predictable effects on the economy. The liberalization is, crucially, one sided. Haiti must "reform," eliminating tariffs in accord with the stern principles of economic science—which, by some miracle of logic, exempt U.S. agribusiness; it continues to receive huge public subsidies, increased by the Reagan administration to the point where they provided 40 percent of growers' gross incomes by 1987. The natural consequences are understood and intended: a 1995 USAID report observes that the "export-driven trade and investment policy" that Washington mandates will "relentlessly squeeze the domestic rice farmer," who will be forced to turn to the more rational pursuit of agroexport for the benefit of U.S. investors, in accord with the principles of rational expectations theory.[55]

By such methods, the most impoverished country in the hemisphere has been turned into a leading purchaser of U.S.-produced rice, enriching publicly subsidized U.S. enterprises. Those lucky enough to have received a good Western education can doubtless explain that the benefits will trickle down to Haitian peasants and slum dwellers—ultimately. Africans may choose to follow a similar path, as currently advised by the leaders of "global meliorism" and local elites, and perhaps may see no choice under existing circumstances—a questionable judgment, I suspect. But if they do, it should be with eyes open.

The last example illustrates the most important departures from official free-trade doctrine, more significant in the modern era than protectionism, which was far from the most radical interference with the doctrine in earlier periods either, though it is the one usually studied under the conventional breakdown of disciplines, which makes its own useful contribution to disguising social and political realities. To mention one obvious example, the Industrial Revolution depended on cheap cotton, just as the "golden age" of contemporary capitalism has depended on cheap energy, but the methods for keeping the crucial commodities cheap and available, which hardly conform to market principles, do not fall within the professional discipline of economics.

One fundamental component of free-trade theory is that public subsidies are not allowed. But after World War II, U.S. business leaders expected that the economy would collapse without the massive state intervention during the war that had finally overcome the Great Depression. They also insisted that advanced industry "cannot satisfactorily exist in a pure, competitive, unsubsidized, 'free enterprise' economy" and that "the government is their only possible savior" (*Fortune, Business Week,* expressing a general consensus). They recognized that the Pentagon system would be the best way to transfer costs to the public. Social spending could play the same stimulative role, but it has defects: it is not a direct subsidy to the corporate sector, it has democratizing effects, and it is redistributive. Military spending has none of these unwelcome features. It is also easy to sell, by deceit. President Truman's Air Force secretary put the matter simply: we should not use the word *subsidy,* he said;

the word to use is *security*. He made sure the military budget would "meet the requirements of the aircraft industry," as he put it. One consequence is that civilian aircraft are now the country's leading export, and the huge travel and tourism industry, aircraft based, is the source of major profits.[56]

It was quite appropriate for Clinton to choose Boeing as "a model for companies across America" as he preached his "new vision" of the free-market future, to much acclaim. A fine example of really existing markets, civilian-aircraft production is now mostly in the hands of two firms, Boeing–McDonald and Airbus, each of which owes its existence and success to large-scale public subsidy. The same pattern prevails in computers and electronics generally, automation, biotechnology, communications, in fact just about every dynamic sector of the economy.[57]

There was no need to explain this central feature of "really existing free market capitalism" to the Reagan administration. They were masters at the art, extolling the glories of the market to the poor at home and the service areas abroad while boasting proudly to the business world that Reagan had "granted more import relief to U.S. industry than any of his predecessors in more than half a century"—in reality, more than all predecessors combined—as they "presided over the greatest swing toward protectionism since the 1930s," shifting the U.S. from "being the world's champion of multilateral free trade to one of its leading challengers," the journal of the Council on Foreign Relations commented in a review of the decade. The Reaganites led "the sustained assault on [free-trade] principle" by the rich and powerful from the early 1970s that is deplored in a scholarly review by GATT secretariat economist Patrick Low, who estimates the restrictive effects of Reaganite measures at about three times those of other leading industrial countries.[58]

The great "swing toward protectionism" was only a part of the "sustained assault" on free trade principles that was accelerated under "Reaganite rugged individualism." Another chapter of the story includes the huge transfer of public funds to private power, often under the traditional guise of "security," a "defense buildup [that] actually pushed military R&D spending (in constant dollars) past the record levels of the mid-1960s," Stuart Leslie notes.[59] The public was terrified with foreign threats (Russians, Libyans, etc.), but the Reaganite message to the business world was again much more honest. Without such extreme measures of market interference, it is doubtful that the U.S. automotive, steel, machine tool, semiconductor industries, and others, would have survived Japanese competition or been able to forge ahead in emerging technologies, with broad effects through the economy.

There is also no need to explain the operative doctrines to the leader of today's "conservative revolution," Newt Gingrich, who sternly lectures seven-year-old children on the evils of welfare dependency while holding a national prize for directing public subsidies to his rich constituents. Or to the Heritage Foundation, which crafts the budget proposals for the congressional "conservatives" and therefore called for (and obtained) an increase in Pentagon spending beyond Clinton's increase to ensure that the "defense industrial base" remains solid, protected by state power, and offering dual-use technology to its beneficiaries to enable them to dominate commercial markets and enrich themselves at public expense.

All understand very well that free enterprise means that the public pays the costs and bears the risks if things go wrong—for example, bank and corporate bailouts that have cost the public hundreds of billions of dollars in recent years. Profit is to be privatized, but cost and risk socialized, in really existing market systems. The centuries-old tale proceeds today without notable change, not only in the United States, of course.

Public statements have to be interpreted in the light of these realities, among them, Clinton's current call for trade-not-aid for Africa, with a series of provisions that just happen to benefit U.S. investors and uplifting rhetoric that manages to avoid such matters as the long record of such approaches and the fact that the U.S. already had the most miserly aid program of any developed country even before the grand innovation. Or to take the obvious model, consider Chester Crocker's explanation of Reagan administration plans for Africa in 1981. "We support open market opportunities, access to key resources, and expanding African and American economies," he said, and want to bring African countries "into the mainstream of the free market economy." The statement may seem to surpass cynicism, coming from the leaders of the "sustained assault" against "the free market economy." But Crocker's rendition is fair enough, when it is passed through the prism of really existing market doctrine. The market opportunities and access to resources are for foreign investors and their local associates, and the economies are to expand in a specific way, protecting "the minority of the opulent against the majority." The opulent, meanwhile, merit state protection and public subsidy. How else can they flourish, for the benefit of all?

To illustrate "really existing free market theory" with a different measure, the most extensive study of transnational corporations found that "virtually all of the world's largest core firms have experienced a decisive influence from government policies and/or trade barriers on their strategy and competitive position" and "at least twenty companies in the 1993 Fortune 100 would not have survived at all as independent companies, if they had not been saved by their respective governments," by socializing losses or simple state takeover when they were in trouble. One is the leading employer in Gingrich's deeply conservative district, Lockheed, saved from collapse by $250 million in government loan guarantees. The same study points out that government intervention, which has "been the rule rather than the exception over the past two centuries, . . . has played a key role in the development and diffusion of many product and process innovations—particularly in aerospace, electronics, modern agriculture, materials technologies, energy and transportation technology," as well as telecommunications and information technologies generally (the Internet and World Wide Web are striking recent examples), and in earlier days, textiles, steel, and of course energy. Government policies "have been an overwhelming force in shaping the strategies and competitiveness of the world's largest firms."[60] Other technical studies confirm these conclusions.

As these examples indicate, the United States is not alone in its conceptions of "free trade," even if its ideologues often lead the cynical chorus. The gap between rich and poor countries from 1960 is substantially attributable to protectionist measures of the rich, the *UN Development Report* concluded in 1992. The 1994 report concluded that "the industrial countries, by violating the principles of free trade, are costing the developing countries an estimated $50 billion a year—nearly equal to the total flow of foreign assistance"—much of it publicly subsidized export promotion.[61] The 1996 global report of the U.N. Industrial Development Organization estimates that the disparity between the richest and poorest 20 percent of the world population increased by over 50 percent from 1960 to 1989 and predicts "growing world inequality resulting from the globalization process." That growing disparity holds within the rich societies as well, the U.S. leading the way, Britain not far behind. The business press exults in "spectacular" and "stunning" profit growth, applauding the extraordinary concentration of wealth among the top few percent of the population, while for the majority, conditions continue to stagnate or decline. The corporate media, the Clinton administration, and the cheerleaders for the American Way generally proudly offer themselves as a model for the rest of the world; buried in the chorus of self-acclaim are the results of deliberate social policy during the happy period of "capital's clear subjugation of labor," for example, the "basic indicators" just published by UNICEF,[62] revealing that the U.S. has the worst record among the industrial countries, ranking alongside of Cuba—a poor Third World country under unremitting attack by the hemispheric superpower for almost forty years—by such standards as mortality for children under five and also holding records for hunger, child poverty, and other basic social indicators.

All of this takes place in the richest country in the world, with unparalleled advantages and stable democratic institutions, but also under business rule, to an unusual extent. These are further auguries for the future, if the "dramatic shift away from a pluralist, participatory ideal of politics and towards an authoritarian and technocratic ideal" proceeds on course, worldwide.

It is worth noting that in secret intentions are often spelled out honestly, for example, in the early post–World War II period, when George Kennan, one of the most influential planners and considered a leading humanist, assigned each sector of the world its "function": Africa's function was to be "exploited" by Europe for its reconstruction, he observed, the U.S. having little interest in it. A year earlier, a high-level planning study had urged "that cooperative development of the cheap foodstuffs and raw materials of northern Africa could help forge European unity and create an economic base for continental recovery," an interesting concept of "cooperation."[63] There is no record of a suggestion that Africa might "exploit" the West for its recovery from the "global meliorism" of the past centuries.

If we take the trouble to distinguish doctrine from reality, we find that the political and economic principles that have prevailed are remote from those that are proclaimed. One may also be skeptical about the prediction that they are "the wave of the future," bringing history to a happy end. The same "end of history" has confidently been proclaimed many times in the past, always wrongly. And with all the sordid continuities, an optimistic soul can discern slow progress, realistically I think. In the advanced industrial countries, and often elsewhere, popular struggles today can start from a higher plane and with greater expectations than those of the past. And international solidarity can take new and more constructive forms as the great majority of the people of the world come to understand that their interests are pretty much the same and can be advanced by working together. There is no more reason now than there has ever been to believe that we are constrained by mysterious and unknown social laws, not simply decisions made within institutions that are subject to human will—human institutions, which have to face the test of legitimacy and, if they do not meet it, can be replaced by others that are more free and more just, as often in the past.

Skeptics who dismiss such thoughts as utopian and naive have only to cast their eyes on what has happened right here in the last few years, an inspiring tribute to what the human spirit can achieve and its limitless prospects—lessons that the world desperately needs to learn and that should guide the next steps in the continuing struggle for justice and freedom here too, as the people of South Africa, fresh from one great victory, turn to the still more difficult tasks that lie ahead.

NOTES

This article was originally delivered as the Davie Lecture at the University of Cape Town, South Africa, in May 1997, and later published in *Pretexts* (Cape Town), no. 1, 1998, and in *Z Magazine* (Sept./Nov. 1997) 18 Millfield Street, Woods Hole, MA 02543; www.Znet.org.

1. UNICEF, *The State of the World's Children 1997* (Oxford: Oxford University Press, Oxford, 1997); UNICEF, *The Progress of Nations 1996* (New York: UNICEF House, 1996).
2. Thomas Friedman, *New York Times (NYT)*, June 2, 1992; National Security Adviser Antony Lake, *NYT*, Sept. 26, 1993; historian David Fromkin, *NYT Book Review*, May 4, 1997, summarizing recent work.
3. On the general picture and its historical origins, see, inter alia, Frederic Clairmont's classic study, *The Rise and Fall of Economic Liberalism* (Asia Publishing House, 1960), reprinted and updated (Penang and Goa: Third World

Network, 1996); Michael Chossudovsky, *The Globalization of Poverty* (Penang: Third World Network, 1997). Clairmont has been an UNCTAD economist for many years; Chossudovsky is a professor of economics at the University of Ottawa.

4. John Cassidy, *New Yorker,* Oct. 16, 1995; Harvey Cox, *World Policy Review,* spring 1997; Martin Nolan, *Boston Globe (BG),* March 5, 1997; John Buell, *The Progressive,* March 1997. The sample is liberal-to-left, in some cases quite critical. The analysis is similar across the rest of the spectrum but generally euphoric.

5. John Liscio, *Barron's,* April 15, 1996.

6. Bernays, *Propaganda* (New York: Liveright, 1928), chaps. 1–2. See M. P. Crozier, S. J. Huntington, and J. Watanuki, *The Crisis of Democracy: Report on the Governability of Democracies to the Trilateral Commission* (New York: New York University Press, 1975).

7. Richard Cockett, "The Party, Publicity, and the Media," in Anthony Seldon and Stuart Ball, eds., *Conservative Century: The Conservative Party since 1900* (Oxford: Oxford University Press, 1994); Harold Laswell, "Propaganda," *Encyclopedia of the Social Sciences,* vol. 12 (New York: Macmillan, 1933). For quotes and discussion see my 1997 Huizinga lecture "Intellectuals and the State," reprinted in *Toward a New Cold War* (New York: Pantheon, 1982). Also at last available is some of the pioneering work on these topics by Alex Carey, in his *Taking the Risk Out of Democracy* (Sydney: University of New South Wales Press, 1995; Urbana: University of Illinois Press, 1997).

8. Ibid.; Elisabeth Fones-Wolf, *Selling Free Enterprise: The Business Assault on Labor and Liberalism, 1945–1960* (Urbana: University of Illinois Press, 1995). Also, Stuart Ewen, *PR!: A Social History of Spin* (New York: Basic Books, 1996). On the broader context, see my "Intellectuals and the State" and "Force and Opinion," reprinted in *Deterring Democracy* (London: Verso, 1991).

9. Editorial, *New Republic,* March 19, 1990.

10. Sanford Lakoff, *Democracy: History, Theory, Practice* (Boulder: Westview, 1996), 262f.

11. J. Toye, J. Harrigan, and P. Mosley, *Aid and Power,* vol. 1 (London: Routledge, 1991), 16, cited by John Mihevc, *The Market Tells Them So* (London: Zed, 1995), 53. On the Leninist comparison, see my essays cited in note 8 and *For Reasons of State* (New York: Pantheon, 1973), introduction.

12. Carothers, "The Reagan Years," in A. Lowenthal, ed., *Exporting Democracy* (Baltimore: Johns Hopkins University Press, 1991). See also his *In the Name of Democracy* (Berkeley: University of California Press, 1991).

13. Cited by Gordon Wood, *The Radicalism of the American Revolution* (New York: Vintage, 1991), 190.

14. Lance Banning, the leading scholarly proponent of the libertarian interpretation of Madison's views, citing Gordon Wood. For further discussion and

sources, see my *Powers and Prospects* (Boston: South End, 1996), chap. 5; and "Consent without Consent," *Cleveland State Law Review* 44, no. 1 (1996).

15. Frank Monaghan, *John Jay* (Bobbs-Merrill, 1935), 323.

16. *Survey of Current Business* 76, no. 12, Dec. 1996 (U.S. Department of Commerce, Washington, D.C.).

17. Morton Horwitz, *The Transformation of American Law, 1870–1960* (Cambridge, Mass., Harvard University Press, 1992), chap. 3. See also Charles Sellers, *The Market Revolution* (Oxford: Oxford University Press, 1991).

18. See Michael Sandel, *Democracy's Discontent* (Cambridge, Mass.: Harvard University Press, 1996), chap. 6. His interpretation in terms of republicanism and civic virtue is too narrow, in my opinion, overlooking deeper roots in the Enlightenment and before. For some discussion, see among others my *Problems of Knowledge and Freedom* (New York: Pantheon, 1971), chap. 1; several essays reprinted in James Peck, ed., *The Chomsky Reader* (New York: Pantheon, 1987); and *Powers and Prospects,* chap. 4.

19. See Carey, op. cit., and "Force and Opinion."

20. For details, see my *Turning the Tide* (Boston: South End, 1985), chap. 11 (and sources cited), including long quotes from Figueres, whose exclusion from the media took considerable dedication. See my *Letters from Lexington* (Monroe, N.H.: Common Courage, 1993), chap. 6, on the record, including the long obituary in the *New York Times* by its Central America specialist and the effusive accompanying editorial, which again succeeded in completely banning his views on Washington's "crusade for democracy." On media coverage of Nicaraguan and Salvadoran elections, see Edward Herman and Noam Chomsky, *Manufacturing Consent* (New York: Pantheon, 1988), chap. 3. Even Carothers, who is careful with the facts, writes that the Sandinistas "refused to agree to elections" until 1990.

21. Another standard falsification is that the long-planned elections took place only because of Washington's military and economic pressures, which are therefore retroactively justified.

22. On the elections and the reaction in Latin America and the U.S., including sources for what follows, see *Deterring Democracy,* chap. 10.

23. Original emphasis, op. cit.

24. For details, see, inter alia, Richard Garfield, "Desocializing Health Care in a Developing Country," *Journal of the American Medical Association* 270, no. 8 (Aug. 25, 1993); my *World Orders, Old and New* (New York: Columbia University Press, 1994), 131f.

25. Kinsley, *Wall Street Journal (WSJ),* March 26, 1987; *New Republic,* March 19, 1990. For more on these and many similar examples, see *Culture of Terrorism,* chap. 5; *Deterring Democracy,* chaps. 10, 12.

26. Greenway, *BG,* July 29, 1993.

27. *NYT,* May 2, 1985.

28. Ruth Leacock, *Requiem for Revolution* (Kent, Ohio: Kent State University Press, 1990), 33.

29. David Sanger, "U.S. Won't Offer Testimony on Cuba Embargo," *NYT,* Feb. 21, 1997. The actual official wording is that the "bipartisan policy since the early 1960s [is] based on the notion that we have a hostile and unfriendly regime 90 miles from our border, and that anything done to strengthen that regime will only encourage the regime to not only continue its hostility but, through much of its tenure, to try to destabilize large parts of Latin America," so that Cuba is a national security threat to the U.S. and to Latin America—much as Denmark has been to Russia and Eastern Europe. Morris Morley and Chris McGillion, *Washington Report on the Hemisphere* (Council on Hemispheric Affairs, June 3, 1997).

30. David Sanger, "Playing the Trade Card: U.S. Is Exporting Its Free-Market Values through Global Commercial Agreements," *NYT,* Feb. 17, 1997. On the same day, *Times* editors warned the EU not to turn to the W.T.O. on Washington's sanctions against Cuba. The whole affair is "essentially a political dispute," they explain, not touching on Washington's "free-trade obligations."

31. Sofaer, *The United States and the World Court,* U.S. Department of State, Bureau of Public Affairs, Current Policy, no. 769 (Dec. 1985).

32. For detailed review of the very successful subversion of diplomacy, hailed generally as a triumph of diplomacy, see *Culture of Terrorism,* chap. 7; and my *Necessary Illusions* (Boston: South End, 1989), appendix IV.5 (pp. 84ff., above).

33. Letter, *NYT,* Feb. 26, 1997.

34. *Foreign Relations of the United States, 1961–63,* vol. 12, American Republics, 13f., 33.

35. Piero Gleijeses, "Ships in the Night: The CIA, the White House and the Bay of Pigs," *Journal of Latin American Studies* 27, part 1 (Feb. 1995), 1–42; Jules Benjamin, *The United States and the Origins of the Cuban Revolution* (Princeton: Princeton University Press, 1990), 186ff. On recent polls by a Gallup affiliate, see *Miami Herald* Spanish edition, Dec. 18, 1994; Maria Lopez Vigil, *Envío* (Jesuit University of Central America, Managua), June 1995 (reviewed in my "Passion for Free Markets," *Z Magazine,* May 1997); *Profit over People* (New York: Seven Stories Press, 1998), 81.

36. See *World Orders, Old and New,* 131ff. On the predictions and the outcome, see economist Melvin Burke, "NAFTA Integration: Unproductive Finance and Real Unemployment," *Proceedings from the Eighth Annual Labor Segmentation Conference,* April 1995, sponsored by Notre Dame and Indiana Universities. Also, *Social Dimensions of North American Economic Integration,* a report prepared for the Department of Human Resources Development by the Canadian Labour Congress, 1996. On World Bank predictions for Africa, see Mihevc, op. cit., also reviewing the grim effects of consistent failure—grim for the population, that is, not for the Bank's actual constituency. That the record

of prediction is poor, and understanding meager, is well-known to professional economists. See, for example, Paul Krugman, "Cycles of Conventional Wisdom on Economic Development," *International Affairs* 71, no. 4, Oct. 1995. He is, however, a bit selective in exempting professional economists from his withering censure.

37. Helene Cooper, "Experts' View of NAFTA's Economic Impact: It's a Wash," *WSJ,* June 17, 1997.

38. Editorial, "Class War in the USA," *Multinational Monitor,* March 1997; Bronfenbrenner, "We'll Close," ibid., based on the study she directed, "Final Report: The Effects of Plant Closing or Threat of Plant Closing on the Right of Workers to Organize." The massive impact of Reaganite criminality is detailed in a report in *Business Week,* "The Workplace: Why America Needs Unions, but Not the Kind It Has Now," May 23, 1994.

39. Levinson, *Foreign Affairs,* March–April 1996; *Workshop,* Sept. 26–27, 1990, Minutes, 3.

40. OECD, *Multilateral Agreement on Investment: Consolidated Texts and Commentary* (OLIS, Jan. 9, 1997; DAFFE/MAI/97; Confidential). Scott Nova and Michelle Sforza-Roderick of Preamble Center for Public Policy, Washington, "M.I.A. Culpa," *The Nation,* Jan. 13; Martin Khor, "Trade and Investment: Fighting Over Investors' Rights at W.T.O.," *Third World Economics* (Penang) Feb. 15; Laura Eggerston, "Treaty to Trim Ottawa's Power," *Toronto Globe and Mail,* April 3; Paula Green, "Global Giants: Fears of the Supranational," *Journal of Commerce* (Canada), April 23; George Monbiot, "A Charter to Let Loose the Multinationals," *Guardian* (U.K.), April 15, 1997. On the outcome and its significance, see *Profit over People,* chaps. 6–7.

41. Kenneth Roth, Executive Director, HRW, Letter, *NYT,* April, 12, 1997.

42. See Paul Farmer, *The Uses of Haiti* (Monroe, Me.: Common Courage Press, 1994); *World Orders, Old and New,* 62ff.; my "Democracy Restored," *Z Magazine,* Nov. 1994; NACLA, *Haiti, Dangerous Crossroads* (Boston: South End, 1995).

43. "Democracy Restored," citing John Solomon, AP, Sept. 18, 1994 (lead story).

44. Nick Madigan, "Democracy in Inaction: Did Haiti Fail US Hope?" *Christian Science Monitor,* April 8, 1997; AP, *BG,* April 8, 1997.

45. John McPhaul, *Tico Times* (Costa Rica), April 11, May 2, 1997.

46. Bairoch, *Economics and World History* (Chicago: University of Chicago Press, 1993).

47. Vincent Cable, *Daedalus* (spring 1995), citing *UN World Investment Report 1993* (which, however, gives quite different figures, noting also that "relatively little data are available" [164f.]). On the U.S. and Mexico, see David Barkin and Fred Rosen, "Why the Recovery Is Not a Recovery," *NACLA Report on the*

Americas, Jan.–Feb. 1997; Leslie Crawford, "Legacy of Shock Therapy," *Financial Times,* Feb. 12, 1997 (subtitled "Mexico: A Healthier Outlook," the article reviews the increasing misery of the vast majority of the population, apart from "the very rich"). On post-NAFTA intrafirm transactions, see William Greider, *One World, Ready or Not* (New York: Simon and Schuster, 1997), 273, citing Mexican economist Carlos Heredia.

48. 1992 OECD study cited by Clinton's former chief economic adviser, Laura Tyson, *Who's Bashing Whom?* (Institute for International Economics, Washington, D.C., 1992).

49. Alfred Chandler, *The Visible Hand* (Cambridge, Mass.: Belknap Press, 1977).

50. John Brewer, *Sinews of Power* (New York: Knopf, 1989).

51. Radhakamal Mukerjee, *The Economic History of India: 1600–1800* (Allahabad: Kitab Mahal, 1967); C. A. Bayly, *The New Cambridge History of India* (Cambridge: Cambridge University Press, 1988); Dietmar Rothermund, *An Economic History of India* (London: Croom Helm, 1993); Bairoch, op. cit.

52. Hutton, *The State We're In* (London: Jonathan Cape, 1995), 128f. On the wartime revival of the U.S. economy, laying the basis for postwar economic growth, see Gregory Hooks, *Forging the Military-Industrial Complex* (Urbana: University of Illinois Press, 1991).

53. See, inter alia, Gerald Haines, *The Americanization of Brazil* (Wilmington, Del.: Scholarly Resources, 1989); Nathan Godfried, *Bridging the Gap between Rich and Poor* (Westport, Conn.: Greenwood, 1987); Michael Weis, *Cold Warriors and Coups d'Etat* (Albuquerque: University of New Mexico Press, 1993); David Rock, *Argentina* (Berkeley: University of California Press, 1987), 269, 292f.

54. On Colombia, see Walter LaFeber, "The Alliances in Retrospect," in Andrew Maguire and Janet Welsh Brown, eds., *Bordering on Trouble* (Bethesda, Md.: Adler and Adler, 1986). On Kenya, see Michael Phillips, "U.S. Is Seeking to Build Its Trade with Africa," *WSJ,* June 2, 1997. On Mexico, see David Sanger, "President Wins Tomato Accord for Floridians," *NYT,* Oct. 12, 1996.

55. See my *Year 501* (Boston: South End, 1993), chap. 8, and sources cited; Farmer, op. cit.; *Labor Rights in Haiti,* International Labor Rights Education and Research Fund, April 1989; *Haiti after the Coup,* National Labor Committee Education Fund (New York), April 1993; Lisa McGowan, *Democracy Undermined, Economic Justice Denied: Structural Adjustment and the AID Juggernaut in Haiti* (Development Gap, Washington, D.C., Jan. 1997).

56. *Turning the Tide,* chaps. 4–5; Frank Kofsky, *Harry Truman and the War Scare of 1948* (New York: St. Martin's Press, 1993); *World Orders, Old and New,* chap. 2.

57. Ibid.

58. Ibid, citing Secretary of the Treasury James Baker; Shafiqul Islam, *Foreign Affairs, America and the World* (winter 1989–90); Low, *Trading Free* (New York: Twentieth Century Fund, 1993), 70ff., 271.

59. Leslie, *The Cold War and American Science* (New York: Columbia University Press, 1993), introduction.

60. Winfried Ruigrock and Rob van Tulder, *The Logic of International Restructuring* (London: Routledge, 1995), 221–22, 217.

61. For discussion, see Eric Toussaint and Peter Drucker, eds., *IMF/World Bank/WTO, Notebooks for Study and Research* (Amsterdam: International Institute for Research and Education, 1995), 24–25.

62. UNICEF, *State of World's Children 1997.*

63. UNICEF, *State of World's Children 1997*; Kennan, PPS 23, Feb. 24, 1948 (FRUS, vol. 1, 1948), 511; Michael Hogan, *The Marshall Plan* (Cambridge: Cambridge University Press, 1987), 41, paraphrasing the May 1947 Bonesteel Memorandum.

5

UNMASKING A PEDAGOGY OF LIES: A DEBATE WITH JOHN SILBER

> *Jeremy Paxman* (BBC's Radio 4): You don't deny [that the bombing of Cambodia] was secret though? . . . This was a secret operation against a neutral country.
>
> *Henry Kissinger:* Come on now Mr. Paxman, this was fifteen years ago, and you at least have the ability to educate yourself about a lie in your own program.
>
> *Paxman:* What's factually inaccurate?
>
> *Kissinger:* That's outrageous.

In the above exchange, Henry Kissinger once again demonstrates that if you are the intellectual mouthpiece of the doctrinal system, you can easily dismiss impertinent historical facts by simply labeling them as "lies" while remaining assured that the doctrinal system will not only protect you but also reward you. In fact, Kissinger can comfortably and arrogantly dismiss the historical facts because, according to Chomsky, "if you're following the party line you don't have to document anything; you can say anything you feel like. . . . That's one of the privileges you get for obedience. On the other hand, if you're critical of received opinion, you have to document every phrase." Even though we now have irrefutable evidence of Kissinger's inglorious involvement in the secret carpet bombings of Laos and Cambodia, which killed thousands of innocent people, including women and children, he continues to enjoy enormous rewards as an "expert," with authority and access to those institutions charged with the responsibility of shaping public opinion. His inglorious support of Augusto Pinochet, who destroyed the democratically elected socialist government of Salvador Allende and killed along the way more than 3,000 people, cannot be denied. His complicity with the Indonesian government's invasion of East Timor is well documented. The Indonesian invasion unleashed a genocide of monstrous proportions in East Timor which continues to the present day with the outrageous carnage euphemistically labeled "ethnic cleansing" by Western "experts," while Western powers conveniently sit on the sidelines and watch the final solution in East Timor. Instead of being charged with crimes against humanity by the War Crime Tribunal, Kissinger continuous to make pronouncements regarding the NATO bombing of Kosovo.

Once intellectuals are adapted to the doctrinal system and rewarded by it, it becomes increasingly less difficult for them to live within a lie and ignore the true reality, even when faced with documented historical evidence. Nowhere is this more evident than in the debate that follows between Noam Chomsky and John Silber. When Chomsky proceeded to expose the contradictions and hypocrisy of the U.S. policy in El Salvador, by citing the wholesale slaughter of El Salvadorans by ultraright death squads supported and trained by the United States, Silber angrily dismissed Chomsky's documented evidence by calling him a "systematic liar." Chomsky's evidence speaks for itself. We now have learned from the U.N. Truth Commission the truth Chomsky has been trying to tell us all along, as the U.N. commission findings clearly show:

1. Between 200 and 500 peasants slaughtered at El Mozote in 1981; man accused: the late Colonel Domingo Monterrosa
2. Archbishop Oscar Romero, shot dead while he said mass in 1980; man accused: the late Robert d'Aubuisson
3. Six Jesuit priests, a housekeeper, and her fifteen-year-old daughter murdered in 1989; man accused: General Rene Emilio Ponce, who until October 1993 was El Salvador's defense minister
4. Three nuns and an American laywoman raped and killed in 1980; man accused: General Vides Casanova, a former defense minister.

David Nyhan, a *Boston Globe* reporter writes that the two American journalists, Raymond Bonner from the *New York Times* and Alma Guillermoprieto from the *Washington Post,* "were attacked by name" in a now infamous *Wall Street Journal* editorial. "Overly credulous," said the journal. That's editorial-pagese speak for "Those two leftie-symp journalists are in the tank to the commies." In a passage that would eventually result in getting Bonner yanked off the El Salvador beat, the journal encouraged the men who ran the *Times* to mistrust their own reporter, who'd been "poking around among the skeletons."

We now have documented evidence that Bishop Romero's assassination was ordered by Robert d'Aubuisson, the man who was given the red carpet treatment in Congress by Jesse Helms, the Republican Senator from North Carolina, and other ideologues who supported and still support unimaginable atrocities in Latin America. Yet there is no mechanism to make individuals like John Silber, the former president of Boston University, accountable for their intellectual dishonesty and moral irresponsibility.

Because there is no accountability requirement if one supports the party line, not only Silber could continue to lie about the atrocities committed in El Salvador with the full support of the United States; he can also arrogantly and systematically attack anyone who dares to speak the truth. Because Silber is part of a system that "is captive to its own lies," he can arrogantly falsify everything and be rewarded and promoted by the doctrinal system to the status of leader, educator, and philosopher with little if any evidence to support such status. By carefully reading the debate between Noam Chomsky and John Silber that follows, we begin to see that the greater the rewards received, the more dogmatic the defense of the doctrinal system becomes. Silber's dogmatic defense of the indefensible doctrinal system in his debate with Chomsky needs no further comment.

> *Chris Lydon* (host): Our guests are as far apart on the contra question as American intellectuals can be—John Silber, the president of Boston University, was a member of the Kissinger Commission that diagnosed a security threat in Central America; Noam Chomsky, the language theorist at

MIT, argues in his new book, entitled *Turning the Tide,* that U.S. intervention in Central America is the acute case of our general misuse and misrule of the Third World.

I would like you to begin, President Silber. Address yourself to the waverers, if there are any, in the U.S. Senate. Why would you vote for the contra money?

John Silber: Well, the Senate of the United States has traditionally been in favor of supporting democratic forces as opposed to totalitarian forces. And if they continue that practice, they are going to vote against the Sandinistas and they are going to vote in favor of the contras. On October 15 the Sandinistas passed an edict that suspends the protection against the search of homes without a warrant, that suspends the privacy of mail and allows for the censorship of mail. They suspended the right of free assembly. They have suspended all freedom of the press. They have continued their harassment of their people and suspended virtually all democratic rights. The October 15 decree is much more restrictive and comprehensive than the decree that Hitler passed on February 28, 1933, when he ended the democratic republic of Weimar. Once you see this totalitarian nature of the regime, which was apparent since 1979 in September and has continued ever since then, it is time for the Senate of the United States to support the Democrats.

Lydon: Noam Chomsky, in a short speech to the U.S. Senate, why would you be agin the contra money?

Noam Chomsky: Well, as even the most ardent supporters of the contras now concede, this is what they call a proxy army, which is attacking Nicaragua from foreign bases, is entirely dependent on its masters for directions and support, has never put forth a political program, has created no base of political support within the country, and almost its entire top military command is Somozist officers. Its military achievements so far consist of a long and horrifying series of very well documented torture, mutilation, and atrocities, and essentially nothing else. Administration officials are now openly conceding in public that the main function of the contras is to retard or reverse the rate of social reform in Nicaragua and to try to terminate the openness of that society. The state of siege, for example, which was imposed last fall and which is very mild, I should say—there is much political opening in Nicaragua, as everyone there up to the American ambassador will tell you—that corresponds roughly to the state of siege which has been in place in El Salvador since early 1980, except in El Salvador it has been associated with a huge massacre of tens of thousands of people. Destruction of the press, so on and so forth. Whereas in Nicaragua it is a reaction to a war that we are carrying out against them with precisely the purpose of trying to retard social reform and to restrict the possibilities of an open and developing society. That is a cruel and savage policy, which we should terminate.

Silber: Are you going to continue that series of plain falsehoods? That's a series of falsehoods the likes of which I've never seen compacted in such a small period of time. The massacres that have occurred in Nicaragua have been the massacres by the Sandinistas of the Miskito Indians. The repression there is massive. It is more serious than anything we have seen in Central America or in any Latin American country to date. It is a genuine dictatorship imposed there. And to describe the leaders of the contras as being supporters of Somoza is simply fabrication. Robelo, Cruz, Calero, Chamorro are not Somozistas and never have been. And when you take the leadership of the army of the contras—some of them were members of the National Guard—but then if you are going to object to that, which would be highly unreasonable because that was an army that was not simply followers, or Somozistas, it is important to remember that Modesta Rojas, the vice chairman of the air force of the Sandinistas, was also a member of the National Guard, and a very large number of members of the National Guard are the ones who are coordinators of the block committees that imposed the dictatorship by the Sandinistas. This is a series of distortions and fabrications, and the effort of the Sandinistas to discredit the contras by the manufacture of atrocities is now a point that has been very well documented.

Lydon: Noam Chomsky's turn to respond to, among other things, to the original picture of the totalitarian . . .

Chomsky: . . . Let's just first start by talking about the facts. I stated again that the military leadership of the contras is almost entirely drawn from the top, from the Somozist National Guard.

Silber: . . . Somoza's soldiers . . .

Chomsky: Forty-six out of forty-eight of the top military commanders according to Edgar Chamorro—this is the top military commander . . .

Silber: . . . soldiers are . . .

Chomsky: Excuse me. Now look, I let you go on. Did I let you?

Silber: You engage in a series of fabrications of truth, and it's time that somebody . . .

Chomsky: May I?

Silber: . . . had the opportunity of correcting your historical misstatements while you're still around . . .

Chomsky: Mr. Silber has a very good reason for not wanting me to talk . . .

Silber: . . . Mr. Marcos, Mr. Marcos . . .

Chomsky: . . . and that is he knows what the truth is and he doesn't want me to . . .

Silber: . . . no, no, no, it's because you have distorted the truth long enough.

Chomsky: May I have a chance to say what . . .

Silber: . . . No, just let me finish. It is Marcos. Marcos is the very army that helped Aquino into power, so when you try to take on the National Guard, as if the National Guard was Somozistas, you misstate the case.

Lydon: . . . But let him make the case. It's . . .

Silber: . . . You also overlook the fact that there are plenty of National Guard members who are supporting the Sandinistas.

Lydon: Mr. Chomsky . . .

Silber: Now you go ahead and distort the truth again.

Chomsky: Now let me, see, here you're having an action. A good example of totalitarianism, and that is to ensure that the opposition . . .

Silber: I'm the first one that stopped your monopoly on misinformation.

Chomsky: The idea that I have a monopoly of misinformation of the American press is a little ridiculous.

Silber: No, it's not . . .

Chomsky: Really? I control the American press? Let me repeat. Let's go back to the facts: Forty-six out of the forty-eight top military commanders of the contras are Somozist officers. You can find that in the congressional report. You can find that from Edgar Chamorro who is the CIA-appointed spokesman. That's exactly what I said, and it's exactly true. As to the idea that the Sandinistas have carried out massacres on a par with those that we have been carrying out in Central America, this is really astonishing!

In El Salvador, the number of people massacred since 1978 or since 1979 when we moved in in force is on the order of 60,000. In Guatemala, where we incidentally have been supporting it all the way through with military aid which never terminated and are now supporting it enthusiastically, the number of people massacred is on the order of 100,000.

Mr. Silber referred to the Miskito Indians, who were badly treated; I should say, the figures are that approximately sixty or seventy were killed. Whereas in contrast, about 5,000 or 6,000 people have been killed—and I don't mean killed, this is not your garden variety killing; this is torture, murder, and mutilation, massively documented in great detail—by our forces. Now there are crimes of the Sandinistas, there is no doubt, but they are undetectable in comparison with the crimes that we have supported . . .

Lydon: I'd like to go back to two central arguments this thing turns on. One is that Sandinista Nicaragua poses a security threat to the United States and to this hemisphere. Secondly, we owe it to the so-called Democrats and the democratic notion to help people who are carrying our standard in the region. John Silber, are these equal arguments, and do you support them both?

Silber: Well, I don't support the presence of about 6,500 Soviet and Cuban troops in Nicaragua. I don't support the presence of twenty-four armed helicopter gunships supplied by the Soviet Union to Nicaragua, or 150 battle tanks, or about

1,200 trucks and 300—

Lydon: . . . But where is the notion that it is a security threat to this country?

Silber: Well, it's not a security threat yet. And neither was Hitler a security threat when he suspended all freedoms of the Germans on February 28, 1933. He wasn't even a security threat that was serious in 1936 when he rearmed the Rhineland. But by the time that the Allies got around to recognizing that he was a threat, it cost us tens of millions of lives and it took six years in which to defeat him.

Now, at the present time we can put an end to the Sandinista dictatorship in Central America without using a single American life. All we have to do is help pay for the firemen. There is a fire going on down there. We don't have to put the fire out. But we're asked to pay for the firemen. If we wait, if we decide to do nothing until the Soviets establish a land base there and it develops, as it will develop if we allow it to happen, we will then have to face the fact of a possibility of war. It is not a present threat, it is a vector. If people don't have sense enough to understand that a small fire in a room is a threat, not because it's a small fire but because small fires have a way of becoming big fires, then we haven't learned anything from history.

Lydon: It's Noam Chomsky's turn on the question of the security threat to the hemisphere and to this country.

Chomsky: Well, to talk of Nicaragua as a security threat is a bit like asking what threat Luxembourg poses to the Soviet Union. Mr. Silber mentioned Hitler, and I am old enough to remember Hitler's speeches in which he talked about the threat to Germany posed by Poland from which Germany had to defend itself. And even that's unfair to Hitler to draw that example. It is quite true that Nicaragua is now Soviet-armed and heavily armed. And the reason is that it is being attacked by a superpower which has specifically blocked every other source of supply. For example, up until the May embargo last year, 20 percent of Nicaraguan trade was with the Soviet bloc. Prior to that, its arms were coming from everywhere.

We then blocked the arms from everywhere else. As we intensified the war, they do exactly what the U.S. government wants them to do, namely, to divert resources from the social reforms which we really fear, and they turn them towards militarization. The idea that Nicaragua could attack—I might add that the countries of Latin America regard this as hysterical lunacy. Every country, all the Contadora countries, all the support countries, which include all of the relatively democratic countries in Latin America, are pleading with us to call off the war against the country. They understand perfectly well exactly what it's doing. It's forcing them to be a militarized state, and it's creating a danger of a wider war in the region. If we want to get the Soviet tanks out of Nicaragua, and there are very few, and the Cuban advisers out, what we should do is very simple, and everyone in the government knows it. Call off the war, and they will return to what they were doing before we attacked them—namely, creating the most effective reforms in the hemisphere, which were widely praised by the World Bank, the Inter-American Development Bank, organizations like OXFAM, which described them as unique in their experience in seventy-six developing countries . . .

Lydon: We're running out—

Chomsky: . . . which we have retarded and stopped by this attack.

Lydon: We are running so far over time that we might just as well keep going. I want you to deal with the question of democracy and our responsibility to aid the cause. You criticized the Sandinistas, but do you really want to embrace the contras as a vehicle of democracy?

Silber: Absolutely. And let's dispense with the myth somehow that these were lovely Democrats until we drove them into the hands of the Soviet Union by our opposition. That is a myth. That is a fabrication of history that Mr. Chomsky knows is false. As a matter of fact, when the revolution came to an end in July of 1979, the Sandinistas came to Washington, after having pledged to the Organization of American States that they would hold free elections. They then received $117 million in loans, they received credit from the World Bank through the intercession of the United States. They were very well received and very well treated. And on September of 193—ah, 1979—they already began their process of repression. So the notion that we drove them into the hands of the Communists is utterly false. It's a fabrication.

Lydon: But the question is "Are the contras a vehicle for democracy?"

Silber: The contras do not have overt support among the Nicaraguan people at the present time inside Nicaragua, for one obvious reason. Hitler's opponents did not have any obvious support in Germany after Hitler had taken over that country. In a totalitarian state the opposition does not have any effective voice. You don't find that effective voice in the Soviet Union now either. You have isolated groups of refuseniks. But in Nicaragua you have a leadership: Robelo, Cruz, Chamorro, Calero—those are major figures, major democratic figures who opposed Somoza, and many of them went to jail, and they are literally followed by thousands of people who are opposing the Sandinista dictatorship. To try to write these people off as totalitarian and to come up with that trumped-up nonsense about the atrocities that those people have committed is just a good example of doublethink. This is just a 1984 exercise by Mr. Chomsky for which he has already established a worldwide reputation. It's rubbish.

Lydon: Mr. Chomsky, when you hear this call to come to the rescue of democracy and democratic forces, what do you answer?

Chomsky: I would be delighted if the United States were to reverse its long-standing policies of opposing democratic forces throughout Central America and begin to support those forces.

Now, to return to Nicaragua and to return to the real world, I never described the Sandinistas as perfect Democrats or whatever your phrase was. What I did was quote the World Bank, OXFAM, the Jesuit Order, and others who recognize that what they were doing was to use the meager resources of that country for the benefit of the poor majority. That's why health standards shot up. That's why literacy shot up. That's why agrarian reform proceeded, the only place in the region. That's why subsistence agriculture improved and consumption of food increased, and that's why we attacked them. It had nothing to do with democracy.

Now, I also did not say that Cruz and Robelo committed atrocities. In fact, Cruz and Robelo sit in Washington and don't do anything. They are figureheads who we concocted. The people who commit atrocities are the contra forces led by the National Guard. And of all the figures you mention, one is involved: namely, Calero, who is an ultra-right-wing businessman and represents the extremist, narrow business forces in Nicaragua.

Now, if we had the slightest concern with democracy—which we do not in our foreign affairs and never have—we would turn to countries where we have influence, like El Salvador. Now, in El Salvador they don't call the archbishop bad names; what they do is murder him. They do not censor the press; they wipe the press out. They sent the army in to blow up the church radio station. The editor of the independent newspaper was found in a ditch mutilated and cut to pieces with a machete.

Silber: Don't you ever—

Chomsky: . . . May I continue? I did not interrupt you . . .

Silber: Don't you ever want to put a time value on anything you say . . .

Chomsky: Excuse me, that was 19—

Silber: . . . Or do you just want to lie systematically on television?

Chomsky: I'm talking about . . . I'm talking about . . . I'm talking about 198—

Silber: . . . You are a systematic liar . . .

Chomsky: . . . Did these things happen, or didn't they?

Silber: These things did not happen in the context in which you suggest at all.

Chomsky: . . . Really?

Silber: . . . And when you suggest that Cruz is simply a figurehead and does nothing, you overlook the fact that Arturo Cruz was the ambassador of the Sandinistas to the United States.

Chomsky: Yes, and he has always . . .

Silber: And he was the head banker of the Sandinistas . . .

Chomsky: Exactly—in the United States.

Silber: . . . Until he finally broke with them when he found out that they were utterly totalitarian. You are a phony, mister, and it's time that the people read you correctly.

Chomsky: Well, it's clear why you want to divert me from the discussion . . .

Silber: No, it's not. It's because we get tired of rubbish!

Chomsky: Excuse me. Arturo Cruz, exactly as I said, was in the United States, he was brought to . . .

Silber: Why was he in the United States?

Chomsky: He was in the United States and he defected in the United States. He was brought back to Nicaragua, as a political figure, because the business-based opposition there had no credible candidate. He did not participate in the elections, as he could have, in part because . . .

Silber: . . . He couldn't because he was broke . . .

Chomsky: May I continue?

Silber: No, because you're lying again.

Lydon: I've got to cut you both off.

Chomsky: I didn't say anything yet.

Silber: The Turbas [pro-Sandinista street militia] were the ones who prevented Cruz from participating in the elections . . .

Chomsky: That's another fabrication. But let's continue with . . .

Lydon: Except we can't. I'm afraid we're out of time. You've given President Reagan a tough act to follow on Sunday night. We thank you both, John Silber and Noam Chomsky.

Chomsky: Yeah, OK.

The following are supplemental excerpts from related works by Chomsky:

The fall of [Nicaraguan dictator] Somoza in 1979 aroused fears in Washington that the brutal dictator of El Salvador might be overthrown, leading to loss of U.S. control there as well. The second and still more threatening development was the growth of "popular organizations" in the 1970s: Bible study groups that became self-help groups under Church sponsorship, peasant organizations, unions and the like. There was a fearsome prospect that El Salvador might move towards a meaningful democracy with opportunities for real popular participation in the political process. . . .

The Carter Administration reacted to these threats in El Salvador by backing a coup led by reformist military officers in October 1979, while ensuring that the most reactionary military elements retained a position of dominance. . . .

In February 1980, Archbishop Romero pleaded with President Carter not to provide the junta with military aid, which, he observed, "will surely increase injustice here and sharpen the repression that has been unleashed against the people's organizations fighting to defend their most fundamental human rights." . . .

But increasing the repression, destroying the people's organizations and preventing independence were the very essence of U.S. policy, so Carter ignored the Archbishop's plea and sent the aid, to "strengthen the army's key role in reforms." . . .

In March 1980, Archbishop Romero was assassinated. A judicial investigation was initiated, headed by Judge Atilio Ramírez. He accused General Medrano, the death squad organizer and U.S. favorite, and rightwing leader Roberto d'Aubuisson of hiring the assassins, and shortly after fled the country after death threats and an attempt on his life. . . . Judge Ramírez concludes that "it is undoubtedly the case that from the very beginning, they were involved in a kind of conspiracy to cover up the murder." . . .

In June, the university was shut down after an army attack that left many killed, including the rector, and facilities looted and destroyed. . . .

Meanwhile, the independent media were eliminated by bombings and terror, another prerequisite for "free elections" to legitimate the client regime. The editor and a journalist [of *La Crónica del Pueblo*] were found with their bodies hacked to pieces with machetes, and *[El Independiente]* closed after three attempts to assassinate the editor, threats to his family, occupation of the offices by armed forces, and the arrest and torture of staff members. The Church radio station was repeatedly bombed, and shortly after Reagan's election, troops occupied the Archdiocese building, destroying the radio station and ransacking the newspaper offices. . . .

On October 26, 1980, Archbishop Romero's successor, Bishop Rivera y Damas, condemned the armed forces' "war of extermination and genocide against a defenseless civilian population"; a few weeks later, Duarte hailed the armed forces for "valiant service alongside the people against subversion" as he was sworn in as civilian president of the junta. [*Turning the Tide* (Boston: South End, 1985), 102–07]

During the Salvadorian election [the *New York Times, Time, Newsweek,* and CBS News had not] even mentioned the destruction by physical violence and murder of *La Crónica* and *El Independiente,* or the toll of murdered journalists. [Edward Herman and Noam Chomsky, *Manufacturing Consent* (New York: Pantheon, 1988), 129]

INDEX

ABOUT THE AUTHOR AND EDITOR

Noam Chomsky, author of more than eighty books, is Institute Professor in the Department of Linguistics and Philosophy at the Massachusetts Institute of Technology. His seminal work in linguistics has been cited and debated for five decades, influencing disciplines as diverse as philosophy, sociology, biology, and cognitive sciences. His prolific writings on politics and international affairs are read around the world, in many languages. He lives in Lexington, Massachusetts.

Donaldo Macedo, is Professor of English and a Distinguished Professor of Liberal Arts and Education at the University of Massachusetts, Boston. He has published extensively in the areas of Creole languages, critical literacy, bilingualism, and multiculturalism. His publications include: *Literacy: Reading the Word and the World* (with Paulo Freire, 1987), *Literacies of Power: What Americans Are Not Allowed to Know* (1994), and *Ideology Matters* (coauthored with Paulo Freire, forthcoming). His work has been translated in several languages.